CONSUMERS AND CONSUMPTION IN COMPARISON

COMPARATIVE SOCIAL RESEARCH

Series Editor: Fredrik Engelstad

Recent Volumes:

Volume 18:	Family Change: Practices, Policies, and Values, 1999
Volume 19:	Comparative Perspectives on Universities, 2000
Volume 20:	The Comparative Study of Conscription in the Armed Forces, 2002
Volume 21:	Comparative Studies of Culture and Power, 2003
Volume 22:	The Multicultural Challenge, 2003
Volume 23:	Comparative Studies of Social and Political Elites, 2007
Volume 24:	Capitalisms Compared, 2007
Volume 25:	Childhood: Changing Contexts, 2008
Volume 26:	Civil Society in Comparative Perspective, 2009
Volume 27:	Troubled Regions and Failing States: The Clustering and Contagion of Armed Conflicts, 2010
Volume 28:	The Nordic Varieties of Capitalism, 2011
Volume 29:	Firms, Boards and Gender Quotas: Comparative Perspectives, 2012
Volume 30:	Class and Stratification Analysis, 2013
Volume 31:	Gender Segregation in Vocational Education, 2015
Volume 32:	Labour Mobility in the Enlarged Single European Market, 2018
Volume 33:	Bureaucracy and Society in Transition: Comparative Perspectives, 2018
Volume 34:	Elites and People: Challenges to Democracy, 2019
Volume 35:	Social Democracy in the 21st Century, 2020
Volume 36:	A Comparative Historical and Typological Approach to The Middle Eastern State System: Taking Stein Rokkan's Ambitions Beyond Europe, 2024

COMPARATIVE SOCIAL RESEARCH VOLUME 37

CONSUMERS AND CONSUMPTION IN COMPARISON

EDITED BY

EIVIND JACOBSEN
Oslo Metropolitan University, Norway

PÅL STRANDBAKKEN
Oslo Metropolitan University, Norway

ARNE DULSRUD
Oslo Metropolitan University, Norway

AND

SILJE ELISABETH SKULAND
Oslo Metropolitan University, Norway

emerald PUBLISHING

United Kingdom – North America – Japan
India – Malaysia – China

Emerald Publishing Limited
Emerald Publishing, Floor 5, Northspring, 21-23 Wellington Street, Leeds LS1 4DL

First edition 2025

Reprints and permissions service
Contact: www.copyright.com

British Library Cataloguing in Publication Data
A catalogue record for this book is available from the British Library

ISBN: 978-1-83549-315-1 (Print)
ISBN: 978-1-83549-314-4 (Online)
ISBN: 978-1-83549-316-8 (Epub)

ISSN: 0195-6310 (Series)

Printed and bound by CPI Group (UK) Ltd, Croydon, CR0 4YY

CONTENTS

LIST OF REVIEWERS

Nan Bakkeli	Oslo Metropolitan University
Jon Ivar Elstad	Oslo Metropolitan University
Fredrik Engelstad	University of Oslo
Bente Halkier	Copenhagen University
Are S. Hermansen	University of Oslo
Arno von Hootegem	University of Oslo
Piia Jallinoja	Tampere University
Unni Kjærnes	Oslo Metropolitan University
Lise Kjølsrød	University of Oslo
Anne Krogstad	University of Oslo
Lars Mjøset	University of Oslo
Judith Nyfeler	University of St.Gallen
Liza Reisel	University of Oslo
Laura Seppanen	Finnish Institute of Occupational Health
Dale Southerton	University of Bristol
Niklas Sørum	University of Gothenburg
Terhi-Anna Wilska	University of Jyväskylä

ABOUT THE EDITORS

Dr Eivind Jacobsen is a previous Director of Consumption Research Norway (SIFO), Oslo Metropolitan University (Norway). He is trained in Sociology and Science studies. He has published widely on consumer issues related to food, food provisioning, food consumption as well as on marketing, and retailing.

Dr Pål Strandbakken is Researcher at Consumption Research Norway (SIFO). He is trained as a Sociologist and has published on sustainable consumption, social theory and participatory democracy.

Arne Dulsrud is Research Professor at Consumption Research Norway (SIFO). His current research focuses on food security and sustainability with a global approach, encompassing projects in both India and Latin America. His most recent project addresses how processes of digitalization impact household consumption practices.

Silje Elisabeth Skuland is the Head of research for the research group Consumption Policy and Economy at Consumption Research Norway (SIFO). She holds a PhD in Sociology from the University of Oslo. She has researched on food practices and economic differences, packed lunch, health and safe food practices, loan problems and children's and youth consumption. Silje is especially interested in children's and young people's lives.

ABOUT THE CONTRIBUTORS

Johanna Sofia Adolfsson is a Researcher at the Centre for Development and the Environment, University of Oslo. Adolfsson is a Cultural Psychologist with an overarching research focus that investigates the dominant role of Western psychological theory and practice in global development policy and intervention, including a focus on the individualization of human ways of being.

Andreea Ioana Alecu is a Senior Researcher at Consumption Research Norway (SIFO). Alecu is a Political Scientist currently working on topics related to the impact of policy design and implementation on different forms of social inequalities. Her PhD dissertation examined social divisions in access to social capital and their influence on interpersonal trust.

Mattia Andreola is a PhD candidate in Agrifood and Environmental Sciences at the University of Trento. During his doctoral studies, Andreola focused on the sociology of food and agriculture and contributing to the 'Nutrire Trento' project, the local urban food policy. As part of his PhD, Andreola gained valuable experience as a Visiting Researcher at Consumption Research Norway (SIFO), where he broadened his expertise in the sociology of consumption and quantitative methods. He is currently involved in the NUECity project, studying new urban economies through the analysis of online platforms and lifestyles in food, mobility and care.

Julia Brannen is an Emerita Professor of the Sociology of the Family, Thomas Coram Research Unit, UCL Institute of Education, London, and a Visiting Professor at the University of Sussex. A Fellow of the Academy of Social Science, she has an international reputation for methodology and international research on family lives. Recent work with Professor Rebecca O'Connell concerns families and food poverty in Europe.

Kia Ditlevsen is an Associate Professor in Sociology of Food and Eating at Department of Food and Resource Economics, University of Copenhagen. Ditlevsen is a Qualitative Sociologist interested in social inequality, social difference and everyday food practices. Her recent work explores class differentiated food cultures in a Nordic welfare state and gendered food practices.

Jamie Evans is a Research Fellow at the Personal Finance Research Centre, University of Bristol. He is a Human Geographer whose research focuses predominantly on the financial wellbeing of low- and middle-income households in the United Kingdom, exploring issues of financial inclusion, fintech, the poverty premium and consumer vulnerability. His applied policy work has been used by UK Government organizations, including the Money and Pensions Service and Financial Conduct Authority.

Francesca Forno is an Associate Professor at the University of Trento (Italy), Department of Sociology and Social Research. She has published and done research on political consumerism, collaborative consumption, eco-social innovation and alternative food networks (AFNs). She is currently leading the project FOODEMOCRACY – Investigating and experimenting with how food policies work.

Arve Hansen is a Senior Researcher at Centre for Development and the Environment, University of Oslo, where he leads the centre's research group on sustainable consumption and energy equity. His research focuses on consumption and sustainability, both in affluent societies and emerging economies. His recent work includes Consumption and Vietnam's New Middle Classes (Palgrave 2022) and Consumption, Sustainability and Everyday Life (Palgrave, 2023; edited with Kenneth Bo Nielsen).

Vilde Haugrønning is a Researcher at Consumption Research Norway (SIFO). She holds a Master's from the Centre for Environment and Development (SUM) at the University of Oslo and a Bachelor's degree in Social Anthropology and Visual Culture from NTNU. She has previously researched food consumption in Norwegian households and is currently doing her PhD on clothing consumption, gender and sustainability.

Ingrid Haugsrud is a PhD student at Consumption Research Norway (SIFO). Her research interests lie within sustainable consumption – especially related to clothing in everyday life, theories of care, wardrobe studies and consumption and childhood.

Marie Hebrok is a Research Professor at Consumption Research Norway, Oslo Metropolitan University. Hebrok is a Design Researcher interested in the relationships between design and sustainable consumption practices. She is currently leading the project *REDUCE – rethinking everyday plastics* and working on the project *IMAGINE – contested futures of sustainability*. Her recent work has revolved around food practices and product durability.

Nina Heidenstrøm is a Senior Researcher at Consumption Research Norway, Oslo Metropolitan University. Heidenstrøm is a Sociologist interested in how consumption organizes everyday life and the importance of consumption to sustainability and risk management. She is currently leading the research project *IMAGINE – Contested Futures of Sustainability*. Her recent work has revolved around imaginaries, food consumption and household preparedness.

Elaine Kempson is an Emeritus Professor of Social Policy and Personal Finances at the University of Bristol and a Visiting Professor at OsloMet University. She is known, internationally, for her work on financial inclusion, payment problems, financial capability and most recently financial well-being. She is currently researching the links between mental health and payment problems.

Unni Kjærnes is retired from position as Research Professor at Consumption Research Norway (SIFO). As Sociologist, Kjærnes has worked on a range of issues on consumption and consumer policy. Topics include changes in eating habits, trust and power, food security and sustainable regulation. She has coordinated a large number of projects in Norway, the Nordic countries and Europe.

Sabina Kuraj is a Researcher at Consumption Research Norway, Oslo Metropolitan University. Kuraj is a Political Scientist interested in the relationships between agricultural policy and sustainable food consumption. She is currently part of two research projects: DISCo – Digital infrastructures for sustainable consumption: Redirecting, reorganizing, reducing and reimaging consumption funded by the Belmont Forum, and NKJ – A Nordic-Baltic framework for sustainable food systems funded by The Nordic Joint Committee for Agricultural and Food Research (NKJ). Her recent work has revolved around sustainable food production and consumption and food security.

Mikko Laamanen is a Research Professor at Consumer Research Norway (SIFO). His research focuses on the everyday politics of technology, inclusion and social change; his current projects examine inclusive digital platforms, alternative consumption communities and sustainability in arts. His research has been published in *Current Sociology*, *Information Communication & Society*, *International Journal of Consumer Studies*, *Journal of the Academy of Marketing Science*, *Journal of Marketing Management* and *Social Movement Studies*.

Rebecca O'Connell is a Professor of Food, Families and Society at the Centre for Research in Public Health and Community Care (CRIPACC), University of Hertfordshire and Visiting Professor at the Thomas Coram Research Unit, UCL Institute of Education. Her research examines the economic, social and cultural determinants shaping what children and families eat and the part food plays in their everyday lives. Recent work with Julia Brannen concerns families and food poverty in Europe. She is currently co-leading a project, *Adapt-Ed*, that is co-designing improvements to food in special schools with children with special educational needs and disabilities, their families and other stakeholders (NIHR163616).

Christian Poppe holds a PhD degree in Sociology. He is a Senior Researcher at Consumption Research Norway (SIFO). His research interests include personal finance, borrowing practices, debt problems and debt settlements. He has contributed to the Russia Trust Fund-funded *Financial Capability* project, where he served as a consultant for the World Bank. Poppe managed two projects funded by the Norwegian Research Council: *Financialization of Social Welfare*, and *Debt Problems, Ill-Health and Work Market Marginalisation*. Poppe recently conducted several studies to assess households' financial well-being during the cost-of-living crisis.

Alexander Schjøll is the Head of Research for the research group on textiles and food at Consumption Research Norway (SIFO). Schjøll is an Economist interested in food habits, retailing of food and consumers' perception of animal welfare. He is currently leading a project on marketing of unhealthy food towards juveniles in social media.

Kamilla Knutsen Steinnes is a PhD candidate in Behavioural Analysis at Consumption Research Norway (SIFO). Steinnes is a Psychological Researcher interested in consumer behaviour in digital platforms, the commercialization of digital spheres and how market dynamics influence social relations and gendered consumption patterns. Her doctoral project explores the interplay between identities, consumption and game design in video games.

Hanne Torjusen is a Postdoctoral Fellow at Consumption Research Norway (SIFO). Torjusen is a Nutritionist with a particular interest in the health and sustainability issues of consumption practices and food and fibre systems. Previous research includes the impact of organic food consumption in pregnancy on the health of mother and child, based on the Norwegian Mother and Child Cohort Study, and multidisciplinary, international collaborations, such as the EU-funded projects Welfare Quality, Organic-PLUS, Strength2Food and FOOdIVERSE. She is currently engaged in Amazing Grazing, a Norwegian project on sheep rangeland grazing systems.

Per Arne Tufte is a Sociologist and an Associate Professor at Oslo Business School, Oslo Metropolitan University, and has a background as a Researcher at Consumption Research Norway (SIFO). His main fields of research are household economics, financial counselling, welfare policy and animal welfare. He has also published several contributions on research methods and explanations in the social sciences.

Gunnar Vittersø works as a Senior Researcher at Consumption Research Norway (SIFO). He holds a PhD in Human Geography from the University of Oslo. His research interests are in studies of sustainable consumption with a special focus on social transformation of the food system including studies of everyday food practices and alternative food networks. Vittersø has participated in several EU-funded projects with interdisciplinary approaches among others including methods on involvement of citizens and stakeholders.

Stefan Wahlen is a Professor of Food Sociology at the University of Giessen in Germany. His current research focuses on food culture and eating in the sense of doing food, as well as organizational and sociopolitical dimensions of food. Stefan is the Coordinator of the European ERA-net project 'FOOdIVERSE', which aims to uncover the role of diversity for a more sustainable and resilient food system. He is a member of the steering committee of the 'Sustainable Consumption Research and Action Initiative' in Europe (SCORAI-Europe) and a co-editor of the journal *Consumption and Society*, published by Bristol University Press.

Ulrikke Wethal is a Researcher at the Centre for Development and the Environment, University of Oslo. Wethal is a Human Geographer by training, and her research focuses mainly on how to change systems of consumption and production in more sustainable directions, including research projects on meat consumption, circular practices and the role of local governments in promoting sustainable consumption.

ABOUT THE CONTRIBUTORS

FOREWORD

Within the social sciences, the study of consumers and consumption has gained momentum these last years. Consumption has been on the radar of sociologists ever since the classics in the later part of the 19th century (more on this in the Introduction). However, as a research field in its own, with its own canon, journals, curriculums and PhD programmes, it's relatively new. It started out in the early 90s within a small network of mostly Nordic and British researchers, confined to European Sociological Associations (ESA) RN5. Famously, in the first interim network meeting in Bergen in 1992, all the participants could be seated in two taxis. This contrasts to the last interim meeting, also this held in Norway (at Consumption Research Norway SIFO, in Oslo), where participants numbered more than 150 and came from all of Europe, and even some from Asia and the United States.

To the contributors to this issue, consumption is a broad phenomenon encompassing activities related to acquisition, modification, use, repair, and finally the disposal of goods and services. As such, consumption is about much more than shopping or choosing products in markets, most frequently in focus in the marketing literature. Moreover, to be a consumer is for us a part-time role where people engage in such activities. In other words, for us – the contributors for this volume – no one is a consumer in essence, but everyone enrolls and performs consumer roles daily.

Consumption and the enactment of consumer roles is currently deeply entangled in all kinds of big social questions. The English sociologist David Evans (2022) writes on connecting consumption and the social.

- Consumption is a key reference point for understanding macro-social processes of organization and change.
- Consumption is a societal phenomenon to be understood through recures to "social" in contrast to the methodological individualism found in marketing and behaviourism.
- Consumption is linked to today's big societal challenges, like climatic change, health, etc. both as contributor and site for solutions.

Through this volume, we would like to show these three points by means of a set of articles applying a comparative approach to different consumption practices. The various papers compare consumption across nations, and consumption areas, thereby demonstrating the contextual embedding and situatedness of consumption and consumers and the necessity to study them in relation to production, politics and various forms of regulations.

The editors would like to thank the reviewers for their time and friendly advice, and the Editorial Board headed by Professor Emeritus Fredrik Engelstad, both for the invitation to produce this issue, and for support and advice during the process. We would also like to thank the publisher, Emerald, for its professional flexibility, and Consumption Research Norway (SIFO) for offering time and administrative resources. SIFO – for short – is currently the largest European social science–based institute solely engaged with consumer research. It is therefore somewhat appropriate that a large number of the contributors work there.

INTRODUCTION: CONSUMPTION IN THE SOCIAL SCIENCES

Pål Strandbakken, Eivind Jacobsen, Arne Dulsrud and Silje Elisabeth Skuland

Oslo Metropolitan University, Norway

CONSUMERS AND CONSUMPTION IN SOCIAL RESEARCH

It's a truism that we live in a consumer society. Consumption, often understood as the private acquisition and use of goods acquired through monetary exchange in markets, is almost everywhere, engulfing the everyday life of large parts of the human population. For some, consumer society is a synonym for capitalist society, promising affluence, and freedom, but also economic differences, alienation, decadence, littering and waste. Hence, the concept is heavily loaded morally and politically and at the heart of almost every major current political debate (Sulkunen, 2015, p. 150).

The concept is often also used to pinpoint who is in charge of everything, notably the consumer. They are supposed to be 'always right' and thus the one producers and sellers must bow to. However, if the consumer is King, then they are also the ones to blame and shame, for cultural flattening, for resource depletion, for nature and climate crises, for exploitation of the southern working poor, and so on and on. As such, the consumer has been the hero of the political and economic liberals and the villain of the left and sometimes also by the more aristocratic inclined right. This has also had its effects on post-war consumption research. The often left-leaning sociologists have mostly shunned consumption as a research topic, while the more liberal economists and of course the marketing researchers have embraced it.

Hence, today, most consumer research is done in business schools and marketing departments of private firms.[1] This research aims to understand consumers, improve brand management and feed into various forms of corporate decision-making processes. The methodological palette of this research is diverse, feeding on most of the methods in general use in the social and psychological

Consumers and Consumption in Comparison
Comparative Social Research, Volume 37, 1–12

Published under exclusive licence by Emerald Publishing Limited
ISSN: 0195-6310/doi:10.1108/S0195-631020240000037001

sciences. Theoretically though, it mostly ascribes to *psychological and social-psychological models* of the consumer. Consumers are mostly portrayed as individual utility seekers with somewhat restricted rationality. Central to this literature is a focus on *choices* consumers make in *markets*, how these are made and/or arranged. Even though marketing researchers may study how wants, desires and preference are made and developed, their moment of truth is very much the buy/not buy decision of individuals. As such, consumers tend to be portrayed as information processors and decision-makers, driven by rational considerations and various kinds of sentiments. The latter often implies that consumers are seen as subject to biological-evolutionary-derived cognitive biases distorting rational decision-making and opening the door for manipulation and hence room for persuasion, which marketing is all about.

Another major strand of academic consumer literature is preoccupied with the aggregate effect of individual choices, known as *demand*, that is 'the combined quantity that buyers wish to purchase at any conceivable price' (see any textbook, for instance Begg et al., 2003, p. 26). Demand is – of course – together with its twin concept of *supply* and its cousin *price*, the basic building blocks of economics. In this literature, consumers are mostly studied through aggregates supposed to reveal actual *consumer behaviour* in markets. In other words, in this literature, the consumer as such is a black box whose inner life only can be derived from how they prioritize within the limits of their restricted buying power. Besides sharing marketing-researchers attentiveness to choices in markets – understood as transactions, economists also share their concern for how the rationality of these choices tend to be distorted. Transaction costs and information asymmetries pave the way for power imbalances where consumers often end up as the weaker part.

Most of the contributions of this volume belong to a third strand of research, notably sociological consumer research. This strain of research has very much developed in the last 30 years or so, very much within a loose network of European sociologists (cf., European Sociological Association (european-sociology.org). Here, consumption is understood as more broadly entangled in the everyday life and practices of individuals, families and households. In this regard, sociologists aren't only concerned with decision-making in markets but also with the use and ultimate disposal of the products acquired. Acquisition can take place in markets but may just as well be the effect of gifting or other ways of passing goods and services through social networks. Of course, in market-based societies/economies, much acquisition is made through markets where people participate as shoppers. This is understood as a part-time role entangled with other statuses, like being a parent, and activities, like preparing for dinner (Strandbakken, 2018). The use-face of consumption is hard to distinguish from modern life itself. Consumer goods are props in the roleplays and activities of everyday life. Hence, the goods themselves are also social in the very sense of the word, carrying social scripts involving functional as well as normative aspects of use. Some of this research tangent on the humanities, where they study the goods in themselves, as cultural objects with distinct meanings and significance.

Today, this is a growing and thriving field of research, increasingly involving researchers from adjacent disciplines, like anthropology, geography and history and other parts of the world. But in sociology, it started much earlier.

CONSUMPTION IN SOCIOLOGY

Sociology has, since the formative years, had a strong production focus. There has probably also existed a rather naïve idea or 'feeling' that production is a serious and masculine affair, while consumption is superficial and feminine. Sociologists of all political leanings tend to have followed Marx in insisting on the primacy of the economic substructure, known as 'historical materialism.' It is necessary, however, to point to the rather obvious point, that *consumption is the reason why anything is produced.* A slight contempt for consumption among social critics, environmentalists and others tends to obscure this fact. Such critics also need to be reminded that 'consumption' is something more that the clothes shopping of young women. The term 'lifestyle' might seem better when we want to address the whole pattern and volume of consumption in modern countries, but the consumption term works well in conjunction with production.

Even with the aforementioned production focus, classical sociology *did* address consumption from the beginning, but this has gained less attention. Too often, contemporary discourse over consumption is dominated by economists and their focus on demand and consumer rationality. For a sociology of consumption, it is vital to transcend these perspectives, and a good starting point might be to consider some of the contributions from the founding fathers. We will single out contributions from Thorstein Veblen, Georg Simmel and Max Weber that still are theoretically interesting. Karl Marx' differentiation between people's needs and wants also remains relevant, but the concept is changing slightly because it will have to be based on a *social minimum* or sufficiency rather than a biological definition.

Veblen

The *Theory of the Leisure Class: An Economic Study of the Evolution of Institutions* (Veblen, 1899/1994) was published in 1899, and it is basically a political-polemical treatise. But the book introduces ideas and insights that are useful for analyzing some of the more irrational aspects of status competition. In a comparative perspective, it is worth noting that he compared the rich East Coast upper class with what was then regarded as primitive tribes. In an epoch strongly influenced by different versions of social Darwinism, this was a shocking approach and a very interesting use of comparative social research. Beyond this polemic, Thorstein Veblen's lasting contribution is the term *conspicuous consumption*, which remains in the vocabulary of sociologists today. Veblen's work also anticipates some themes and perspectives that appear in Bourdieu's famous study of consumption and lifestyles in *Distinction* (1984b).

Simmel

Georg Simmel's most consumption relevant contribution is his analysis the mechanisms around *Fashion* (1904), where he addresses the trickle-down effects and the interplay between differentiation and imitation between different social strata. Simmel's description of the fashion mechanism may have some similarities with Max Weber's *ideal types* (Strandbakken, 2017), or even with the 'models' used by economists. These two opposing principles transform fashion (in a broad sense of the term) into a mighty social force. Even if the term is trickle-*down*, Simmel mainly describes an upwards striving, where groups and individuals imitate and pursue lifestyles and status symbols of their superiors. The interplay between differentiation and imitation in a specific historical situation is described by the design historian Adrian Forty:

> A constant succession ow new designs was produced in small quantities for middle-class women who wished to be dressed in patterns that had not yet been reproduced on the cheaper fabrics worn by working-class women. It is hard to pin down exactly how the patterns for the middle-class differed from those for the working class and whether they indicated anything about the differences that were supposed to exist between the two classes. In any case, many fashionable designs were subsequently reproduced by the manufacturers on cheap cotton, a practice which both attracted working-class customers wanting to follow the fashion, and caused owners of dresses in the first, expensive printing of a pattern to discard them, because they had become 'common', and to buy new ones. (Forty, 1995, pp. 74–75)

If your approach to class and class conflict has only two strata, upper and lower, you have a situation where the upper only differentiates and the lower only imitates. In a more empirical and realistic model, you will have many strata, and all of the in-between groups will engage in the double praxis of imitating upwards and differentiating downwards. But the top and the bottom groups will have only one motive for their behaviour. This last observation comes from McCracken (1986, p. 94) and is not part of Simmel's article, but it is a development of a theory that remains interesting and relevant more than a century after its formulation.

Another, slightly consumption relevant contribution from Simmel is the essay *The Metropolis and Mental Life* (1903/1971), where he in a surprisingly modern language analyses the transition from slow rural to fast urban ways of life, not similar to the perspectives Walther Benjamin explores in the *Arcades Project* (Benjamin, 1999).

Weber

Max Weber was critical of his Marxist contemporaries that wanted to reduce stratification to only a question of economics. In *Economy and Society* (1978), he introduces a three-dimensional class analysis where he differentiates between wealth, honour and power. Interesting in this context is the emphasis on honourable lifestyles, connected to the idea of *Stand* or status group. The social status of the nobility was in the early modern period not based on its wealth, as it was surpassed by elements of the bourgeoisie. The nobility's superiority was signalled through its consumption and lifestyle (again rather similar to Bourdieu's distinction between cultural and economic capital as described in *Distinction*). At the philosophical level, Marx' class theory probably is superior; ultimately status and power will result from economics, but as an empirical tool for sociological analysis, Weber's approach seems more useful.

THE CONSUMPTION THEME IN MODERN SOCIOLOGY

Prehistory

Even with the classical contributions mentioned above, the sociology of consumption is a rather more recent phenomenon. Frank Trentmann's major work *Empire of Things* (2019), with the elaborate subtitle *How We Became a World of Consumers From the Fifteenth Century to the Twenty-first*, studies the consumption phenomenon through history, but the interesting academic, or partly academic, study of consumption, taking off in the 1960s, tended to concentrate on the post WWII Western societies, characterized by affluence and mass consumption.

In the beginning, studies of consumption were closely connected to the consumer movement. Two of the most interesting studies were Ralph Nader's *Unsafe at Any Speed* (1965), addressing automobile safety, and Vance Packard's *The Waste Makers* (1960), about planned product obsolescence. Neither writer was trained as a sociologist, they were lawyers and journalists, respectively, but their contributions informed and guided early sociological consumer research. Packard actually worked very close to sociology; he addressed class questions in *The Status Seekers* (1959) and marketing in *The Hidden Persuaders* (1957). The critique of 'consumer society' also gained momentum from the emerging environmental consciousness, at the time exemplified by Rachel Carson's *Silent Spring* (1962). This early consumer sociology was oriented towards value for money, consumer rights (Kennedy, 1962), safe products, nutritious food etc. It was politically relevant, but theoretically rather underdeveloped; often based on shallow rational actor models from economics, and the empirical research often utilized quite simple quantitative common sense based studies.

In an article from 2015, Jukka Gronow dismisses this tradition altogether, and claims that *'the sociology of consumption did not really establish itself as a recognized field of social studies until the 1980s and early 1990s'* (Gronow, 2015, p. 41). There existed, however, a parallel academic tradition, where sociologists and philosophers engaged in radical social critique inspired by the upheavals in the 1960s; a neo-Marxist sociology criticizing Western – especially Americanized lifestyles – for its superficiality, its materialism and so on, also contrasted to class differences inside nation states and the huge differences between the rich and poor nations. This early 'critical sociology' was much inspired by perspectives from the Frankfurt School; Horkheimer, Adorno and Marcuse and their 'critical theory'.

One shortcoming with the Frankfurt School, however, is its lack of contact with popular culture. Its practitioners, and their epigons, tended to be isolated in a kind of high culture ivory tower. This gave them an intellectual platform and a 'critical standard' but kept them out of touch with major cultural and political upheavals in the late 1960s and early 1970s.

Here, the British 'cultural studies' tradition becomes relevant. Richard Hoggart and Stuart Hall founded the *Centre for Contemporary Cultural Studies* at the University of Birmingham in 1962. Their theoretical point of departure was the critical theory of the Frankfurt School, but with one important exception:

> British cultural studies systematically rejected high/low culture distinctions and took seriously the artefacts of media culture, thus overcoming the elitism of the Frankfurt School. (Kellner, 1997, p. 144)

In the first 20 years, the Birmingham sociologists pursued a leftist political agenda; aiming at a reconstruction of Marxism and studying themes like feminism, gay liberation, working class subcultures, etc. But in the 1980s, cultural studies underwent a change, to a large degree inspired by postmodernism:

> . . .to celebrations of the popular, the pleasure of consumption and affirmation of a postmodern global culture of multiplicity and difference which lead many in cultural studies to uncritical celebration of 'popular culture'. (Kellner, 1997, p. 147)

The sociology of consumption that Gronow represents was very much born of the tension between the mundane consumer movement emphasis on use value and value for money on the one hand and a postmodern enthusiasm for symbolic value and 'signs' (Gronow, 2015). Gronow and Warde (Eds.). *Ordinary Consumption* from 2001 formulates an empirical critique of cultural studies and of a sociology of consumption that has been too obsessed with the spectacular, with individual choice, with identity and with conspicuous consumption.

THE PRACTICE THEORETICAL TURN

The concept of 'practice', and the theoretical reasonings behind it, has a long and rather complicated history in the social sciences. The list of writers who have been called practice theorists is impressing; it includes not only de Certeau, Foucault, Latour, Giddens and Bourdieu but also philosophers like Heidegger and Wittgenstein in addition to Weber and the early Marx. In our context, however, it seems more correct to start with a new set of contributions, linked to Schatzki (1996) and Reckwitz (2002). Reckwitz' definition goes like this:

> A 'practice' (Praktik) is a routinized type of behaviour which consists of several elements, interconnected to one other: forms of bodily activities, forms of mental activities, 'things' and their use, a background knowledge in the form of understanding, know-how, states of emotion and motivational knowledge. (Reckwitz, 2002, p. 249)

According to him, 'the social' is situated in the practice, and he suggests that the practice should be the smallest unit of the analysis. It is more interesting to study the practice than to study individuals. Without forgetting that the carriers of the (often uncoordinated) practices are individual human beings.

The practice-oriented sociology is often concerned with the body, its routines, etc. This might be seen as an attempt to transcend the classical western distinction between body and mind. According to Reckwitz, the body is never just an instrument that the actor must use to act (p. 251). Terms like body, bodily practices, knowledge, things and routines are central, without us claiming that these terms originated within the practice theoretical tradition. The terms are often employed, however, and often in combination.

A bodily practice, like eating with a knife and fork, dancing, skiing, etc., is a result of training and repetition. For these examples, it is more meaningful to claim that one *is* a body than that one *has* a body. You will never learn to play the guitar by memorizing where to put your fingers in the different chords, as mental knowledge, and then command your body to perform. Everybody knows this; the relevance here is that practice theory tries to be aware of and to consider it in the analyses (see also Gram-Hanssen, 2011).

Specific social practices contain or use specific forms of *knowledge*, but the kind of knowledge that is most often addressed inside practice theory is the implicit, often culturally specific 'tacit' knowledge. According to Reckwitz, even a phenomenon like falling in love presupposes some degree of knowledge about culture, about how to understand oneself and how to understand the other. This kind of knowledge is related to Giddens' non discursive, practical consciousness (Giddens, 1984a, 1984b). Again, this insight does not originate with practice theory, but it is something that practice theoretical sociology tries to take account of.

The Reckwitz quote above highlights routines. It is a matter of how practices appear to be routinized, in the interplay between bodily practices, knowledge and equipment or things. According to this perspective, routinization is the nature of social structure (Reckwitz, p. 255). The different practices use gear and artefacts adapted to the specific activities. As leisure activities, one might mention downhill skiing, golf, fishing and off-road cycling, all depending on specialized equipment. This focusing on the thing, or the product, is a focus on the social. This is also potentially a take on the questions of growth in consumption. *'The activity generates wants, rather than the other way around'* (Warde, 2005, p. 137. See also Heidenstrøm & Strandbakken, 2012, p. 39). The practices we engage in will often depend on equipment/products purchased in the market. This goes for prestigious activities like mountain climbing, gourmet cooking and violin playing too, and not only for the – in the tabloids – much despised stupefying mass consumption.

PRACTICE THEORY IN THE STUDY OF CONSUMPTION AND EVERYDAY LIFE

It is in the combination of the above-mentioned concepts and perspectives that we might identify a 'practice theoretical turn' in the sociology of consumption. Alan Warde's 2005-article *Consumption and Theories of Practice* was a turning point in this regard. Based on the insights from Schatzki and Reckwitz he searched for a new theoretical basis and a programme for the study of consumption, its drivers and organization (p. 132).[2] He pointed to the fact that practice theory neither is individualistic nor holistic. As such, it facilitates for studies of consumption as a phenomenon between freedom and determinacy, between choice and structure.[3] Social practice theory also suits Warde's ambition of studying the ordinary and common rather than the spectacular and as such allows for considering use value and symbolic value simultaneously (after Heidenstrøm & Strandbakken, 2012, p. 37). To support such a position between economists', use value and cultural theorists' symbolic value, Warde gives this long and comprehensive definition of consumption:

> ... I understand consumption as a process whereby agents engage in appropriation and appreciation, whether for utilitarian, expressive or contemplative purposes, of goods, services, performances, information or ambience, whether purchased or not, over which the agent has some degree of discretion. (p. 137)

Warde adds that consumption is not in itself a practice, but that consumption is a moment in most practices. Much of the contemporary European sociology of consumption works inside or is heavily influenced by this practice theoretical turn. So is also several of the contributions to this volume.

COMPARATIVE CONSUMER RESEARCH

At the end of the day, all social science is comparative. You cannot study poverty without some sort of critical standard to compare it with, affluence, theoretical income and fortune equality, etc. The educational choices of girls are interesting when compared to those of boys, or compared with girls' educational choices 30 years ago, or compared with the situation in other countries. We compare across nations, across classes, across ethnicity, gender or at different times. Weber compared regions dominated by Protestants to regions dominated by Catholics. The simple point is that the isolated fact is rather meaningless until it is compared to another fact.

So, the term 'comparative sociological research' should probably be reserved for contributions where the comparative aspect is highlighted and made explicit. The most influential contribution to the sociology of consumption is beyond doubt Pierre Bourdieu's *Distinction. A Social Critique of the Judgement of Taste* (1984a), which was published in France in 1979. Much consumer sociology is dialogue with Bourdieu, and at least until the 'practice turn' (Warde, 2005), it seemed hard to get beyond his theoretical approach.

Bourdieu's material is mainly about the French class system in the early 1970s, most notably the consumption habits and the distribution of economic and cultural capital between different sections of the French elite. His research design, his methods (correspondence analysis) and his theoretical perspectives have been transferred to other national settings, yielding some very interesting results.

ABOUT THE CONTRIBUTIONS IN THIS ISSUE

This issue comprises nine articles about a mixed bouquet of consumer- and consumption-related topics, applying different theoretical and methodological approaches. The contributors belong to different disciplines within the range of the social sciences and humanities, though sociologists dominate the field. Despite the differences, the contributions all share a concern for how consumption and the performance of consumer roles are linked to and makes a difference for wider societal issues. They all explicitly use comparisons to explore this, but what's being compared variates. Some compare consumers or households in different countries or different cities. Others compare different fields of consumption, and others again compare different ways of provisioning and consuming. One article compares different theoretical approaches to consumption, cf. Adolfsson et al.

The first two articles deal with living conditions, economic deprivation and poverty comparing two distinct welfare-state models (cf. Esping-Andersen), the Scandinavian social-democratic and the liberal British. In the first article, Poppe et al. ask how well welfare states protect households in a cost-of-living crisis, comparing the United Kingdom and Norway using survey data measuring financial well-being. Even though there are similarities between the two when it comes to how the effects of the crisis was mitigated, the analysis shows that the respective countries have been fairly faithful to their welfare state models. The United Kingdom has stuck to modest universal transfers, supplied with various means-tested as well as non-means-tested and on-off payments. Norway has on the other hand been equally true to its social-democratic model, marked by universalism, long-lived price subsidies and non-means-tested schemes. Despite this, the empirical analysis shows that the fall in financial well-being was greater in Norway than in the United Kingdom.

The second article, by Brannen et al., uses interview data to study how lone-parent households with a disability or long-term health condition in the United Kingdom and Denmark handle domestic food provisioning and food insecurity. Taking a comparative case approach, it examines parents' strategies and identifies factors or mechanisms operating at different levels that enhance or reduce food security in these households. In both countries the households interviewed rely on the support from family and friends to get by, with some in the United Kingdom also being forced to turn to charity for food. The paper points to evidence that Britain provides insufficient financial support for these households. These food security differences are reflected in the different depth and rates of poverty between the two countries.

In the third article, Andreea Alecu examines cross-national variations in consumer trust. The study employs multilevel hierarchical models on four rounds of surveys covering 30 European countries in the 2014–2020 period. In doing so, it partly accounts for national-level institutional and policy variation, by employing country and year fixed effects. In sum, the study suggests a link between trust in public authorities and markets.

In the fourth article, Wahlen et al. examine the experiences of local activists involved in the food movement scene in Germany (Cologne), Italy (Rome), and the United Kingdom (Bristol), with the objective of comparing strategies in localizing food movement politics and seeking scale for collective action though institutions. Specifically, it delves into the grassroots-driven, bottom-up development of food policies by neo-materialist movement organizations (NMMOs) asking why food has become a central focus, what these organizations do and who participates and how and why strategies for working with local institutions are implemented.

Food consumption and sustainable food system transition is also in focus in the fifth article by Vittersø et al. By a comparison of Europeans' valuations of chicken meat, they discuss social and contextual conditions for consumption change. The study is based on national representative surveys carried out in seven European countries, and concerns peoples' valuations of indirect quality factors related to e.g. place of origin, animal welfare, and production methods (organic, breed). The article concludes that despite integration of markets and harmonization of regulations, consumer roles are shaped quite differently across Europe. These contextual conditions, thus, need to be taken into account when formulating policies for consumption change.

In the sixth article, Haugrønning and Haugsrud explore the influence of gender on clothing consumption and the impact on differences in clothing volumes between men and women. Based on a qualitative and quantitative wardrobe study, they employ theories of social practice with theories on gender performance to examine the relationship between gender and clothing consumption in 15 households in Norway. The study contributes to a better understanding of the social conventions and gender dynamics that shape clothing consumption patterns. Moreover, it underscores the need to consider the implications of gender in sustainable clothing consumption and challenges the prevailing studies on clothing and fashion that often overlook the nuanced practices and actions that influence clothing volumes.

Gender is also the main focus in the seventh article, by Steinnes, looking at young players in online games. Through 41 *play-along* interviews with children and youth aged 10–24 years, she seeks to understand how consumption patterns shape and reinforce gender identities in games, and by which market mechanisms gendered consumption patterns are maintained. The findings are discussed in terms of how gendered consumption influences membership in the gaming culture and encourages the promotion of inclusion in game design and gaming platforms.

The eight article, by Adolfsson et al., explores the differences and similarities of social practice theory and psychological approaches to consumption, popularly known as 'nudge' theory, with the aim to explore the room for breaking out of disciplinary silos and investigate potentials for cross-field pollination. They address this through the empirical case of continuity and change in meat consumption. They demonstrate that while cross-pollination between nudge and practice theories could potentially increase political attention as well as be used to deliver more precise and tailored interventions, the diverging ontological underpinnings of these directions of thought significantly reduce the potential for further co-development.

The ninth and last article, by Hebrok and Heidenstrøm, examines prevailing Western imaginaries of future food consumption. Drawing on a combination of qualitative interviews and online ethnography, the article provides an analysis of the socio-technical imaginaries embedded in two competing Norwegian food provisioning platforms. They identify two distinct imaginaries: One revolving around a technology-enabled efficiency regime characterized by affordable prices, convenience, and a diverse range of familiar food items. The other centred on a community-enabled quality regime, emphasizing ethics, sustainability, co-creation, nutrition, and variation in food offerings. By shedding light on divergent imaginaries of future food consumption, they contribute to a deeper understanding of the socio-technical dynamics influencing food choices and provisioning.

NOTES

1. The global revenue of the market research industry exceeded 81 billion US dollars in 2022 and has grown more than twofold since 2008. The leading market research companies include Nielsen Holdings (US), Kantar (UK), IQVIA (US), Ipsos (France) and GfK Group (Germany). IQVIA was the largest market research company worldwide in terms of revenue in 2021 (Statista, 2024) https://www.statista.com/statistics/242477/global-revenue-of-market-research-companies/.

2. These paragraphs are based on Heidenstrøm and Strandbakken (2012) thoroughly discussion of Warde's article. There they also elaborate on how Warde is positioning his perspectives in relation to Bourdieu (1984a, 1984b, 1990) and Giddens (1984a, 1984b, 1991).

3. On this agency – structure duality in practice theory as applied in consumption research, see also Spargaaren, 1997.

REFERENCES

Begg, D., Fischer, S., & Dornbusch, R. (2003). *Economics* (7th ed.). McGraw-Hill

Benjamin, W. (1999). *The arcades project*. Belknap Press.

Bourdieu, P. (1984a). *Distinction. A social critique of the judgement of taste*. Harvard University Press.

Bourdieu, P. (1984b). *Distinction*. Routledge.

Bourdieu, P. (1990). *The logic of practice*. Stanford University Press.

Carson, R. (1962). *The silent spring*. Houghton Mifflin.

Forty, A. (1995). *Objects of desire: Design and society since 1750*. MW Books Ltd.

Giddens, A. (1984a). *The constitution of society. Outline of the theory of structuration*. University of California Press.

Giddens, A. (1984b). *The constitution of society*. Polity.

Giddens, A. (1991). *Modernity and self-identity. Self and society in the late modern age*. Stanford University Press.

Gram-Hanssen, K. (2011). Understanding change and continuity in residential energy consumption. *Journal of Consumer Culture*, *11*(1), 61–78.

Gronow, J. (2015). Main currents in recent consumer studies. In P. Strandbakken & J. Gronow (Eds.), *The consumer in society*. Abstrakt Forlag.

Gronow, J., & Warde, A. (2001). *Ordinary consumption*. Routledge.

Heidenstrøm, N., & Strandbakken, P. (2012). *Air to air heat pumps in Norwegian households Technological and market development, media analysis, and the use of practice theory to study consumption*, Project note no. 19-2012 SIFO.

Kellner, D. (1997). Social theory and cultural studies. In D. Owen (Ed.), *Owen red: "Sociology after postmodernism"*. Sage.

Kennedy, J. F. (1962, March 15). John F. Kennedy: Special message to the congress on protecting the consumer interest. *presidency.ucsb.edu*. Archived from the original on 14 September, 2018. Retrieved March 8, 2013.

McCracken, G. (1986, June). Culture and consumption: A theoretical account of the structure and movement of the cultural meaning of consumer goods. *Journal of Consumer Research*, *13*(1), 71–84.

Nader, R. (1965). *Unsafe at any speed: The designed-in dangers of the American automobile*. Grossman Publishers.

Packard, V. (1957). *The hidden persuaders*. Longmans, Green & Co.

Packard, V. (1959). *The status seekers*. David McKay Company, Inc.

Packard, V. (1960). *The waste makers*. David McKay Company, Inc.

Reckwitz, A. (2002). Toward a theory of social practices: A development in culturalist theorizing. *European Journal of Social Theory*, *5*(2), 243–263.

Schatzki, T. (1996). *Social practices: A Wittgensteinian approach to human activity and the social*. Cambridge University Press.

Simmel, G. (1903/1971). Simmel, Georg, "the metropolis and mental life". In D.Levine (Ed.), *Georg Simmel on individuality and social forms* (p. 324). Chicago University Press.

Simmel, G. (1904, October) Fashion. *International Quarterly*, *10*(1), 130–155; "Fashion", American Journal of Sociology, n. 62, 1957 [Philosophie der Mode, Pan-Verlag, Berlin 1905].

Spaargaren, G. (1997). *The ecological modernisation of production and consumption: Essays in environmental sociology*. Dissertation, Wageningen: Department of Environmental Sociology. Wageningen University.

Strandbakken, P. (2018). The study of consumption in sociology – Beyond utility theory. In S. Leiulfsrud (Ed.), *Concepts in action. Conceptual constructivism*. Brill Academic Publishers.

Sulkunen, P. (2015). The consumer society and the social bond: The neoliberal turn in Norway. In P. Strandbakken & J. Gronow (Eds.), *The consumer in society*. Abstrakt Forlag.

Trentmann, F. (2019). *Empire of things: How we became a world of consumers, from the fifteenth century to the twenty-first*. Harper.

Veblen, T. (1899/1994). *The theory of the leisure class*. Macmillan.

Warde, A. (2005). Consumption and theories of practice. *Journal of Consumer Culture*, *5*(2), 131–153.

Weber, M. (1978). *Economy and society*. University of California Press.

FINANCIAL WELL-BEING AND THE WELFARE STATE: EFFECTS OF THE COST-OF-LIVING CRISIS IN THE UNITED KINGDOM AND NORWAY

Christian Poppe[a], Jamie Evans[b], Elaine Kempson[b] and Per Arne Tufte[a]

[a]*Oslo Metropolitan University, Norway*
[b]*University of Bristol, UK*

ABSTRACT

From 2021, prices began to rise sharply in many European countries without incomes keeping up. Under such circumstances, households partly depend on government intervention to moderate the effects of inflation. Segments of the population will also depend on welfare schemes to stay financially afloat and avoid severe detriment and poverty. This article asks how well welfare states protect households in a cost-of-living crisis. Based on Esping-Andersen's regime theory, two countries are investigated: the United Kingdom and Norway, which represent the liberal and the social-democratic model, respectively. The empirical analysis shows that both countries introduced first- and second-level measures to mitigate the cost-of-living crisis at the household level. The fall in financial well-being was greater in Norway than in the United Kingdom due to late and less generous second-level targeted payments to vulnerable households. However, while such support may alleviate the difficulties of dealing with price increases, it tends to be time-limited, while high prices persist following periods of rapid inflation. In conclusion, the ideal would be to have generous first-level permanent transfers that protect people's standard of living and to adjust the provisions promptly to compensate as prices increase.

Keywords: Welfare states; financial well-being; regime theory; affordable housing; social policy

Consumers and Consumption in Comparison
Comparative Social Research, Volume 37, 13–37

ISSN: 0195-6310/doi:10.1108/S0195-631020240000037002

INTRODUCTION

In contrast to the COVID crisis, which at the household level was an income shock, the subsequent cost-of-living crisis is an expenditure shock. From 2021, prices began to rise sharply in many European countries without incomes keeping up. Moreover, it was not about price increases on peripheral goods and services but on life necessities such as energy, food and housing. Generally, when prices run wild, households partly depend on government intervention to moderate the effects of inflation and eventually bring it under control, and partially adapt by changing their consumption patterns. Segments of the population will also depend on welfare schemes to stay financially afloat and avoid severe detriment and poverty. Given almost two years of rising prices, this article asks how well households are protected from the effects of the cost-of-living crisis. The question is not least relevant since welfare programs are primarily designed to protect people against income shocks. So, how well are people protected from expenditure shocks?

To answer this question, we look empirically at how households have fared in two welfare states: Norway and the United Kingdom. The two countries were chosen because of their different approaches to welfare. In Esping-Andersen's terms, they represent two different welfare regimes. This article's central assumption is that such regimes provide the countries belonging to them with social policy values and principles, which partly account for the different routes they choose to mitigate the effects of the cost-of-living crisis.

ESPING-ANDERSEN'S REGIME THEORY AND BEYOND

In his groundbreaking book, *The Three Worlds of Welfare Capitalism* (Esping-Andersen, 1990), Esping-Andersen identified three welfare regimes: the *liberal*, the *conservative* and the *social-democratic*. The typology is grounded in the neo-Marxist theory of decommodification (cf. Béland et al., 2021) – i.e., the degree to which welfare regimes '... emancipate individuals from market dependence' (Esping-Andersen, 1990, p. 22) – and the power resource theory, the central thesis being that working-class action can modify capitalism to empower workers (Deeming, 2017, p. 415). One crucial point is that Esping-Andersen defined welfare regimes as a total configuration of welfare measures and not a matter of individual welfare schemes. The typology and its theoretical rationale have proved relevant across many policy areas (Béland et al., 2021, p. 788).

Esping-Andersen's welfare regimes are ideal-typical constructions and empirically measurable. Each country is classified according to how well or poorly they fit with selected welfare indicators. At the country level, cultural and ideological guidelines for handling social problems influence the configuration of welfare schemes. In broad terms, while conservatism believes that the state and the market should not undermine the responsibility of the family to take care of its members and reproduce community values, liberalism claims that a good society must be based on individual freedom on the market and that the state must not interfere with the autonomy of individuals. Socialism, conversely, claims that government intervention in the market is necessary to ensure the well-being of families and the common good. In democracies, where voters express varying ideological preferences in elections, these influences can be thought of as forming a Venn diagram where the common denominator is to ensure some level of welfare. Overlaps and fluid transitions exist between individual countries' welfare schemes. At the same time, the social-political consequences for the citizens are significant across the regimes (Fanning, 2021).

This article is limited to how two countries, the United Kingdom and Norway, have fared during the cost-of-living crisis. They are typical representatives of the liberal and social-democratic welfare regimes respectively. According to Esping-Andersen (1990:26), welfare provision in the former is characterised by '... means-tested assistance [and] modest universal transfers or social-insurance plans', predominantly available only to low-income state dependants under strict and typically stigmatising entitlement rules. The underlying principle is the liberal work ethic, where the level of performance is equal to '... the marginal propensity to opt for welfare instead of work.' In contrast, the social-democratic regime is comparatively more generous, committed to full employment and far-reaching income protection to create the highest possible welfare for all rather than a minimum level for the few who fall outside the labour market (Esping-Andersen, 1990, p. 27). Within this regime, universalism and decommodification are the dominant principles in social policy, supported by '... a strongly interventionist state used to promote equality through a redistributive social security system' (Bambra, 2007, p. 1098).

It falls outside the scope of this article to refer to the colossal academic literature that Esping-Andersen's book has triggered. However, we shall briefly mention two discussions relevant to our analysis. The first concerns the measurement of welfare regimes and the extent to which the three ideal types are stably observable or whether there are other types and additional welfare configurations to consider. Extensive literature reviews have shown that depending on which indicators are included in the measurement instrument, the countries chosen for the analysis tend to fall into varying welfare regimes and form more regimes than those identified by Esping-Andersen. Moreover, while some studies find that the approach is tenable, others have rejected it since only some countries consistently fall into one and only one regime type. In our context, however, it is well worth noting that across these studies, the UK and Norway consistently fall into different categories, mainly those identified by Esping-Andersen. And where the analyses result in other typologies, their labels support the original classification of the two countries. To illustrate, while the United Kingdom is placed in categories such as 'radical', 'basic security', 'low decommodification', and 'low generosity', Norway's position is characterised as 'universalist', 'encompassing', 'high decommodification' and 'high generosity' (cf. Bambra, 2007; Powell et al., 2020).

The second discussion revolves around many studies taking Esping-Andersen's conceptualisation for granted, setting out to criticise or improve it without asking whether something has changed since the book was published in 1990.

One particularly important point from this literature is that the financialisation of the economy, leading to increased individualism, market orientation and largely loan-financed access to welfare for households, has altered the nature of the welfare configuration in the liberal regime and that we are now dealing with a neo-liberal welfare regime (Deeming, 2017). It has drawn social policy away from universality towards a leaner welfare state and extended use of market mechanisms to distribute social and financial well-being to the citizens. It has further implied more means-testing and use of support schemes that are conditional on the recipients assuming a significant share of responsibility for the situation that has arisen (Giddens, 1999). Moreover, the level of state welfare measures has been based on a sharpened minimalist view that it should pay to work. Some countries, notably the UK, have focused more and more on the 'squeezed middle' (working middle-class households) rather than the needs of people experiencing poverty (Deeming, 2017). These ideas have not only changed the liberal regime but also, to a more modest degree, influenced the development of the social-democratic model.

WELFARE STATE CONFIGURATION

Before addressing how well the UK and Norway protect their citizens in a cost-of-living crisis, we should first, in line with Esping-Andersen, look at the overall welfare state configuration as it forms a baseline for living standards across social groups and determines the households' resilience when crises occur. However, it is beyond the scope of this article to provide full-fledged descriptions of all areas of the welfare state since the two systems contain a multitude of arrangements. Rooted in two different regimes, the United Kingdom and Norway are very different in areas such as health and education. Our approach to analysing the welfare effects of the cost-of-living crisis is to look at the principal divisions between the two systems through the lens of two areas: *pensions* and *working-age income replacement provision*. In doing that, regime theory suggest that we should focus on the principles of universality versus targeted assistance and the levels of generosity that define the schemes.

The cost-of-living crisis is strongly related to changes in prices. Fig. 1 shows that the Headline consumer price index has risen by 16% in the United Kingdom and 11.8% in Norway from January 2021 to March 2023. In the same period, the Food CPI (including food and non-alcoholic beverages) increased by 25.8% in the United Kingdom and 10.1% in Norway. Energy CPI rose by 83.7% in the United Kingdom and 43.2% in Norway. Generally, the price level has increased more in Britain than in Norway. It is, in particular, the case for food and energy. We also see that energy prices, particularly in Britain, have increased substantially more than food prices in this period. There is also evidence from the Household Cost Indices that prices increased faster for lower-income households at the start of the cost-of-living crisis as energy bills rose (and later for middle-to-higher income households due to mortgage costs rising).[1]

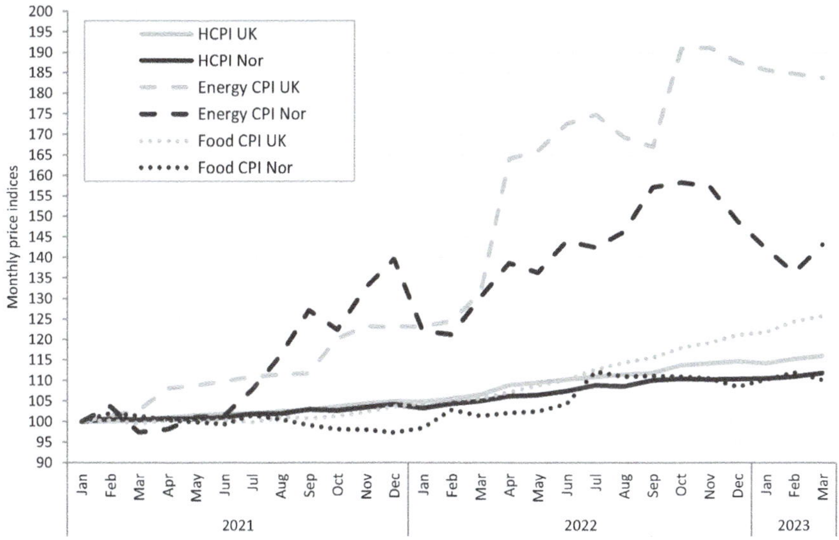

Fig. 1. Monthly Price Indexes (Headline Consumer Price Index, Food CPI and Energy CPI) in the United Kingdom and Norway 2021–2023. *Notes:* https://www.worldbank.org/en/research/brief/inflation-database (Jongrim, H., Ayhan Kose, M., & Ohnsorge, F. (2021). *One-stop source: A global database of inflation.* Policy Research Working Paper 9737, World Bank).

Moreover, when assessing generosity, we must also consider that the income and cost levels differ in the United Kingdom and Norway. Among other things, exchange rates, interest rates, inflation, and different composition of household costs in the two countries complicate such comparisons, but they can still give us an impression. According to the OECD figure (Table 1), the median equivalised annual disposable income in 2021 in Norway was around 80% higher than in the United Kingdom, while the cost of living using the Harmonised Consumer Prices Index was roughly one-third higher (in 2022). Looking at real change in hourly wages, there is an adverse change in both countries, but the reduction is more significant in Britain (−2.7%) than in Norway (−2.4%).

Considering living costs, estimated monthly living costs (without rent) are about 30% higher in Norway than in Britain. On average, childcare accounts for a substantially larger share of wages in Britain. In addition, we see that the increase in living costs is higher in Britain.

A careful interpretation is that these figures indicate that the income level is higher, and the change in real income was less negative in Norway compared to the United Kingdom. Relatively speaking, living costs are higher in Norway, but they do not outweigh differences in income between the two countries, and the recent increase in the cost of living has been higher in Britain.

Regarding welfare arrangements, the Norwegian system is relatively generous compared to the United Kingdom. State pensions, unemployment benefits and

Table 1. Basic Statistics on Incomes and Cost of Living in Norway and the United Kingdom.

		UK	Norway
Income[a]	Median equivalised annual disposable income 2021 in €[b]	24,029€	44,080€
Real wage change[c]	Change in real hourly wages between Q1 2022 and Q1 2023	−2.9%	−2.4%
Inequality and poverty[d]	Income inequality	0.35 (top quarter)	0.29 (bottom quarter)
	Poverty ratio (total)	0.117 (average)	0.079 (bottom third)
	Poverty ratio (children)	0.127 (average)	0.067 (bottom third)
	Poverty ratio – aged 66+	0.145 (average)	0.038 (very low)
Unemployment[e]	Unemployment rate – aged 15+	4.8% (2021)	4.4% (2021)
		3.7% (2022)	3.2% (2022)
Net replacement rate of benefits in unemployment 2022[f]	Single person, no children	50%	78%
	Single person, two children	62%	93%
	Couple, no children, partner out of work	57%	77%
	Couple, two children, partner out of work	64%	91%
	Couple, no children, partner has average wage	66%	87%
	Couple, two children, partner has average wage	69%	92%
Net replacement on retirement[g]	Individual net pension entitlement divided by net pre-retirement earnings, taking account of personal income taxes and social security contributions paid by workers and pensioners	49.0%	55.7%
Cost of living	Estimated monthly costs without rent 2023[h]		
	• Family of four	2,966.0€	4,033.5€
	• Single person	869.7€	1,127.9€
	Childcare costs of couple on average wage's income 2022[i]	29%	8%
	Cost of living increase April 2023	7.8%[j]	6.9%[k]

[a]https://stats.oecd.org/index.aspx?queryid=66670

[b]Median income is converted by the average exchange rate in 2021: £1 = €1.1633 and NOK 1 = €0.09839.https://www.ecb.europa.eu/stats/policy_and_exchange_rates/euro_reference_exchange_rates/html/index.en.html

[c]https://www.worldbank.org/en/research/brief/inflation-database (Jongrim, H., Ayhan Kose, M., & Ohnsorge, F. (2021). *One-stop source: A global database of inflation*. Policy Research Working Paper 9737, World Bank).

[d]https://www.euronews.com/next/2023/08/21/real-wages-are-down-in-europe-which-countries-have-seen-the-biggest-changes-in-salaries

[e]https://www.ilo.org/shinyapps/bulkexplorer2/?lang=en&segment=indicator&id=UNE_2EAP_SEX_AGE_RT_A

[f]https://stats.oecd.org/Index.aspx?DataSetCode=NRR

[g]https://www.oecd-ilibrary.org/sites/75fed0dc-en/index.html?itemId=/content/component/75fed0dc-en

[h]Cost of Living (numbeo.com).

[i]Benefits and wages – Financial disincentive to enter employment with childcare costs – OECD Data.

[j]https://www.ons.gov.uk/economy/inflationandpriceindices/articles/costofliving/latestinsights

[k]https://ec.europa.eu/eurostat/databrowser/view/prc_hicp_manr/default/table?lang=en

disability benefits, for example, are typically paid at 61–63% of previous income (the number of qualifying years varies slightly from benefit to benefit). In the United Kingdom, the state pension is also universal, and for new retirees, it is not means-tested, except for the pension credit, which is a means-tested benefit for those of pensionable age on low income. The state pension is, however, a flat rate and much less generous than the Norwegian state pension. UK pensioners are actively encouraged to take out private pensions. In Norway, old age pensions consist of a fixed basic pension, an additional pension, and a mandatory civil service or company pension, all based on previous income. A full retirement pension for public sector employees born before 1954 is 66% of the income basis. If we look at the proportion of individual net pension entitlements to net earnings before retirement, the United Kingdom has a lower replacement rate (49%) than Norway (55.7%).

Table 1 shows that the unemployment rate went down from 2021 to 2022 in both countries, but the rate is higher in the United Kingdom (4.7% compared to 4.2%). Regarding unemployment allowance, in the United Kingdom, the provisions are means-tested at the household level, and most new claimants would receive Universal Credit. It is much less generous than the sums their counterparts in Norway will receive under the primarily social insurance-based system. Taking the simple case of a single person with no dependants over 25 years becoming unemployed in the United Kingdom in April 2023, he or she would receive a maximum standard rate of €418.51 a month, which would be reduced if the household had any income or savings above €6,810.[2]

In Norway, unemployment allowance is calculated at the individual (as opposed to the household) level. There is a ceiling set at 62.4% of previous income and a maximum payout at €62,297 a year (2023), given that the person had an income of a minimum €15,574 in the last 12 months, or a minimum €31,148 in the last 36 months. For a medium monthly salary of €4,173 the allowance would be €2,604 a month (the calculation basis is the best of income last year or the average of the last 3 years).[3,4] If a person has insufficient qualifying years, they are entitled to social assistance, which is means-tested.

Table 1 illustrates the outcomes of these differences. For example, the net average replacement rate for an unemployed person with no children is 50% in the United Kingdom, compared with 78% in Norway. The corresponding rates for lone parents with two children are 62% and 93%. While for a couple with two children and a partner earning the average wage, they are 69% and 92%, respectively.

Overall, the indicators in Table 1 show that income in general is higher in Norway than in the United Kingdom. Living costs are higher in Norway but in proportion to income lower than in the United Kingdom, and the increase in living costs is also relatively lower. In addition, welfare arrangements are more generous in Norway compared to the United Kingdom. The consequence of these differences can be seen in inequality and poverty measures. In Norway, income inequality, as measured by the Gini coefficient, is 0.26, putting it in the bottom quartile of countries. In the United Kingdom, it is 0.35, meaning the country is in the top quartile. While the overall poverty ratio is 0.084 in Norway, the corresponding rate is 0.112 in the United Kingdom, putting Norway in the bottom third of countries while the United Kingdom is at the average level. The difference in poverty ratios for pensioners is even higher: 0.044 (very low) and 0.131 (average), respectively. In other words, the UK population was potentially more exposed to the cost-of-living crisis than their Norwegian peers.

MITIGATING THE EFFECTS OF THE COST-OF-LIVING CRISIS

In a seminal article, Hall (1993) points out that policymaking is a learning process where decision-making at t_1 is a response to measures implemented at t_0 and their consequences. State policymakers operate customarily within a framework of ideas and standards that specify the goals and instruments and the very nature of the problems they are meant to address. In each policy area, a specific possibility space – according to Hall, a *policy paradigm* – is established that is routinised and fixed but which, under rare conditions, can be challenged and lead to replacing current overarching goals with entirely new policies. When dealing with systemic challenges and calls for political action, three alternative routes are available to policymakers. *First-order* responses involve *modification of basic instrument settings* in the light of experience and new knowledge, while overall policy goals remain the same. Decisions of the *second order* imply keeping the overall goals but *replacing or adding policy instruments* and fine-tuning their settings. *Third-order* responses, by contrast, rarely occur but involve a move from one policy paradigm to another, i.e. *simultaneous changes of goals, the palette of instruments and their settings.*

The cost-of-living crisis undoubtedly has revealed systemic weaknesses in the state's safety net and has the potential to drive a larger part of the population into poverty. Extensive media coverage, popular protests and pressure from political alliances could, in principle, have forced a paradigm shift in social policy. But our data show that this has yet to happen in Great Britain and Norway – or any other Nordic countries belonging to Esping-Andersen's the social-democratic model, for that matter (Greve et al., 2023). Third-order responses require a fundamental change in overall visions for societal development, such as the turn to monetarism in Great Britain in the early 1980s (Hall, 1993) or the broad anchoring of the financialisation of the economy across conservative and socialist divides in the Nordic countries in the 80s and 90s (Sulkunen, 2015). It changed the aims and structure of the welfare schemes, which in both countries were to varying degrees linked to the principle of lower eligibility, i.e. the benefits must be lower than the lowest wages in working life.

Table 2 gives an overview over measures in the United Kingdom and Norway to reduce the effects of energy and general cost-of-living inflation on households 2021–2023. If we relate those measures to Hall's theoretical framework, we see that both Norway and the United Kingdom have used first- and second-order responses to mitigate the cost-of-living crisis. Under their respective paradigms' conceptual basis and objectives, standard instruments were adjusted, and new ones temporarily implemented. Table 2 classifies the measures in the two countries as *universal*, *targeted non-means-tested*, and *targeted means-tested*, respectively.

First-order responses include adjustments of basic welfare instruments such as pensions, unemployment benefits, disability benefits and child benefits for single parents and families with children generally. In the United Kingdom, such

Table 2. Measures to Reduce the Effects of Inflation on Households 2021–2023.

	UK	*N*
General Cost of Living Support		
Universal	*April 2022:* Increase in the amount a worker can earn before national insurance Contributions (a form of taxation) has to be paid.	*May 2022:* The calculation base (*G*) in the national insurance increased by 4.77% (below inflation rate). *May 2023:* The calculation base (*G*) in the national insurance increased by 6.41% (above inflation rate).
Targeted – non-means-tested pensioners	*April 2022:* State pension annual increase (3.1% – well below the inflation rate) *April 2023:* State pension annual increase (10.1% – above the inflation rate) *December 2022 One off cost of living payment: (£300) to all pensioner households (A further £300 payment was made in December 2023)*	*May 2022:* Annual increase in minimum pension corresponding to average wage and price growth (3.53% – below inflation rate). *February 2023:* Increased minimum pension for single pensioners (€350 per month). *May 2023:* Annual increase in minimum pension corresponding to average wage and price growth (6.41% – above inflation rate).
Targeted – non-means-tested disabled	*April 2022:* Annual increase in the Personal Independence payment and Attendance Allowance – to cover the additional costs of disability/social care respectively (3.1% – well below the inflation rate) *April 2023:* Annual increase in the Personal Independence payment and Attendance Allowance – to cover the additional costs of disability/social care respectively (10.1% – above the inflation rate) *September 2022: One-off cost of living payment (£150) for those on non-means-tested disability benefits (a further £150 payment was made in autumn 2023)*	*May 2022:* Disability benefit annual increase in step with increased *G* (4.77% – below the inflation rate) *May 2023:* Disability benefit annual increase in step with increased *G* (6.41% – above inflation rate) *February 2023: One-off payments to persons with disability benefits (€3260).*
Targeted – non-means-tested unemployed		*May 2022:* Unemployment benefit annual increase in step with increased *G* (4.77% – below inflation rate) *May 2023:* Unemployment benefit annual increase in step with increased *G* (6.41% – above inflation rate)

(Continued)

Table 2. *(Continued)*

	UK	*N*
Targeted – non-means-tested families w/children		*March 2023:* Increased child support for children <6 years (from €90 to €95 per month) *March 2023*: Increased child benefit for single parents (from €90 to €218 per month), special tax allowance removed. *July 2023:* Increased toddler allowance for single parents (from €58 to €59 per month)
Targeted – means tested	*April 2022*: Annual increase in means-tested benefits for disabled people, unemployed and others (3.1% – well below inflation rate). *April 2023*: Annual increase in means-tested benefits for disabled people, unemployed and others (10.1% above inflation rate) *February 2022:* £150 (local) council tax rebate *for households in the lowest four tax bands.. And funding for local councils to give assistance to vulnerable people on low incomes in higher council tax bands.* ***July 2022 – April 2023****: three flat rate one-off cost-of-living payments totalling £950 for those on Universal Credit and certain means-tested benefits (July 2022: £324; November 2022 £324; April 2023 £300)*	*June 2022:* Social assistance annual increase (3.4% – below inflation rate). *June 2023:* Social assistance annual increase (10% – above inflation rate) *2022–2023:* Increased housing benefits for low-income families *January 2023: One-off payments to social assistance recipients (€88)* ***January 2023:*** *Additional one-off payments to social assistance recipients with children (€88 per child)* ***February 2023:*** *One-off payment to pensioners with minimum pensions (€88)*
Energy-specific		
Universal	***October 2022:*** *introduction of the Energy Price Guarantee (EPG) – automatically limited the amount charged per unit of gas or electricity, but no reduction in the daily standing charge. This continued until July 2023 when it was revised to make it a reduction in the standing charge.* ***October 2022–March 2023****:* Energy Bills Support Scheme (EBSS) – *a £400 payment to all households* via *their energy supplier made in six monthly payments.* ***October 2022:*** *Alternative Fuel Payments Alternative Fund – £200 one-off payments for households who use alternative fuels (such as heating oil) for heating. Low-income families with pre-payment metres should have received vouchers for £400, but not all did*	***December 2021****: Energy support covering 55% of monthly mean price per kilowatt-hour above NOK 0.875 (inc. VAT) up to 5,000 kwh.* ***January 2022****: Support rate was increased to 80%. Expanded to housing cooperatives and condominiums.* ***September 2022****: Support rate increased to 90%* ***September 2023****: Energy support rate changed from monthly average price to hourly average price.* ***2022–2023****: Reduced electricity charge (elavgift) per kWh Introduction of winter change for January-March*

Table 2. *(Continued)*

	UK	N
Targeted – non-means-tested	***2021:*** *pre-existing one-off Winter Fuel Payment (£150) paid to pensioners annually in December*	***Autumn 2022****: Students living away from home could apply for an extra energy grant of total NOK 1,500.*
Targeted – means-tested	***2021:*** *pre-existing one-off Winter Fuel Payment (£300) paid annually in December to low-income pensioners, people receiving means-tested out of work benefits or in low waged employment receiving tax credits* ***2021:*** *pre-existing Warm Home Discount a reduction of £140 on energy bill to approximately 3 million low-income households* ***November 2022–January 2023:*** *the amount was increased to £150*	***December 2022 – April 2023:*** *Extra energy support for housing benefit recipients (€88 or €131 per month, plus extra €13 for each additional person in the household). About 100,000 households.*

Notes: First-order responses (non-italic), and second-order responses (italic).

instruments have been up-rated during the cost-of-living crisis, but with a six-month time lag between the date when inflation was calculated and the date of implementation. So, when inflation was rising, they were under-compensated. In Norway, cost-of-living support typically came as up-adjusted rates on universal and targeted benefits, several of which followed from the annual rise of the basic amount (the so-called G) for calculating many types of social insurance. On average, the *G* increase was about the same as the growth in wages in 2022 but lower than inflation and exceeded the increase in both wages and inflation in 2023.[5] Moreover, a political tug-of-war in the Parliament led to a boost in some benefits beyond the routine increase of the *G* amount (see Table 2). Despite this, many workless households suffered financial loss since inflation since 2021 has yet to be covered in full by the up-adjusted benefit rates.

Second-order responses are crucial because they are typical crisis measures and not intended to last when normal times are back. In both countries, they include price subsidies and cash transfers (see Table 2). The most important price subsidising measure in the United Kingdom was universal payments to protect households against energy inflation. The UK energy price subsidy was the Energy Price Guarantee, which limited energy price rises to 27% in October 2022 – as opposed to the 80% rise that households would have otherwise faced.[6] Energy prices were also subsidised via a universal flat rate payment from the government to energy companies, who deducted it from bills over several months in winter 2022/23. A modest increase in existing targeted energy bill cash transfers, mostly means-tested, supplemented these schemes. Norway's more generous, long-lived universal price subsidy scheme came one year earlier than in the United Kingdom and has lasted to date. In 2022, it covered, on average, some 43% of energy bills for households living in the South-West where inflation was highest.[7] Additional energy support to recipients of housing benefits was given as targeted means-tested support for the winter 2022–2023. The subsidy scheme has been particularly important for low-income households and other vulnerable groups such as disabled people, single parents, and housing benefit recipients (Dalen & Halvorsen, 2022).

In addition to price subsidies for energy inflation, both countries have implemented one-off cash payments for particularly vulnerable groups. The targeted (and largely means-tested) one-off cost-of-living cash transfers in the United Kingdom came earlier and were much more generous than the Norwegian ones (see Table 2). The different approaches to using cash transfers are consistent with the two countries' respective welfare models.

The measures against the cost-of-living crisis came late. Apart from the Norwegian universal energy subsidy and some one-off payments to vulnerable groups facing energy-poverty in the United Kingdom, they predominantly only occurred during autumn/winter 2022/23, i.e. just over a year after prices started to rise. Both countries have yet to compensate households for the price increase from 2021. The delays in compensating people for inflation tend to leave people on low incomes with severe financial difficulties that are difficult to reverse.

METHODS AND DATA

We analyse cross-sectional, nationally representative survey data of households in Norway and the United Kingdom, collected at three time points between 2021 and 2023. The UK data were collected online using YouGov's consumer panel in October 2021 (N = 5,770), July 2022 (N = 5,716) and May 2023 (N = 5,766), while Norwegian householders from Norsk Gallup's panel were surveyed online in June 2021 (N = 1,938), June to August 2022 (N = 4,200) and March 2023 (N = 3,446).[8,9] While there was a four-month gap between each country's surveys in 2021, we consider both to be reflective of a (mostly) post-lockdown, pre-cost-of-living-crisis situation. The surveys in both countries were aligned from inception, both using adapted versions of an approach to measure financial well-being first conceptualised by Kempson et al. (2017).

Both sets of surveys asked a set of core questions (translated into their respective languages) about how households are coping with their day-to-day finances and credit commitments and the extent to which they have the financial resilience to meet unexpected expenses or cope with income shocks. These questions form the basis of a financial well-being score computed for all respondents, which runs from 0 to 100 – with 0 representing the worst a respondent could possibly score and 100 representing the best. This score is constructed by recoding each financial well-being question so that all run in the same direction, with low values representing 'poor' financial well-being and high values representing high levels of financial well-being. Confirmatory principal component analysis (Hair et al., 2014 Chapter 14) is then used to ensure that the grouping of variables form a coherent single underlying measure of 'financial well-being.' The variables grouped together here were: assessment of current financial situation; how much of a struggle to pay for food and other necessities;

how much of a struggle to pay bills and other commitments; arrears including payment holidays on bills and household commitments; ability to cover an unexpected bill equivalent to a month's income; how long could make ends meet if experienced a fall in income of a third or more; and amount held in savings. Factor scores are then estimated and re-scaled from 0 to 100 (Kempson et al., 2017; Poppe & Kempson, 2023a).

This enables a comparison of financial well-being of households in the United Kingdom and Norway at each time point in 2021, 2022 and 2023, predominantly through descriptive statistics. Further sub-group analysis is also conducted where equivalent socio-economic or demographic variables were collected in both countries and at all time points, thus enabling deeper understanding of the way in which financial well-being had changed for different types of households in either country over the course of the cost-of-living crisis. In particular, we consider gross annual household income (categorised into comparable bands across the two countries based on the average exchange rate for 2022), workless households (where neither the respondent nor their partner were in work and where they were also not retired or in full-time study), and by age group (comparing those aged 67 or over, i.e. pension age in Norway, with those aged 18–66).

RESULTS

Analysis of financial well-being scores reveals that, on average, Norwegians had considerably higher levels of financial well-being than Britons prior to the cost-of-living crisis, with mean financial well-being scores of 81.3 and 66.5 respectively (Table 3). In both countries, mean scores reduced from 2021 to 2023 – by 8.6 points in Norway and 7.1 points in the United Kingdom. Examining medians presents a slightly different pattern, with median scores declining to a greater extent in the United Kingdom (by 10.5 points, compared with 7.7 in Norway). This suggests that different parts of the financial well-being distribution in each country may have experienced differing impacts over the course of this period.

Figs. 2 and 3 explore this in more detail. Fig. 2 shows the average financial well-being score for each 5% of the population (in terms of financial well-being score) in each country in 2021 and 2023. It demonstrates that Norwegian households were had considerably higher levels of financial well-being than their UK counterparts in all but the top 5% of households in both 2021 and 2023, but that the decline in financial well-being has been larger for those towards the lower end of the distribution. In contrast, the decline in financial well-being in the United Kingdom has been more evenly distributed, with those just above the top half seeing the most significant declines.

This is shown more clearly in Fig. 3, which also gives the change in average scores for each 5% vingtile between each individual survey wave (rather than just the change over the whole period). In both countries this shows a substantial decline in financial well-being between 2021 and the summer of 2022, in line with the energy crisis triggered by the Russian invasion of Ukraine, but there were somewhat diverging patterns from that point to spring 2023. While in Norway,

Table 3. Average Financial Well-being Score (0 = Low, 100 = High) in the United Kingdom and Norway at Each Survey Wave.

Country	Time Point	Mean	Median	Standard Deviation	*N*
Norway	June 2021	81.3	87.2	18.2	1,938
	June/August 2022	74.0	79.7	21.7	4,200
	March 2023	72.8	79.5	23.4	3,446
	Change 2021 to 2023	−8.6	−7.7	5.2	
UK	October 2021	66.5	70.3	25.6	5,770
	July 2022	60.5	62.0	27.5	5,716
	May 2023	59.4	59.8	25.8	5,766
	Change 2021 to 2023	−7.1	−10.5	0.1	

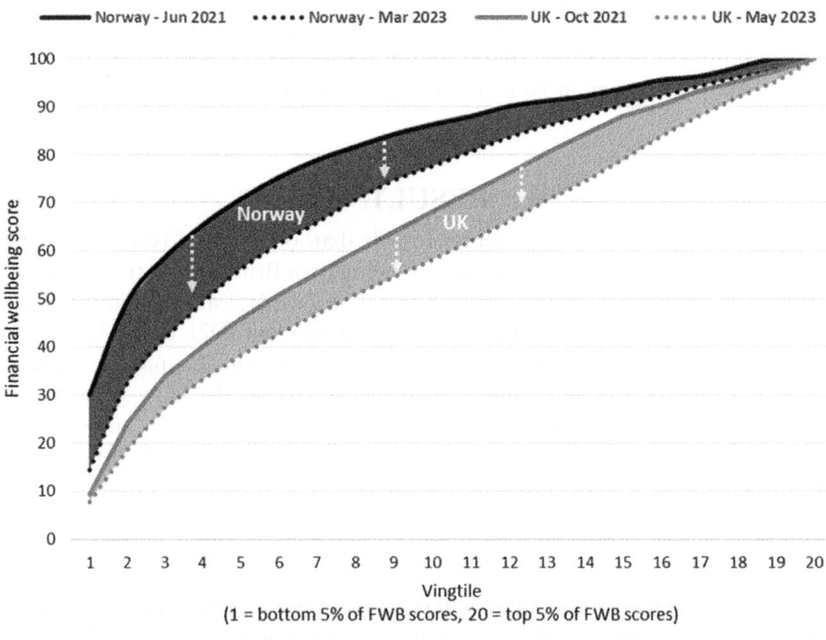

Fig. 2. Mean Financial Well-being Scores for Each Vingtile (5% Group of the Population Based on Financial Well-being Score), in Norway and the United Kingdom in 2021 and 2023. *Notes:* Unweighted sample sizes as follows: Norway – Jun 2021 = 1,938, Mar 2023 = 3,446; UK – Oct 2021 = 5,770, May 2023 = 5,766.

financial well-being continued to decline most among those at the bottom of the distribution, in the United Kingdom those in the bottom 15% actually saw an improvement in financial well-being scores, with those further up the distribution seeing falls – though not to the same extent as seen in the previous period.

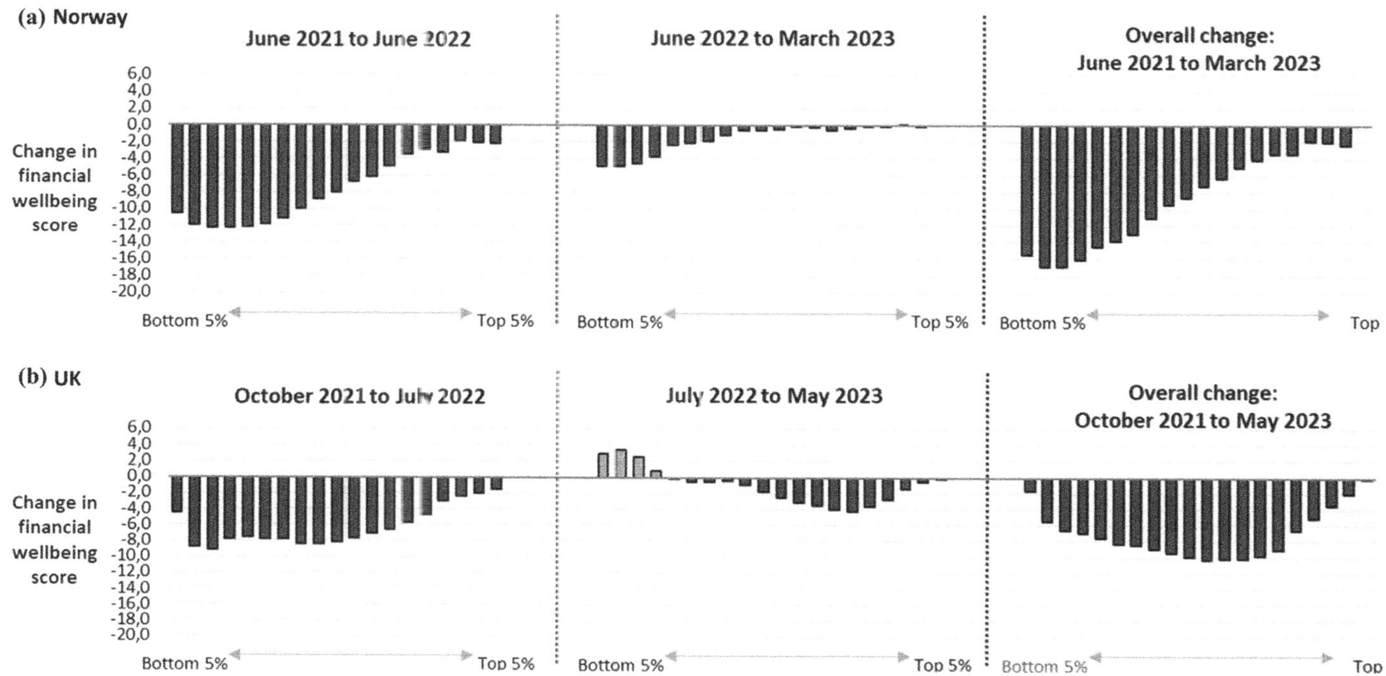

Fig. 3. Change in the Mean Financial Well-being Score of Each Vingtile (5% Group of the Population Based on Financial Well-being Score), in Norway and the United Kingdom Between Different Time Points (2021–2023). (a) Norway, (b) UK. *Notes:* Unweighted sample sizes as follows: Norway – Jun 2021 = 1,938, Jun 2022 = 4,200, Mar 2023 = 3,446; UK – Oct 2021 = 5,770, Jul 2022 = 5,716, May 2023 = 5,766.

Table 4 breaks down mean financial well-being scores further within each country, considering changes over time for different income groups, for workless households where neither the respondent or partner was in work, retired or a full-time student, and for those of pensionable age. Regarding income, we use raw income before housing costs (BHC) and not income equivalised for household size.[10] The income breakdown reveals a similar pattern to those previously shown, whereby those on the lowest incomes (below 200,000 NOK/£15,000) saw a greater decline in financial well-being in Norway than they did in the United Kingdom. It is still noteworthy, however, that low-income households in Norway score five points higher than their counterparts in the United Kingdom.

Similarly, workless households in Norway saw a larger fall in financial well-being score (10.5-point decline) than in the United Kingdom (6.0-point decline), though mean scores still remain substantially higher overall for this group in Norway (50.9, compared with just 36.0 in the United Kingdom). The picture for pensioner households is somewhat different. It shows that, in both countries, pensioners' mean financial well-being scores are far higher than those for workless households, albeit higher in Norway than in the United Kingdom. In this case, though, the fall in financial well-being was lower in Norway than in the United Kingdom. Moreover, the decline for Norway's pensioners was a great deal lower than it was for the country's workless households. In the United Kingdom, it was slightly higher .[11]

WELFARE DETRIMENTS

Table 5 shifts focus from our composite financial well-being score to the crisis's consequences for the two populations' living conditions. It largely demonstrates considerably worse outcomes for UK households than those in Norway regarding financial outcomes and increased shares with reduced living conditions related to energy and food. It applies both among the population as a whole and specifically to workless households.

When prices accelerate, households risk ending up in a precarious financial situation – some immediately because they lack buffers, others later because they use up their reserves and eventually have nothing left to go on. After two years of sharp price increases, more than two out of ten households in the United Kingdom and more than one out of ten in Norway constantly struggle to pay for food and other necessary expenses. And the proportion ended up in payment problems approached two out of ten households in both countries, with the United Kingdom having a slightly higher proportion than Norway.

Furthermore, when the prices of essential goods and services rise sharply simultaneously, many people must prioritise scarce resources and reduce consumption to break even. It applies not least to critical consumption areas such as energy and food. Although many have room to manoeuvre, financially weak households are at risk of suffering severe welfare detriments.

Regarding energy, the table shows that after two years of price increases, many households have suffered welfare detriments in terms of turning down the

Table 4. Mean Financial Well-being Scores by Income, Workless Household Status and Age Group, By Country and Time point.

		Norway				UK			
		Jun 2021	Jun–Aug 2022	Mar 2023	*Change 2021 to 2023*	Oct 2021	Jul 2022	May 2023	*Change 2021 to 2023*
Annual gross household income	Under 200,000 NOK/Under £15,000	65.3 (59)	64.5 (79)	51.2 (87)	*−14.1***	49.0 (760)	45.6 (815)	46.2 (806)	*−2.7**
	200,000–399,999 NOK/ £15,000–£34,999	69.3 (204)	58.2 (472)	56.8 (375)	*−12.5***	64.4 (1,717)	56.2 (1,641)	56.6 (1,622)	*−7.8***
	400,000–599,999 NOK/ £35,000–£49,999	80.6 (350)	70.7 (747)	69.5 (610)	*−11***	69.6 (887)	63.9 (912)	63.3 (923)	*−6.3***
	600,000–799,999 NOK/ £50,000–£69,999	81.4 (290)	77.6 (666)	75.4 (507)	*−6.0***	73.8 (618)	68.0 (646)	65.3 (668)	*−8.5***
	800,000–1,199,000 NOK/ £70,000–£100,000	84.6 (493)	77.6 (1,062)	77.1 (870)	*−7.5***	77.2 (396)	73.1 (388)	69.2 (362)	*−8.0***
	1,200,000 NOK or more/£100,000 or more	90.3 (305)	86.6 (623)	84.7 (617)	*−5.5***	82.5 (217)	82.2 (220)	74.9 (276)	*−7.7***
Pensioners	Pensionable age	88.2 (428)	82.3 (928)	83.7 (728)	*−4.4***	78.3 (1,335)	73.5 (1,346)	71.4 (1,413)	*−6.8***
Workless household	Workless household	61.8 (108)	51.0 (246)	50.9 (231)	*−10.8***	42.0 (474)	36.0 (468)	36.0 (467)	*−6.0***

Notes: asterisks denote statistically significant change between 2023 and 2021, whereby $p < 0.05$ = * and $p < 0.01$ = **. Figures showing the change from 2021 to 2023 may not appear to add up correctly due to rounding. Unweighted sample sizes shown in brackets. Pensionable age defined as households where the respondent was aged 67 or above. The income figures exclude those who did not provide their income. Workless households defined as households where neither the respondent nor their partner was in paid work, retired or a student.
Figures in brackets denote unweighted sample size.

Table 5. Effects of the Cost-Of-Living Crisis, by Country in 2023.

	All Households (%)			Workless Households Only (%)			Pension Age Households Only (%)		
Question	UK (May 2023)	Norway (March 2023)	*Difference between UK and Norway*	UK (May 2023)	Norway (March 2023)	*Difference between UK and Norway*	UK (May 2023)	Norway (March 2023)	*Difference between UK and Norway*
Overall Financial Situation Indicators									
Currently struggling to pay for food or other necessary expenses = 'fits very/fairly well'	22.8	11.6	*11.2***	47.9	34.9	*13.0***	12.7	4.9	*7.8***
Ability to meet bills and credit commitments at the moment = 'constant struggle'	14.7	5.3	*9.5***	40.9	20.1	*20.7***	6.1	1.2	*4.8***
Missed at least one payment on household bills or credit commitments	18.3	15.8	*2.5***	35.2	28.5	*6.7***	4.1	5.6	*−1.5*
Actions Taken in Last Six Months to Afford Energy Bills									
Turned down the temperature in your home	57.9	41.1	*16.7***	53.6	50.5	*3.2*	63.2	30.1	*33.1***
Only heated part of your home	33.5	21.0	*12.5***	37.8	28.7	*9.1**	38.3	17.8	*20.5***
Reduced the use of the cooker/oven	42.0	13.9	*28.0***	55.4	33.5	*21.9***	46.8	9.3	*37.5***
Switched electricity/gas consumption (e.g. washing machine, dishwasher) to times of day when the tariff is cheaper	17.9	34.7	*−16.8***	19.8	40.6	*−20.8***	17.7	30.8	*−13.1***
Wearing more clothes than usual to keep warm indoors	58.7	27.2	*31.4***	65.6	40.2	*25.4***	61.8	20.5	*41.2***
Cut back spending on food	32.6	17.2	*15.4***	52.6	29.3	*23.2***	21.5	4.8	*16.7***
Actions Taken to Afford Food/Levels of Food Insecurity									
Cut down on electricity/heating to afford food	21.2	24.7	*−3.4***	46.2	44.2	*2.0*	14.9	11.9	*3.0*
Cut back on other expenses to afford food	23.9	27.8	*−3.9***	47.0	52.7	*−5.7*	13.3	10.4	*2.8*
Accessed a food bank	6.5	3.5	*2.9***	14.6	8.6	*6.0**	1.7	0.4	*1.2**
Received food vouchers/help with food from government body	3.1	3.1	*0.0*	9.2	8.5	*0.7*	0.7	0.1	*0.5*

Food Security Index									
Low or very low levels of food security	23.3	13.3	*10.6***	50.3	31.5	*18.8***	7.0	1.9	*5.1***
Very low levels of food security	5.1	4.5	*0.6*	18.8	13.8	*5.0*	1.2	0.0	*1.2*

Notes: asterisks denote statistically significant differences between UK and Norway, whereby $p < 0.05$ = * and $p < 0.01$ = **. Unweighted sample sizes as follows: All households – UK = 5,766, Norway = 3,446; Workless households only – UK = 461, Norway = 230; Pension age households only – UK = 1,413, Norway = 728. Food security index is an eight-item adaptation of the food security index used within the Family Resources Survey. Households who had done 3–5 of the following things in the past month were considered to have 'low food security', while those who had done 6–8 were considered to have 'very low' food security: Ate less than you felt you should because there wasn't enough money for food; Been hungry but didn't eat because there wasn't enough money for food; Lost weight because there wasn't enough money for food; Missed three or more meals because there wasn't enough money for food; Not eaten for a whole day on three or more occasions because there wasn't enough money for food; Been worried about running out of food before you can afford to buy more; Run out of food and been unable to afford more; Not been able to afford a balanced and healthy diet.

temperature indoors, only heating parts of the home and using the cooker/oven less than they would otherwise have done. Many have also had to wear more clothes indoors than usual to keep warm. Compared with Norway, UK households are worse off on all these welfare indicators. The difference in prevalence varies between 13 and 32 percentage points. Furthermore, a third of UK households have faced the choice between electricity and food and chose to reduce food consumption to afford energy bills, which is twice as many as in Norway. The difference is just as big concerning using energy-intensive devices such as washing machines, dishwashers, and car chargers when electricity prices are lowest. But this time, it is to Norwegian households' disadvantage; this rearrangement of every day routines is much more common in Norway (though it should be noted that this likely relates to time-dependent energy tariffs being much more common in Norway than in the United Kingdom).

In the area of food, the difference between the two countries is considerably smaller. On some welfare indicators, the proportions experiencing deterioration are slightly larger in Norway. On the other hand, while an equal proportion of households received food vouchers or help with food from a government body, larger shares of households in the United Kingdom had accessed a food bank in 2023. This is partly because there are many more of those in that country. But this does not explain why low food security, which is purely poverty-related, is much more widespread in the United Kingdom, although the proportion with very low food security is roughly the same in the two countries.

The same patterns and differences apply to workless households, i.e., those of working age who have no income from work. Since these are groups for which the welfare state traditionally has a special responsibility, it is significant that, in both countries, the proportion is higher compared to the rest of the population. However, Norwegian workless households did better than their UK counterparts on all energy measures, reflecting the higher levels of benefit payments in Norway. But for food there was much less difference and, again, the proportions of households with very low food security were not statistically different.

Regarding pensioner households, the energy indicators suggest pension age households also fared better in Norway than in the United Kingdom. It reflects the more generous Norwegian state pensions, and that, with colder temperatures in Norway, older people are less likely to economise on heating. But on the food indicators, the differences between Norway's and the United Kingdom's pensioner households were much smaller and often not statistically significant.

Moreover, in both countries, pensioners fared much better than workless households in terms of food and the overall financial situation. The same also applied to Norwegian pensioners on the energy indicators. But in the United Kingdom, saving money on energy bills was just as common among pensioners as among workless households of working age. Still, the overall impression is that pensioners are far better protected than the workless in both countries.

CONCLUSION

So, how well are households protected against the effects of the cost-of-living crisis in the United Kingdom and Norway? Let us start by saying that the cost-of-living crisis has yet to lead to any fundamental restructuring of social policy in either of the two countries. The crisis has been handled in both places using first- and second-order responses (Hall, 1993). It means that attempts to mitigate the effects of the crisis have been through a 'business as usual' approach, where traditional instruments have been sharpened, and some new but familiar types of measures have been implemented. In general, our data show that the population in both countries has experienced reduced financial well-being.

Still, there are striking differences in the countries' handling of the cost-of-living crisis. Norway and the United Kingdom belong to different welfare regimes (Esping-Andersen, 1990) and, therefore, have different political mindsets when mitigating the effects of the crisis. While the United Kingdom has stuck to modest universal transfers, with non-means-tested as well as means-tested assistance and one-off payments as the main track, Norway has been equally faithful to the social democratic approach marked by universalism, long-lived price subsidies, and targeted non-means-tested schemes. The difference between the two approaches is well illustrated by the generous price subsidies for energy that both countries introduced. But this measure came late and the universal element of it was short-lived in the United Kingdom, whereas it was introduced early as a long-lasting universal response in Norway.

Given these differences, it is reasonable to expect that the effects of the mitigation measures are different in the two countries and that the different approaches to social policy account for a significant part of these differences. Overall, our data shows that Norwegian households had higher financial well-being for almost all groups, both before and two years into the cost-of-living crisis. It is only at the top end of the well-being continuum that the scores in the two countries are roughly the same. Norwegian households were better prepared to weather the crisis than their British counterparts. This readiness can be traced back to long-term, stable, and generous welfare transfers in the decades leading up to the crisis, partly made possible by high state revenues from the oil industry. Following Russia's invasion of Ukraine in February 2022, the lack of energy in Europe caused oil and gas prices to spike, further enabling a continuous high level of generosity. In addition, higher taxes on energy-producing enterprises with extraordinary profits were introduced. But using state funds for welfare is not a matter of course. The Norwegian approach to the crisis follows from the political mindset characteristic of the social-democratic welfare regime – a willingness to redistribute resources across the population and maintain high public expenditure and increased transfers to households even in times of high inflation.

On the other hand, there has been a drop in financial well-being in both countries. Obviously, Norway and the United Kingdom could have done more to protect households during the cost-of-living crisis. However, this particularly applies to Norway. Between June 2021 and March 2023, the fall was more extensive in Norway and greatest among those with the lowest scores initially.

Moreover, not only was the drop in well-being scores greater on average in Norway than in the United Kingdom, but the analysis shows that between June 2022 and March 2023, the scores actually improved for the bottom 15% of the UK household population, whereas they continued to decline in Norway. Considering the Norwegian state's finances and roots in the social-democratic model, this appears paradoxical, especially when the drop was greatest in the lowest income bands, while better-off households were protected to a greater extent.

A likely explanation lies in the relationship between first- and second-order measures and the principles of social policy embedded in the two welfare regimes. Both countries have implemented a series of first-order measures to mitigate the effects of the crisis. Whether universal, targeted, or means-tested, up-rating such instruments is vital in protecting people from sudden and enduring price rises, provided they are generous enough. Still, as crisis instruments, first-order responses are often insufficient. Although they are routinely increased, they are based on economic data from the previous year or estimated developments in the current year. In times of rapid change, the decision-making basis tends to be incorrect or uncertain, and the measures too late and too scant.

So, to differing degrees, both countries have supplemented first-order responses with second-order crisis policies: price subsidies and targeted cash transfers. However, second-order responses typically lie on the borderlands of policy paradigms. For example, universal price subsidy is basically a foreign element in liberal thinking centring on individual responsibility, limited market intervention and a minimal state (Spicker, 2013). On the other hand, targeted one-off payments are, in principle, inconsistent with the universalist social-democratic model. Therefore, we have seen different second-order practices in the two countries. One-off cost-of-living payments came earlier in the United Kingdom and were more generous than similar measures in Norway. The reverse applied to universal and targeted schemes.

Price subsidies – when they are timely, generous and long-lasting, as in Norway for energy prices – have greater potential than cash transfers to maintain the financial well-being of the population. But where they are universal, they tend to benefit the better off more than people with low incomes. Experience from the United Kingdom suggests that targeted and generous payments to vulnerable households are more effective. Comparing the two countries, the analyses indicate that the lack of focus on one-off payments and other targeted second-order measures in Norway, especially in the early stages of the crisis, was an important reason for the drop in financial well-being among Norwegians with the lowest scores initially. And when these types of measures first arrived, they came too late and were too parsimonious to reverse the trend of falling well-being. It affected the low-income groups the most since they had the least resistance to price increases (Poppe & Kempson, 2023b). Furthermore, when prices spiked, and social benefits did not follow suit, those who depended on social support were hit the hardest (Poppe & Kempson, 2023a). The cost-of-living crisis has thus exposed the Norwegian welfare state's weak ability to protect the poorest against expenditure shocks.

On the other hand, second-order provisions are temporary, designed to be withdrawn once the crisis is over. One-off payments may alleviate the difficulties vulnerable households face dealing with price increases, but they tend to be time-limited while high prices following a period of rapid inflation persist. Moreover, they tend not to compensate adequately for the rising cost of living (Evans et al., 2023). It is demonstrated by the number of people using food banks in the United Kingdom, which goes down when a cost-of-living payment is made, only to return to the same level when the money runs out. The recipients would likely be better off with increases in permanent transfers such as Universal Credit (Morgan, 2023).

In conclusion, the ideal would be to be to have generous first-order benefit levels that protect people's standard of living and to adjust the provisions promptly to compensate as prices increase. However, constantly adjusting payment levels is unrealistic. Therefore, second-order policy responses are always needed, targeting those most in need of protection. Moreover, second-order responses should be consolidated into basic benefit levels as soon as it is practical. On the issue of price controls versus cash transfers, it is probably a matter of practicality. The same goes for universal versus targeted measures.

NOTES

1. Household Costs Indices for UK household groups – Office for National Statistics (ons.gov.uk).
2. Converted by the average exhange rate in April 2023: £1 = €1.1350. https://www.ecb.europa.eu/stats/policy_and_exchange_rates/euro_reference_exchange_rates/html/index.en.html
3. https://www.ssb.no/arbeid-og-lonn/lonn-og-arbeidskraftkostnader/artikler/hva-er-vanlig-lonn-i-norge
4. Alle amounts are converted by the average exchange rate in 2023: NOK1 = €0.08753. https://www.ecb.europa.eu/stats/policy_and_exchange_rates/euro_reference_exchange_rates/html/index.en.html
5. See https://www.regjeringen.no/no/aktuelt/grunnbelopet-og-pensjonene/id2913481/; https://www.smartepenger.no/div/776-inflasjon; https://www.nav.no/grunnbelopet
6. See House of Commons Library (2024) Domestic energy prices. Available at: Domestic energy prices – House of Commons Library (parliament.uk).
7. https://e24.no/energi-og-klima/i/9zXKmq/staten-betalte-naer-33-mrd-i-stroemstoette-i-fjor
8. YouGov's UK Consumer Omnibus panel includes adults aged 18 plus in the United Kingdom who have been pre-recruited from a range of sources, including standard advertising and partnerships with a range of websites. Survey samples are designed to achieve national representation of UK adults in terms of age, gender, social class, and education. A combination of sample quotas and post-stratification weighting. Interlocking quotas are included for education status, age, and gender; for example, to achieve a sufficient sample of males aged 40–49 with a low level of education. Data on survey response rates was not available for the UK surveys. For more information on YouGov's panel, please see: www.yougov.co.uk/about/panel-methodology
9. Norsk Gallup's access panel is a pre-recruited selection of people over the age of 15 who are willing to participate in surveys (currently approx. 40,000 people). The participants are recruited randomly through other telephone (landline and mobile) and postal surveys and form an active panel. A more recent international compilation of non-probability selection and probability selection in panel designs in election surveys

shows that the latter shows better accuracy and is clearly recommendable (Cornesse et al., 2020). Non-response varies somewhat across the samples. In April 2023, 39% of those contacted opened the form. Those who completed the questionnaire make up around 95% of those who opened the form and 37% of all invitations sent out. The corresponding figures for 2022 and 2021 are 31–97–30 and 35–96–34%, respectively. The samples include adults 18–80 years and are designed to achieve national representation in terms of gender, age, place of residence (4 regions) and level of education (2 categories).

10. Raw income (before housing costs (BHC)) is used in preference to equivalised or 'after housing costs' (AHC) measures as data did not exist in all three time points in each country, which would have enabled us to produce such measures. We did, however, explore the impact of such measures for the May 2023 UK survey, where such data did exist. This revealed a reasonably small impact of equivalisation on average financial well-being (FWB) scores for different income quintiles but a slightly more substantial impact when using an AHC measure. For example, for the bottom income quintile, mean FWB changes as follows using different measures: non-equivalised, BHC = 46.4 (out of 100); equivalised, BHC = 45.6; equivalised, AHC = 43.7.

11. Building on this, we explored the extent to which changes in different groups' financial well-being have led to changes in the socio-economic composition of different quintiles of financial well-being over time in either country. Overall, this shows little change in the fundamental composition of each quintile over time in each country.

REFERENCES

Béland, D., Morgan, K J., Obinger, H., & Pierson, C. (Eds.). (2021). *The Oxford handbook of the welfare state*. Oxford University Press.

Bambra, C. (2007). Going beyond the three worlds of welfare capitalism: Regime theory and public health research. *Journal of Epidemiology and Community Health*, *61*(12), 1098–1102. https://doi.org/10.1136/jech.2007.064295

Cornesse, C., Blom, A. G., Dutwin, D., Krosnick, J. A., De Leeuw, E. D., Legleye, S., Pasek, J., Pennay, D., Benjamin, P., Sakshaug, J. W., Struminskaya, B., & Wenz, A. (2020). A review of conceptual approaches and empirical evidence on probability and nonprobability sample survey research. *Journal of Survey Statistics and Methodology*, *8*(1), 4–36. https://doi.org/10.1093/jssam/smz041

Dalen, H. M., & Halvorsen, B. (2022). *konomiske konsekvenser av høye kraftpriser og strømstønad en empirisk studie av stønadsberettigede husholdninger, jordbruks- og veksthusforetak*. Statistisk sentralbyrå.

Deeming, C. (2017). The lost and the new 'liberal World' of welfare capitalism: A critical assessment of Gøsta Esping-Andersen's *the three Worlds of welfare capitalism* a quarter century later. *Social Policy and Society*, *16*(3), 405–422. https://doi.org/10.1017/S1474746415000676

Esping-Andersen, G. (1990). *The three worlds of welfare capitalism*. Polity Press.

Evans, J., Cross, K., & Collard, S. (2023). *Turning a corner? The financial wellbeing of UK households in October 2023*. PRFC, University of Bristol.

Fanning, B. (2021). *Three roads to the welfare state: Liberalism, social democracy and Christian democracy*. Policy Press.

Giddens, A. (1999). Risk and responsibility. *The Modern Law Review*, *62*(1).

Greve, B., Harsløf, I., Van Gerven, M., Nieuwenhuis, R., & Strigén, J. (2023). How have the Nordic welfare states responded to the unexpected increase in inflation? *Social Policy and Society*, *23*(1), 1–13. https://doi.org/10.1017/S1474746423000313

Hair, J. F., Black, W. C., Babin, B. J., & Anderson, R. E. (2014). *Multivariate data analysis* (7th ed.). Pearsons.

Hall, P A. (1993). Policy paradigms, social learning, and the state: The case of economic policymaking in Britain. *Comparative Politics*, *25*(3), 275. https://doi.org/10.2307/422246

Kempson, E., Finney, A., & Poppe, C. (2017). In *Financial well-being. A conceptual model and preliminary analysis. SIFO Project Note 3–2017*. Consumption Research Norway (SIFO).

Morgan, T. (2023, September 23). Cost-of-living payments don't last – Food Bank. *BBC News*. https://www.bbc.com/news/business-66705305

Poppe, C., & Kempson, E. (2023a). *Dyrtid 4: Det er ikke over ennå. Husholdenes økonomiske trygghet i august 2023*. [Cost of living crisis 4: It is not over yet. Financial wellbeing among Norwegian households, August 2023.] SIFO Report 11-2023. Oslo Metropolitan University/Consumption Research Norway (SIFO).

Poppe, C., & Kempson, E. (2023b). *Dyrtid 3: Dyrtid III Husholdenes økonomiske trygghet i mars 2023*. [Cost of living Crisis 3: Financial wellbeing among Norwegian households, March 2023.] SIFO Report 3-2023. Oslo Metropolitan University/Consumption Research Norway (SIFO).

Powell, M., Yörük, E., & Ali, B. (2020). Thirty years of the *three Worlds of welfare capitalism*: A review of reviews. *Social Policy & Administration*, *54*(1), 60–87. https://doi.org/10.1111/spol.12510

Spicker, P. (2013). Liberal welfare states. In B. Greve (Ed.), *The Routledge handbook of the welfare state* (pp. 193–201). Routledge.

Sulkunen, P. (2015). *What is Neo-liberalism? Justifications of deregulating financial markets in Norway and Finland*. SIFO Working Paper 6-2015. Consumption Research Norway (SIFO).

FEEDING THE FAMILY WITH A DISABILITY OR LONG-TERM HEALTH CONDITION: LONE-PARENT FAMILIES AT RISK OF FOOD INSECURITY IN ENGLAND AND DENMARK

Julia Brannen[a], Rebecca O'Connell[b] and Kia Ditlevsen[c]

[a]*UCL Institute of Education, UK*
[b]*University of Hertfordshire, UK*
[c]*University of Copenhagen, Denmark*

ABSTRACT

This chapter contributes to the literature on domestic food provisioning and food insecurity in contemporary Europe, focusing on lone-parent households living with a disability or long-term health condition, either of a parent and/or a child, in the United Kingdom and Denmark. Taking a comparative case approach, it examines parents' strategies to achieve food security through practices of 'domestic food provisioning' that draw on resources within and outside the household. Taking account of the multiple layers of context in which provisioning practices are embedded, this chapter identifies factors or mechanisms that enhance or reduce food security for families living with a disability or long-term health condition. At the micro-level of food preparation, these families experience challenges including cooking and requirements for labour-saving equipment, providing meals that meet the needs of selective eaters (often children), the need to rely on their children's help and for outsourced domestic labour through buying ready-made foods. At the meso-level of procurement and 'physical access' to shops, transport is crucial, with households experiencing differences in service provision. At the macro-level of national welfare systems and 'economic access' to food, this chapter points to

Consumers and Consumption in Comparison
Comparative Social Research, Volume 37, 39–65

ISSN: 0195-6310/doi:10.1108/S0195-631020240000037003

evidence that Britain provides insufficient financial provision for those with a disability or long-term health condition compared with Denmark, differences reflected in the depth and rates of poverty and food insecurity between these countries. However, as the cases in both countries demonstrate, welfare benefits provide insufficient financial resources to access adequate nutritious food or meet customary norms.

Keywords: Disability; chronic health condition; food insecurity; domestic food provisioning; children and families; lone parents; comparative research; case study

INTRODUCTION

This chapter focuses on those living with a disability or long-term health condition who are reliant on social security in the United Kingdom and Denmark, in order to understand how they manage to feed their families. It does so by drawing on the qualitative findings of two studies of food practices in low-income households in the United Kingdom (UK) and Denmark (DK), which have contrasting welfare regimes. Lone-parent families are among the poorest households in the United Kingdom as well as in Denmark (Ditlevsen et al., 2023; O'Connell & Brannen, 2021). Parents' capacity to achieve food security for their children and themselves is examined through the concept of 'domestic food provisioning' that includes accessing and employing resources within the household, in social networks and local services and through income from the state.

An emerging body of research has shown that having a disability, or long-term health condition, that limits activity is associated with higher levels of food insecurity (Coleman-Jensen & Nord, 2013; Loopstra et al., 2019; Schwartz et al., 2019). However, most of these studies have been carried out in North America, and there is a lack of research on what mediates the relationship (Schwartz et al., 2019), with an emphasis on quantitative approaches that fail to examine in depth the dynamics of what happens within households. The academic literature on food insecurity among households living with a disability or long-term health condition in Europe is scarce, with no comparative research on the topic as far as we are aware (Hadfield-Spoor et al., 2022; Schwartz et al., 2019). This is an important gap, since a large and increasing proportion of the European population is classified as having a disability or condition that limits activity (WHO, 2019), and comparative approaches can help shed light on the multi-layered contexts that shape the extent and experiences of food insecurity for different groups (O'Connell & Brannen, 2021).

This chapter begins by defining and discussing food insecurity in the context of the United Kingdom and Denmark. Then, we present the empirical material and the case approach used to analyse how disabilities and health conditions shape food provisioning in low-income, single-parent households. Based on the presented findings, we discuss food provisioning in the participating families and how it is shaped contextually at micro-, meso- and macro-levels.

HOUSEHOLD FOOD INSECURITY

Food security exists when all people at all times have physical, social and economic access to culturally appropriate, nutritious and safe food (FAO, 1996). By contrast, household food *in*security is often defined as the inability 'to consume an adequate quality or sufficient quantity of food for health, in socially acceptable ways, or the uncertainty that one will be able to do so' (Dowler et al., 2001, p. 12). Four criteria or 'pillars', as the UN Committee on World Food Security calls them (CFS, 2009), have to be considered in assessing food security namely availability, access, utilisation and stability; each of these criteria has to be met in order for food security to be achieved.[1]

In most contemporary western societies, there is no shortage in the amount of food *available*. However, in some countries, there are stark inequalities in people's capacity to *access* and *utilise* food in ways that meet their needs for health and social participation. As argued by Amartya Sen (1981) in relation to famine, the problem is not only or primarily one of the unequal distribution of resources but of *entitlements* to those resources and the *capability* or opportunity to utilise them to achieve *functionings* – in this case, to adequate, nutritious meals that meet customary norms.

Food availability, access and the capability to utilise it are determined at the global level, through environmental and political factors such as climate, soil, food systems, war and the international division of labour and employment conditions. At the national level, economic and public policy affects food provisioning through wages, welfare systems and the entitlements they provide. At the local level, community resources including services, charities, kin and informal networks can also be important. However, it is at the household level that most of the work of *domestic food provisioning* is carried out.

DOMESTIC FOOD PROVISIONING

This chapter conceptualises households as resource systems (Brannen & Wilson, 1987/2023) in which their members engage in provisioning processes that are central to biological and social reproduction (Narotzky & Besnier, 2014). Fundamental to household reproductive processes is 'domestic food provisioning', a concept coined by Marjorie DeVault (1991), indicating 'the conjunction of commercial provision and domestic use, with unpaid labour as a crucial intermediating process' (Warde, 2016, p. 26). A useful 'middle range concept', domestic food provisioning includes various aspects of food work involved in 'feeding the family', including planning, procurement, preparation and cleaning up. Food provisioning draws on and makes use of different material and non-material resources that are sometimes referred to in livelihoods approaches as 'assets' or different types of capital; access to resources outside and within households is shaped by 'entitlements' and 'capabilities' that are unequally distributed according to social positioning such as gender and socio-economic position (Sen, 1981). In families with children, mothers traditionally bear most of the burden of responsibility, particularly for managing on restricted resources, though fathers do more food work than in the past (Bowen et al., 2014; Fielding-Singh & Cooper, 2023; Goode et al., 1998; Hanmer & Hearn, 1999; Holm et al., 2015; Scott et al., 1999; Snape et al., 1999; Sung & Bennett, 2007).

Among the 'coping strategies' or ways of 'getting by' employed by parents in the absence of sufficient financial resources is the mobilisation of non-income resources at different levels. At the household level, these may include children's contributions to domestic work and personal resources of time and energy, for example, 'shopping around' for bargains or cooking 'from scratch', i.e. basic ingredients (see O'Connell & Brannen, 2021; Ditlevsen et al., 2023; Ditlevsen et al., forthcoming). Another personal strategy identified in several studies is mothers going without food and other necessities to prioritise the needs of children and partners (Dowler & O'Connor, 2012; Goode et al., 1998; Ridge, 2009) – a practice referred to as 'maternal sacrifice' (Attree, 2005) or 'maternal altruism' (Whitehead, 1984), but which may also include fathers or other carers. Some of these resources and coping strategies are less likely to be available to households in which a parent and/or child has a disability or long-term health condition and, moreover, may increase ill-health and compound health inequalities.

LONG-TERM HEALTH CONDITIONS, DISABILITY AND WELFARE REGIMES

This chapter's empirical focus is upon people who themselves identify as living with a disability or long-term health condition, either their own and/or a child's, how this impacts on parents' financial resources, meaning level of social security and how, in turn, this affects their capacity to feed themselves and their children.

In social science research, there is a lack of consensus on what constitutes a 'disabling condition' – how to define or measure it (Mitra, 2006). While the 'social model of disability', with its attention on environments as disabling, has demonstrated political success for disabled people in society (Owens, 2015), critics have argued for the importance of acknowledging the real impact of people's different embodied experiences (e.g. Crow, 1996). According to the 'biopsychosocial' model of disability (WHO, 2011), disability is understood as an interaction between a person and social context. Debates over definitions of disability are heightened in cross-national research, given differences between countries in the ways and purposes for which disability is assessed and measured (Saleem, 2020).

In European welfare states, the ways in which long-term health conditions are regarded as 'disabling' vary greatly, with the consequence that the principles of entitlement to state support differ (Saleem, 2020).[2] Esping-Anderson's typology of welfare regimes sets out 'the overall way in which welfare is produced and distributed among the state, the market, and the family' (Esping-Andersen, 1990). The United Kingdom, an Anglo-Saxon welfare regime, is characterised by lower levels of spending on social protection, whereas Denmark is considered a Scandinavian welfare regime providing high levels of state support (Bambra &

Eikemo, 2009; Esping-Anderson, 1990). The chapter by Poppe and Kempson et al. in this volume of the journal describes more fully the differences between the welfare systems of the United Kingdom and a Scandinavian country, Norway. We do not propose to duplicate this here but will make several points about benefits for those with an activity limiting condition in the United Kingdom and Denmark.

One way of comparing differences national contexts make to the experiences of people living with disability and limiting health conditions is in terms of 'disability policy systems' (Halvorsen et al., 2017). Drawing on a comparison of 'active citizenship' and disability in nine European countries, Halvorsen et al. (2017) classify countries in terms of whether the following play a comparatively greater or limited role in a country's 'disability-related' public provisions: (1) cash transfers, (2) means testing, (3) services provisions (Halvorsen et al., 2017, 2018).[3,4]According to this typology, Hvinden (2016, p. 26) suggest that the United Kingdom is an example of a country 'with comparatively low levels of spending on cash transfers, comparatively high level of spending on services provision, and a comparatively high degree of means-testing.' Denmark is not included in the study's nine countries. But while 'a unified Nordic disability employment law and policy does not exist' (Arnardóttir et al., 2018), Denmark shares some features with Sweden and Norway that are characterised by 'comparatively high levels of spending on cash transfers and service provisions, with a comparatively low degree of means-testing.'[5]

In determining entitlements to accessing benefits, the United Kingdom operates a 'functional limitation' approach to disability ('fitness' to perform certain tasks), that is administered centrally with assessments conducted by privately contracted assessors. Its entitlement rules are unpredictable and inconsistent (Edmiston et al., 2022). Currently government is proposing further changes to force more disabled people into employment. The three non-means-tested disability cash benefits in the United Kingdom are: Attendance Allowance (for state pension age people), Disability Living Allowance (DLA for those below state pension age who need help with mobility and/or care), Personal Independence Payment (PIP) for people who have difficulty with everyday life who have to reduce their working hours or give up work (PIP is gradually replacing DLA for those of working age). These benefits are not available to all those living with a long-term health condition who are unable to work (or cannot work because of care responsibilities or find the right job), and when they are, are often insufficient for families' living costs (El Dessouky & McCurdy, 2023).

In contrast to the United Kingdom, the contemporary Danish welfare state has been characterised as a country combining a universal, Scandinavian welfare regime and a neoliberal ideology (Vitus et al., 2018). Known for its extensive tax-financed social security system, it has provided citizens with alternative sources of income in case of unemployment (social cash benefits, unemployment benefit or disabilities/sickness (sickness absence benefit, disability pension) (Esping-Andersen, 2002; Nørup, 2020). Social support in terms of cash benefits and services is also provided to cover special needs and expenses related to the disabilities of household members, for example, a child. Municipalities (local government authorities) administer benefits to cover additional expenses (comparable to DLA/PIP and Child DLA). Access to disability benefits is conditioned by a discretionary assessment process in the municipalities.

Like the United Kingdom, the Danish welfare state is in transformation as some of its mitigating effects are removed, resulting in increasing inequality and relative poverty (Ejrnæs et al., 2020). Public cutbacks and limited access to services and assistance have been induced during the last decade (Falster & Ringø, 2023). Further, as in the United Kingdom, Denmark has implemented so-called 'active' social policy reforms aimed to make people return to the labour market and become self-supporting, which affects both the unemployed and people with disabilities and health impairments (Nørup, 2020). Access to disability pensions has been restricted, early retirement pensions are being phased out and social cash benefits (*kontanthjælp*) reduced and made conditional on participation in labour market activation programmes (Nørup & Jacobsen, 2022).

COMPARING FOOD INSECURITY IN THE UNITED KINGDOM AND DENMARK

In the United Kingdom, there is evidence of rising levels of food insecurity among households living with a disability or long-term health condition (Boyle & Power, 2021). The Trussell Trust, the United Kingdom's largest food aid provider, reports that 69% of people referred to a food bank have a disability compared with 26% across the population (Bull et al., 2023). In Denmark, there are fewer national data and less discussion of food insecurity, both generally and among households with disabilities. However, the EU Statistics on Income and Living Conditions (EU-SILC) provides some comparative evidence on both poverty and food insecurity (O'Connell & Brannen, 2021).[6]

Across Europe, as Table 1 shows, the risk of poverty or social exclusion (AROP) among adults (age 16+) living in a household with an income of less than 60% median is significantly higher for people who have some or severe 'activity limitations' than those with none. According to the EU-SILC, in 2018, almost a third (29.7%) of the EU population with an activity limitation was AROP, compared with less than a fifth (18.7%) of people with no limitations (see Table 1).[7]

Comparing the United Kingdom and Denmark, in both countries, those living with an activity limitation are more likely to be living in poverty than those without. However, rates of poverty are considerably higher in the United Kingdom for both those who are living with an activity limitation and those who are not, compared with that in Denmark. In the United Kingdom, a third of people with limitations on their everyday activities because of a health condition are likely to be AROP (32.6%) compared to a sixth among those who are not (16.2%). In Denmark, people with disabilities are still much more likely to be AROP than those without – 25.4% compared to 14.8% – but the proportions are lower and the difference is smaller.

Table 1. Share of People (Age 16+ Years) in the EU, Denmark and the United Kingdom at Risk of Poverty or Social Exclusion by Level of Activity Limitation 2018[a] (EU-SILC).

	Share of People Aged 16 or >			
	At Risk of Poverty or Social Exclusion (AROP)[b]		Cannot Afford Regular Proteins	
2018	Some/severe limitations	No limitations	Some/severe limitations	No limitations
EU 28	29.7	18.7	11.3	5.9
UK	32.6	16.2	7.7	3.5
DK	25.4	14.8	3.3	0.9

[a]2018 is the last year of EU SILC data that includes the United Kingdom; this roughly coincides with qualitative fieldwork for the two projects.
[b]Eurostat Data Browser: Persons at risk of poverty or social exclusion by level of disability (activity limitation), sex and age: https://ec.europa.eu/eurostat/databrowser/view/HLTH_DPE010/default/table?lang=en&category=hlth.hlth_dsb.hlth_dsb_pe

There are few comparative data on food insecurity in Europe; however, the inability to afford a meal containing protein (collected in EU-SILC as an indicator of material deprivation) has been used as a proxy (Davis & Geiger, 2017; Loopstra et al., 2015, 2016). Table 1 shows that, in Europe overall, households living with disability are twice as likely as the general population to report that they are unable to afford regular proteins (at least every other day). In both Denmark and the United Kingdom, the proportion of households reporting they cannot afford to eat proteins regularly is much higher among households living with a disability than without. As indicated by this measure, a greater share of the UK population experiences food insecurity compared to Denmark, both overall and among households with limiting conditions.

METHODS AND DATA

This chapter draws on qualitative research from two studies of food practices in low-income households, in the United Kingdom and Denmark. Both were carried out in the aftermath of the 'austerity' measures introduced by the governments of both countries after the 2008 global financial crisis (O'Connell & Brannen, 2021; Ditlevsen et al., 2023).

The UK study was conducted between 2014 and 2019. It aimed to investigate the ways in which low-income families with children aged 11–15 years managed domestic food provisioning (as discussed earlier) following the UK government's imposition of austerity measures in the wake of the 2008 financial crisis – in practice from 2010 onwards. Forty-five families (including 51 children) were recruited in two sites (an inner London borough and an English coastal town), with the assistance of schools, charities and other organisations.[8] All families were living on low incomes, initially defined subjectively as being below what they needed and subsequently in the analysis based on their incomes (O'Connell et al., 2019; O'Connell & Brannen, 2021).

Semi-structured qualitative interviews and other methods designed to elicit detailed information on income and outgoings, money spent on food and other items and how income and expenditure changed at different times of the month and year. Parents were asked about their daily routines and experiences and their methods of domestic food provisioning – procurement, preparation, planning and consumption – and 'stretching' food (DeVault, 1991) in the context of constrained food budgets. In their interviews, adults and children (separately) were asked to recall what foods and meals they had eaten on the last school and non-school days. Questions were also asked about eating with others inside and outside the home including participants' opportunities for socialising – either to offer or to accept hospitality. In addition, parents and children were asked who or what they thought was responsible for ensuring that families and children had enough decent food to eat and about what the future held in store for them and for families in general. Children were asked about having money of their own, about helping with shopping and other household tasks and about food at home and outside home, including school. Questionnaires were used alongside interviews to collect information and prompt discussion. Parents were given a 'food coping strategies' questionnaire to complete and children filled in a 'food habits module', based on the one used in the international Health Behaviour in School-aged Children (HBSC) study (Vereecken et al., 2005, 2015). Two questions, based on the latter survey, were posed about going to school or bed hungry owing to a lack of food at home. A sub-sample of households participated in photographic kitchen tours and photo-elicitation interviews.

The Danish study, conducted between July 2019 and January 2020, set out to investigate food practices and health in low-income households. Adults (15 men and 15 women) from 30 relatively poor households living all over the country were recruited. As in the UK study, the intention was not initially to investigate food practices in households with members living with a long-term health condition. However, it turned out that many informants in the Danish sample did so: 16 of the participants in the sample were parents (8 fathers, 8 mothers). Of these, 10 were single parents: three fathers and seven mothers. Qualitative in-depth interviews were employed to generate knowledge about food practices, everyday life and understandings of, and engagements in, the healthiness of food and norms surrounding food practices. One adult from each household was interviewed about their social background; everyday life; meal routines; cooking practices and facilities; norms and reflections on food and meals; understandings of, and reflections on, health; and the size of their food budget and economic situation. The interviews were conducted in participants' homes. A semi-structured interview guide was used, allowing the interviewer to follow the pace and order of the interviewee's reflections and narratives (Brinkmann & Kvale, 2018). All interviews were face to face and concluded with a brief series of structured food frequency questions used to measure the healthiness of food eaten (using the Dietary Quality Score (Toft et al., 2017).

While neither study set out to focus on households with a disability or long-term health condition, research participants volunteered why they were unable to do paid work, and how their or their children's health affected day-to-day life and often food and eating. In the UK sample, 20/45 households included a parent and/or child who had a long-term health condition: 16 households with a parent or parents, four of whom were also caring for a child or children with impairments. In four other households, the child had a disability but the parent did not. Of the 20 households that included a parent and/or child with a disability or chronic ill-health, 16 were lone-parent families and four were couples. Among lone-parent families, the most common disability/health issue was poor mental health including anxiety and depression (8/16), followed by problems with backs and legs, characteristic of long-term engagement in manual labour (4/16). Among children, there were a range of conditions; a majority is neurodiverse, with just over half (5/8) diagnosed with autism spectrum disorder (ASD) or attention deficit hyperactivity disorder (ADHD). While some of these parents were in paid employment, the majority was not. However, only a minority was in receipt of disability or sickness-related benefits and so dependent on social security benefits.

In the Danish sample, 22/30 households had one or more members with a long-term health condition. Of the 10 single-parent households, nine were living with disabilities or long-term health conditions. Among the parents, the following conditions were present: Diabetes-1, post-traumatic stress disorder (PTSD), sclerosis, rickets, long-term side effects of thrombosis, fibromyalgia, chronical bowel inflammation, neurodiversity and mental health problems (e.g. depression, anxiety). Among the children, several were neurodiverse, diagnosed with ASD or ADHD. Two of the lone fathers were in low-paid employment; the rest of the Danish lone parents were unemployed and received social cash benefits or a disability pension. Some of the parents on social cash benefits were exempt from the otherwise mandatory participation in labour market activation programmes due to their health condition or their children's need for intensive care. All parents received the universal child benefit (eligible to all parents in DK) and additional child allowance for single parents; some received housing support for their rent (eligible for all with low incomes), and some received support for specific costs related to their disabilities.

The Cases

This chapter takes a case approach. Central to a case-based methodology is its power to make comparisons: the approach allows the researcher to identify the parameters of cases as 'cases of something.' By purposive selection of types of households and by examining their access to different resources, practices of food provisioning and the experience of food in/security can be situated in the social contexts of place – homes, cities, communities and societies (Brannen & Nilsen, 2011). Comparison enables understanding of particular cases situated in the specificities of social conditions and contexts that may not be ideal-typical for a country pattern (Brannen, 2005). The aim therefore is to treat cases as *emblematic* of particular social characteristics, conditions and structural contexts rather than to extrapolate to the general (Thomson, 2009).

In order to identify what makes a difference to the ways in which parents manage food provisioning when they live with a disability or long-term health condition, we aim in this chapter for equivalence between cases. The cases for comparison have been selected according to the following criteria: families headed by a lone parent, experiencing relative poverty and unable to work due to a long-term health condition in the household – either their own or that of their children. To examine families' capacities for food provisioning, we examine the different contexts in which these parents accessed resources to feed their families: the household level, the local level of municipal services and shops and the national level of policies and social security systems.

This chapter focuses on four families. All were headed by lone parents, living with a disability or chronic illness, either their own and/or those of their children, and who were not employed at interview. Three were lone mothers and one a lone father (a Danish case). The parents were all in their thirties, and their children ranged from toddlers to pre-teens. All four were reliant on state benefits of some kind and therefore clustered at the bottom of the income spectrum. Two of the mothers (Fatima [UK] and Laura [DK]) were unable to work and faced difficulties in performing food practices due to their own disabilities, and two parents (Sandra [UK] and Thomas [DK]) were unable to work due to their children's disabilities and faced difficulties in their everyday life due to these. A difference between the cases is ethnicity; these differences reflect the samples of the research which in turn reflect the demography of the areas from which the research participants were drawn. Both UK parents are members of minority ethnic groups (second generation migrants), while the Danish parents are white Danes. There are also differences in terms of the adequacy of their incomes (as indicated by comparison with national reference budgets, Table 2), as we indicate below and discuss further in the case analysis.[9]

Table 2. The Cases: Four Lone-Parent Families in Which the Parent and/or Child Is Living With a Long-Term Health Condition.

Parent pseudonym[a]	Fatima	Sandra	Thomas	Laura
Country, location	UK, London	UK, London	Denmark, urban area	Denmark, rural area
Family type	Lone mother	Lone mother	Lone father	Lone mother
Number of children	2 (girl age 5 and boy age 12)	3 (boy age 5 and girls age 11 months and 11)	2 (boys age 8 and 11)	1 (girl age 11)
Parent ethnicity	Black British	Black British	white Danish	white Danish

Table 2. (*Continued*)

Parent pseudonym[a]	Fatima	Sandra	Thomas	Laura
Income sources	Employment Support Allowance, Disability Living Allowance (DLA), child benefit, child tax credit	Employment Support Allowance, DLA, child benefit, child tax credit	Social cash benefits Child benefit Child allowance (probably housing support – not specified in interview)	Disability pension Support with expenses related to disability Child benefit Child allowance (probably housing support – not specified in interview)
Total income/ reference budget (RB)	£284/week 74% RB	£289/week 50% RB	15.000 Dkr/month 97% RB	13.000 Dkr/month 108% RB

[a]Pseudonyms are used in the case studies to protect the anonymity of participants.

FOUR CASES OF FOOD PROVISIONING IN LOW-INCOME, LONE-PARENT FAMILIES

Fatima, a UK Mother

Fatima is a lone non-employed mother, age 35. She was born and brought up in inner London and is of North African descent. She has two children, a five-year-old daughter and a son aged 12. The boy has mild hemiplegia which affects balance and co-ordination. Fatima has chronic health problems including a degenerative disk disease, arthritis, chronic obstructive pulmonary disease (COPD) and asthma. This means she is in chronic pain and walks with a stick. Because of her health conditions, Fatima has not been in paid work for 11 years. After living in temporary accommodation, the family was housed by the council in a ground-floor maisonette on an inner London housing estate. Most of the housing (rent) costs were covered (she paid £10 per week service charge). Fatima was interviewed twice, 2 years apart. At the first interview, her income was around £284 per week, including Employment Support Allowance and DLA that was intended to provide care for herself, although at the lower level, because she was assessed as mobile. She was also in receipt of the universal benefit – child benefit – and Child Tax Credit, a means-tested benefit – but had recently lost her Income Support that is only available until a child is five when parents are meant to look for work. At the second interview, following an assessment by a private 'health professional' on behalf of the Department of Work and Pensions, Fatima said she had lost her disability benefit following an assessment despite the degenerative disease she suffered from increasingly limiting her mobility. Fatima says this income loss is very significant, amounting to £315 per month and what is left only covers 'the essentials.' At around £284 per week, Fatima's income at her first interview was around three quarters of what a family of this type needs to achieve a socially acceptable standard of living in the United Kingdom (Hirsch, 2015). In addition, she has considerable debt, owing about £400 on catalogues and unpaid bills. At one point, she asked her mother to keep her bank cards and to give her money each week for shopping. At the interview, she staggers repayments, depending on what she can afford, and has given up her credit card.

Even so Fatima prioritises her food budget, which she says is only around £50 per week, for the family of three, regarding expenses such as her electricity and gas bills as more elastic than food. 'Luckily obviously because of my disability as well, I'm a vulnerable so they [companies] can't just cut me off and stuff like that. So I know I can work with that a bit, so …' Her children are entitled to free school meals which help mitigate her constrained food budget. She says she does not cut back on food '. . .you know we get food on the table and everyone's full and stuff like that you know.' Keen to demonstrate they have plenty, she added, 'I've got one cupboard with just like tinned stuff, you know like the chickpeas and the tomatoes … so I can always whip something up regardless … something can always be whipped up.' The importance she placed on 'good food' is underlined by her critical remarks about the way supermarkets cut prices on low quality food such as chicken nuggets instead of healthier food like vegetables. To maximise the food budget, she describes substituting expensive brands of school uniform for cheaper ones.

Fatima shops around for the best deals, and this shapes what she buys, '… you know what's on offer will kind of determine what … you know. Or if there's particular things that I want, and I've kind of got the app on my phone and I'll see who's got it on offer kind of thing.' Because she is unable easily to visit shops she uses apps, 'Yeah basically it'll show you what's kind of on offer, and there's a different app that's called MySupermarket and you can actually select things that you actually like and it'll alert you when they're actually on offer anywhere.' In the supermarkets, Fatima uses loyalty cards and vouchers for food and sometimes for her daughter's school uniform. Her mother has a discount card for a store where they can buy 'a massive box of Fruit Shoots' [fruit flavoured ready-made squash in individual bottles] for £7.

Fatima's chronic ill health impacts both her shopping and cooking practices. She is reliant on help from her 12-year-old son, extended family and friends. To do the shopping, she either uses her taxi card (that entitles her to reduced price taxi fares) or calls on her mother or friends, 'I've got my two best friends that we're on the phone everyday literally.' She also borrows money from them sometimes. Her son helps carry the shopping and sometimes he goes to Sainsburys to get some items. If Fatima shops on her own she says, '*I do couple of shops through the week cos I can't. . . .don't do it all in one go. … And I tend to do it when the kids are at school, otherwise you just get "Mummy can I have this?" "Mummy can I have this?" "Mummy can I have this?" – and then your shopping bill's that long, yeah.* (laughs)'

Because Fatima is not able to stand for long in the kitchen, this affects her cooking practices. She uses an ActiFry (air fryer) that, she says, is both a 'healthy' way to cook and enables her to prepare food quickly (Fig. 1). The children have

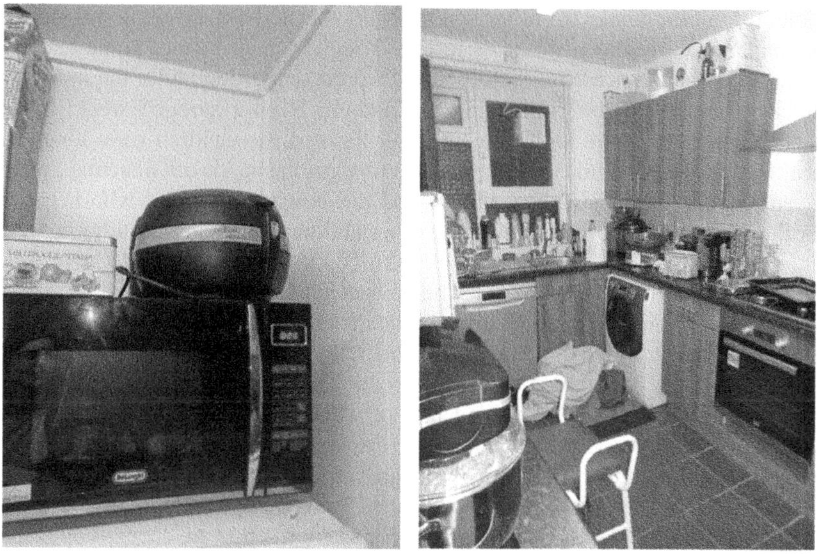

Fig. 1. Fatima's ActiFry and Perching Stool.

pasta and also snacks and the family regularly buys in takeaways (pizza, kebab, KFC). She uses a perching stool while cooking: 'Yeah yeah, the standing round and do the cooking and stuff. Like um … if I'm doing veg and stuff I tend to be sitting down here, I'll bring it all in here and I'll do it. I've got my perching stool in the kitchen so when I'm at the hob and stuff I can use that … but yeah … but I used to love baking and ….' As a consequence, Fatima also often relies on her son to do the cooking, 'I was sick yesterday so he was chef.' This was confirmed in her son. Fatima also said her mother sometimes cooks or brings cooked food round to them. As a consequence of her worsening health, that she describes as 'one thing after the other', *like* 'dominoes', her social life has suffered, '… yeah that's been a big change for me, I was very active, I was you know a very sociable kind of person, go round to friends, families … it's all changed now.' However, she talks to her friends on the phone every day. Sometimes, they come over and bring a takeaway. Her former partner takes the children out occasionally and took them to North Africa in the summer. Overall, she feels better off in comparison to others; 'you know if you look across the country, across the world – there's always someone worse off than you, you know … just thank God for what you've got.'

Sandra, a UK Mother

Sandra is a lone mother aged 29 years (see also Knight et al., 2020). She is Black British, of African-Caribbean heritage. She has a girl aged 11, a boy aged five and an eleven-month-old baby girl. In spite of having a nursing degree, until 2 years ago she was employed by a security firm as a 'bouncer.' Having experienced violent domestic abuse from her son's father, that left her hospitalised, she and her children moved to a women's refuge. They lost their former home and possessions but have since been re-housed in their current ground floor flat in a tower block in inner London. Following the assault, Sandra stopped work, having become pregnant with her youngest child. Two of the children have long-term health or developmental conditions – the baby girl has sickle cell anaemia and the 5-year-old boy is autistic. The 11-year-old girl is a 'young carer' who helps her mother with the cooking and with the other children, for example, administering their medicines.

Sandra is going to apply for disability benefits for two of her children (she is awaiting a final medical report on her son's condition that she needs in order to apply). The household income is around £289, a week made up of Income Support – £95 a fortnight, Child Tax Credit – £154 weekly, child benefit – £40 weekly. Sandra's income is around half of what a family of this type needs to achieve a socially acceptable standard of living (Hirsch, 2015). She also gets Healthy Start vouchers (£8.50 for the youngest child per week) that can be spent on milk and 'healthy foods' like fruit. Her 11-year-old daughter is entitled to and receives free school meals. Most of the housing (rent) costs are covered by benefit (she pays £11 per week but is in arrears). The household's main outgoings include a weekly gas bill of £60 (which was considered high at the time) because the baby needs to be kept warm. Sandra also needs to run a car to take her children to their frequent medical appointments; this is a major expense for her.

Sandra is also in debt from the time she moved on to a zero-hours contract when she was last in paid work; these include parking fees and fines accrued when attending her children's medical appointments; 'I had the money to pay for it to be fair with you, but the money kind of went when he went in hospital, because [...] I had to pay for the parking.' Other debt is for arrears on costly childcare accrued when she used to work nights. Her claim for these costs was rejected by the authorities, and she is paying back around £1,800 debt at a rate of £10 per week, 'because it's like that's another problem. When you're doing shift work and nobody understands that part to it.' Sandra is also repaying debt to the Social Fund (a UK government loan to help people with expenses that are difficult to meet on a low income).

Sandra's food budget is about £35–£40 a week which has to cover a family of four. Healthy Start vouchers cover some of the costs of milk for the children. Sandra shops at a food market about a mile away as it is cheaper than the local shops. She also shops around for deals at her local shops including Tesco, Asda and a stall selling fruit and vegetables at £1 per bowl. She also uses her car to drive to bulk-buy at discount stores with her mother, and for which she has a card.

After Sandra stopped working, she was reluctant to apply for benefits. However, because she has a baby, the health visitor paid her a visit, and Sandra felt forced to turn to her cousin for help: 'because it was affecting my kids and I weren't able to hide it no more ... because my kids they were hungry.' She sought advice from Citizens Advice to help her manage her loan repayments better and has applied to a charity for help with the purchase of floor coverings which the flat lacks; the flat is too cold for the children, two of whom are young and have health conditions. Sandra has also turned to a food bank to help feed the family, an experience she described as shaming. However, because she met others in the same circumstances, it made her realise the seriousness of her situation:

> In order for me to even give my kids milk, breakfast, lunch and dinner that takes money and it took me to go to a food bank to work out this is how bad it's got that we ain't got a penny, because everything's just been sucked dry through whatever debt or whatever thing we owe where we're left with nothing, so yeah I went food bank and I would do it again. I tell you what, I would do it again.

Sandra, often helped by her daughter, makes 'African' and 'Caribbean' dishes containing oxtail, mutton and goat which are more expensive than what she describes as 'English' meals, such as pasta and meatballs, that are low-cost. She now cooks only 'for the day' on the advice of a food bank worker, 'instead of doing this whole big cooking, I now minimise it.'

Although she has brought up her children to eat what they are served, her son's autism means that 'whatever he likes, he gets, sort of thing, because he's really picky with food'. He has particular preferences, and likes his food separated, 'I cooked rice and peas and chicken I think for Sunday dinner and roast potatoes and coleslaw and cabbages and stuff and then he went no, he doesn't want none of that. He wants (laughs) he wants pasta with cheese, coleslaw and the chicken, but he wants them in all different bowls.' She mentions that 'because my son's like, obviously where he's autistic and stuff he just don't, he won't eat certain things... he started to get like really skinny and stuff like that and it's not, you don't do it on purpose.' It got so bad that Sandra became afraid the authorities would take the children from her.

Sandra has a very strong work ethic and would prefer to be employed, 'I'm supposed to protect them and guide them and look after them 'til they're mature enough to do ... I've never had to ask for help and that's what I've learnt [to do] this year.' However, it would be difficult to afford, and find, the necessary childcare for her youngest child, given her long-term health condition, '...there's no point telling people to go to work and the childcare is not sufficient enough to work. It is never ... as I say I've never had a problem getting a job... putting them in childcare is ridiculous. I was paying £280 a week.'

Sandra describes being on benefits as stigmatising, 'It's like people look down at you, people deal with you differently and it shouldn't be like that.' She has cut herself off from the world to the extent that neither she nor her elder daughter socialise. It is significant that the 11-year-old said in her interview that she had forgotten to go to a party to which she was invited and that she 'never' had friends to her home for tea. Sandra blames the costs of childcare and zero hours contracts for their situation: 'My whole life, my whole entire existence went down the hill from there.' Because Sandra wants to be independent, she was slow to go on welfare benefits and doesn't put her trust in other people. She never has friends to her house or goes out with them, 'I don't trust friends as much as I should do. I've cut off all ties on a lot of those sort of social life pattern things as well.'

Thomas, a Danish Father

Thomas is in his 30s. He has been a lone parent for 2 years and takes responsibility for his 2 boys aged 8 and 11. The children no longer have contact with their mother. Thomas has been diagnosed with what he refers to as 'a quite heavy diagnosis that sometimes makes it difficult just to function.' One of his sons is autistic and one has ADHD and they both require a lot of care and parental attention. Thomas is unable to work because of his children's needs that both restrict the household's food consumption practices along with almost all other aspects of everyday life.

Thomas is on social cash benefits, a relatively low means-tested benefit which all citizens in Denmark are entitled to in case of need. At the time of the interview, he had applied for a disability pension and is awaiting the municipality's decision. As long as he is on social cash benefits, his financial situation is precarious. At the interview, he is not required to take part in activation programmes because of his disability and those of his children, but this can be reviewed at any time. The amount Thomas receives in social cash benefits plus specific supplements is just below the Danish reference budget (see endnote x) for a household of his kind (Bonke et al., 2016).

Thomas and his sons live in a rented apartment in a large city, which Thomas hopes to be able to exchange for a larger flat soon. Thomas' current apartment is relatively small and does not easily accommodate the need for space or privacy for its household members, but on the other hand, Thomas finds the rent affordable. Like most rented homes in Denmark, Thomas's apartment is of a reasonable standard although a little worn. Its kitchen facilities and other amenities such as the stove and refrigerator are included in the rent.

Thomas and his family live on a restricted budget. Thomas says that he prioritises food, and that the family does not experience a lack of it. At the same time, the prioritising of foods comes at a cost: Thomas depends on the financial support of his parents to purchase clothes and shoes for his sons and to handle large expenses. Thomas does not think his children experience deprivation. Yet, the family cannot afford vacations; he does not buy new clothing for himself and never purchases what he calls 'expensive foods', such as fish.

Thomas dismisses his own food tastes and preferences and refers to himself as the 'dustbin of the household.' He makes sure he eats leftovers and foods that are about to expire, or he uses them in dishes his sons are willing to eat. Thomas represents a clear case of 'paternal sacrifice' (cf. the concept 'maternal sacrifice' in Attree, 2005) practices, illustrating how such coping strategies can be gender neutral and depend on caregiver responsibilities. He struggles a great deal with getting his sons to eat a variety of foods because they have very restricted preferences that are related to autism and ADHD. This poses a challenge for Thomas not only in terms of avoiding food waste but for his aspirations to serve healthy food and have pleasant family dinners, 'If I think a lot about healthy foods? Yes, all the time. I constantly think "it would be nice to get them to eat more healthily." More vegetables and more variation [...] It annoy me, that it is not really doable.' In addition to restricted food preferences, the son's disabilities also lead to conflict over food and eating situations, making life hard work for Thomas.

Thomas makes use of several strategies to cope with his restricted food budget. He goes to discount supermarkets, and he looks for products that have been reduced due to expiry dates and these determine what he makes for dinner. For non-reduced food products, he checks the expiry dates to make sure the remaining shelf life is long enough, so he does not have to waste food. Food provisioning is challenging for Thomas not only because of his restricted budget but also because he finds it difficult to remember things, and he has a phobia of social interaction. As a result, he also employs strategies to do the shopping. He has a grocery list on his phone, where he writes down what to purchase during the day. In 'bad periods', he says he cannot use the list, and all his planning is lost. He goes to the supermarket in the morning when the supermarket is almost empty, listens to music on his headphones while shopping and uses the self-service check-out to avoid social contact where possible.

Thomas' everyday life is structured around the needs of his children. It requires an effort to take his sons to the supermarket, and he avoids it most days. "He [the oldest boy] is constantly in motion, twirls around and then fall into a thought that pops in his head or in a world that is different from the world the rest of us is in [...] sometimes he can help me select groceries, other times it is a really big task to get him through the store. My youngest is easier, but still very hyper.' On the other hand, Thomas says, he must help his sons to get used to being in the world; so sometimes, he prioritises bringing them along.

Laura, a Danish Mother

Laura is in her late 30s. She is a lone mother and lives with her 11-year-old daughter in a rented house in a new-build housing estate just outside a town in a rural area. Laura has several physical long-term health conditions and PTSD. She was very restricted in her physical activities and suffered from pains in joints and muscles, fatigue and exhaustion.

She lives on a disability pension and has an income just above the Danish reference budget (Bonke et al., 2016). Her housing expenses are relatively high and the household lives on a very tight budget. Keeping within her budget was the major concern for Laura. In her account of her food practices, several methods for saving money stand out: avoiding food waste and stretching food by adding cheap, filling ingredients (such as pasta) to dishes. Like Thomas, Laura's food 'choices' are determined mostly by special offers and reduced prices in the supermarket that determine what they eat for dinner. Laura talks about wanting to include more vegetables in their diet. This is difficult, she explains; because her daughter often does not eat vegetables, it is hard to consume the whole pack. Laura cannot afford to throw away food, 'Once in a while I allow myself tomato – I like that. The problem is that I can only buy at least five at a time. If I am not sure to eat them all, I think it's too expensive to purchase.' The tight budget means that Laura can only purchase foods she is sure will be eaten, and Laura restricts her own food around her daughter's preferences.

Laura used to go fishing. Now, she cannot do that because of her chronic health conditions. She cannot afford to buy fish, which is a relatively expensive food. Occasionally, friends or family bring her fresh fish, and she appreciates that very much.

Because Laura is restricted in her physical activities and easily gets exhausted, she drives to a nearby supermarket and purchases groceries approximately every second day. The expense of running a car is supported by the municipality because of her disabilities.

Everyday domestic work becomes a major daily project for Laura, 'I need to plan my everyday life and ration my energy. I can do a little every day, but not too much', she said. Social events are also draining for Laura, and she often refrains from participating because it would take her several days to recover, days when she could not attend to her daughter.

Laura is a competent cook, but she says she does not enjoy cooking. She cooks because 'it has to be done' and is part of being a responsible parent, just as she feels she must keep to her budget (see also results reported in Ditlevsen et al., forthcoming). She describes how she was brought up 'not to use more than you get.' Laura puts money aside in order to celebrate birthdays and Christmas and makes sure she always has money in a savings account. Yet, her family helps her financially – for example, when she hosted the family Christmas party, her father paid for some of the food, her mother brought the roast and her sister the dessert. She mentions how she had to use her savings to meet urgent household expenses, such as paying a dentist bill and replacing her daughter's worn-out winter boots.

Laura prioritises her spending around her child's needs and likes. They cannot afford to go on holidays, and Laura avoids spending money on herself such as new clothes and leisure activities, 'Last time I was at a café was 17 years ago! I have not seen an adult movie in the cinema in 14 years. Well… it is not something that I moan about. It's just the way it is. And I'd rather not do stuff like that, than have my daughter feel something is missing.'

Laura finds it difficult to accept that she cannot work. She would like to contribute to society, she says, and she misses seeing people. She also reflects on how her situation may affect her daughter and makes an effort to keep on her feet when she is at home, even on days when she is exhausted. 'I do not want her to have an idea that it's normal to just lay on your couch all day… so I don't want her to find me over there. I want her to see me walk around doing things.'

DISCUSSION

The four households selected were all lone parents whose capacity to work was restricted by their own or by their children's disabilities or chronic ill health. They were all reliant on benefits and had constraints on their food budgets and food practices. Comparing the households and how they get by, we can see how access to financial and other resources at different levels of context enables or constrains their capacities to manage food provisioning and so their access to adequate healthy food.

Managing Food Provisioning: The National Policy Level

An important dimension of similarity and difference between the United Kingdom and Denmark concerns entitlements and access to disability benefits that are determined at the national policy level. In the United Kingdom, entitlement to disability benefits is highly restricted as demonstrated in the case of Fatima who had lost her disability benefit following an assessment despite the degenerative disease she suffered from: she was not deemed to be 'ill enough.' She also suffered a reduction in support for one of the children because the child in question had reached an age when her mother was deemed 'able' to work. In the other UK case, Sandra was unable to work because her youngest had sickle cell anaemia, and her middle child is autistic. She was awaiting a report on her son's condition in order to apply for DLA; she had a strong work ethic and wanted to work but was not hopeful about the prospects given limited jobs availability and high costs of childcare. In Denmark, Thomas applied for a disability pension and was awaiting the municipality's decision. In the meantime, he was reliant on social assistance that meant that potentially he will be required at some point to seek employment. This may prove difficult for him in his current situation where he has to deal with his own condition at the same time as take care of his two sons, who require a great deal of parental attention. Laura, on the other hand, experienced a less precarious situation because she is entitled to a disability pension under the Danish welfare system and did not have her economic situation routinely reassessed.

Both in the United Kingdom and Denmark, people living with disabilities are forced to prove they are 'sick enough' to 'deserve' a more permanent and secure benefit that is time-consuming and often involves stressful appeal procedures (Thomas, 2021). Claimants typically have to wait for medical reports to justify their claims, as in the case of Sandra. The difficulties faced by parents in these households were exacerbated by confusing changes to benefits systems, so that parents may not always be aware of what is available to them. Especially in the United Kingdom, new benefits with new criteria are constantly being introduced and others gradually phased out. Changing criteria can mean that those with a disability no longer qualify and suffer significant income losses, as in Fatima's case. In addition, fear of stigma and discrimination made some parents reluctant to claim welfare benefits, as in Sandra's case in the United Kingdom.

Managing Food Provisioning: The Local Level

Here, we refer to the formal and informal support available to the families at the local level. In the United Kingdom, families receiving certain benefits are entitled to free school meals for their school-aged children; this mitigates some of the costs of feeding them during term time. However, not all low-income families are entitled, for example, many who are in paid work. By contrast, there is no such service in Denmark. In the United Kingdom, in the absence of support from the state, charitable support has stepped into the gap (Lambie-Mumford, 2017). However, only Sandra mentioned using charities and a food bank. Local transport was also an issue for some families who had to manage a disability. Laura in Denmark was dependent on a car to do her shopping, the expenses for which were supported by her municipality. In the United Kingdom, Fatima qualified for a taxi card that gave her access to reduced price taxi fares that she sometimes used to help with shopping, while Sandra had to bear the costs of running a car in order to transport her children to their frequent hospital appointments; there was no scheme provided by her local council that would enable her to lease a vehicle at a low cost. In Denmark, while Thomas was not dependent on a car in his everyday life, for Laura, the expense of running a car is supported by the municipality because of her long-term health conditions.

Informal support was dependent on whether family and friends lived close by but also on whether they had sufficient resources and were prepared to share them. Moreover, some parents were reluctant to turn to others as they did not wish to reveal their poor financial circumstances to them and could not reciprocate, with the consequence that they retreated from social participation. For example, Sandra (in the United Kingdom) felt uncomfortable about being unable to pay for herself if she went to eat out with friends; she described herself as lacking trust in people. The Danish participants refrained from social participation with friends because, they said, of their disabilities and due to the need to prioritise limited funds for her children's needs. Thomas and Laura in Denmark talked about getting help from their close relatives. In Thomas' case, his parents' support for essential child clothing enabled him to prioritise food expenditure, while Laura relied on family support on special occasions, such as holiday dinners.

Managing Food Provisioning: The Household Level

The primary constraint on food security in all four households is low income. In the United Kingdom, both Fatima and Sandra reported having debt, a consequence of very low income from state benefits. Thomas and Laura (Denmark) had no debt, suggesting they were in a slightly more secure economic situation. All four parents described difficulties managing to buy sufficient nutritious food on their incomes and can thus be described as facing some level of food insecurity. They were careful in shopping around for the best deals and tried to avoid food waste. While they aimed to buy food that was healthy, in three of the four families, what they ate was largely determined by what was on special offer in the supermarkets; this often meant consuming unhealthy food that was cheaper than healthier food.

People often get by on a low income by treating the food budget as 'elastic'; this means it is squeezed or expanded depending on the costs of other essentials (such as housing and utilities) (Dowler, 2002; Dowler et al., 2001). However, in households in the lowest income groups, there are no further cuts to be made.

This is evident in the cases of the four parents who reported prioritising their food budget over other expenditures. Fatima initially said she prioritised her food budget over electricity bills, but due to her lost benefit entitlement, she had to reduce food expenditure by switching to non-branded and lower 'quality' foods. Thomas also said he prioritised food expenditure, but he was only able to do so because of support from his family with the costs of other basic expenses, such as his children's shoes.

As well as low incomes, the parents' and children's long-term health conditions made food provisioning difficult for them in specific ways. Parents developed strategies for getting by. These included, for example, using a smartphone app for shopping (Fatima), Thomas found shopping difficult himself and also taking his children with him because they were hyperactive. Both Fatima and Thomas experienced difficulties with preparing meals. In Thomas's case, he struggled to balance the need not to waste food with encouraging his children to eat. Fatima had difficulty cooking food because her health made standing for long periods hard and using her hands painful. Both Fatima's son and Sandra's daughter were 'young carers', at times helping with cooking and caring for younger siblings. In three of the families, children's or parents' disabilities meant special diets or equipment were needed. Sandra and Thomas both had difficulties feeding and caring for their children because of the specificities of their disabilities – in Sandra's case trying to keep her baby, who suffered from sickle cell disease, warm and, in Thomas's case, because of his children's restricted food preferences, encouraging his children to eat made participation in family mealtimes difficult.

These challenges required considerable ingenuity and altruism in how parents managed domestic food provisioning and sought to mitigate their food insecurity. They mentioned eating leftovers, going without food themselves and going to lengths to protect their children's material and social needs and wants in order to provide a 'normal' life for them. Thomas talked about the importance of taking the children occasionally to the supermarket as part of their education. Laura said in order to give her daughter a good example, she made sure she was not always lying down at home when her daughter was there. Some parents felt they were 'not successful enough.' Sandra felt guilty about being reliant on benefits because she said she was keen to work but unable to see how this might be possible given the lack of appropriate affordable childcare. By contrast, Fatima took an optimistic view, comparing the family's situation favourably with those worse off than herself and leveraging her poor health as a resource to ensure she did not have to choose between 'heating and eating': 'I'm a vulnerable so they [energy companies] can't just cut me off.'

CONCLUSION

This chapter has suggested that a comparative case-based approach is helpful in understanding how lone parent, non-employed families with a disability or long-term health condition manage to feed themselves. We have shown how all four families struggled with restricted food budgets and particular dimensions of food provisioning. These included a range of challenges related to their specific long-term health conditions: costs related to disabilities that further restricted food budgets and mobility needs that meant in some cases relying on their children's help. Children's selective eating preferences related to their health conditions was another challenge that meant that food was often at risk of being wasted, further restricting parents' ways of managing on a tight budget. Like all low-income families, these parents could not always buy food they deemed 'healthy' and instead relied on lower quality, cheaper food, a situation that was characteristic of the United Kingdom.

We have also shown the ways in which these households' restricted incomes and hence restricted food budgets were sandwiched between the macro level of the state and the local level of relatives and local services. However, these levels are not equal in their impact. The state's insufficient provision of income through its social security benefits and rules of entitlement create the structures within which these households manage, with the United Kingdom having high rates of poverty and food insecurity among people with disabilities compared with Denmark. As the UK cases suggest, benefits are woefully inadequate as reflected in the debt the parents incurred. In Denmark, although benefit levels are higher, the parents still struggled to buy adequate nutritious food.

The local level of services provides a stop gap where the state fails to provide adequately. In the United Kingdom in particular, charities have stepped in, such as food banks, and have become institutionalised. In Denmark, private food bank initiatives and charities have appeared over the last few years but still play a comparably small role. There is little municipal support for parents to access private transport in the United Kingdom to meet the needs of families living with a long-term health condition. While informal support from family and friends can be an important resource for these households, support depends on their having the resources available. The families' health conditions may also make social participation outside the home that centres on food difficult; this may be compounded by the lack the financial means to engage in, and reciprocate, hospitality further excluding the already marginalised. Moreover, withdrawal from social networks can be a self-perpetuating process as families become increasingly isolated and feel increasingly stigmatised.

As the evidence shows, across Europe, families living with a disability or long-term health condition are at greater risk of poverty and food insecurity than those without. Though rates are lower in Scandinavian welfare states, such as Denmark, the spread of neoliberal ideologies means increasing pressure on individuals to engage in the labour market; however, exclusion from suitable paid employment and childcare leaves families living with a disability reliant on benefits that are inadequate. Given the impacts of poor diets on physical and mental health (Firth et al., 2020; Koutoukidis & Jebb, 2019), low-income and food insecurity are likely to compound ill health and health inequalities between those with and without disabilities and long-term health conditions. To address this, governments should ensure the rights of people with disabilities are met, by providing equitable access to suitable employment, childcare and sufficient welfare support. This means taking account of the additional costs of living with disability in setting benefit rates. In the context of rising living costs in many European countries, more generous payments to those living with disability are urgently needed in order for families to feed themselves in ways that meet nutritional targets and customary norms.

FUNDING ACKNOWLEDGEMENTS

The work for the UK study was supported by the European Research Council (ERC) under the European Union's Seventh Framework Programme (FP7/2007–2013), ERC grant agreement number 337977. The work for the Danish study was funded by the Independent Research Fund Denmark, no. 8019-00014b.

NOTES

1. The four commonly cited pillars of food security are 'availability', 'access', 'utilization' and 'stability' (CFS, 2009); more recently, the case has been made for a formal update to include two additional dimensions: 'agency' and 'sustainability' (Clapp et al., 2022).

2. It is important to note that although the terms incapacity and disability are often used interchangeably, they have different meanings. In relation to benefits, disability usually means having an impairment, whereas incapacity concerns being unable to work because of an impairment: '[p]eople can be disabled without being unable to work, and unable to work without being disabled' (Spicker, 2003, p. 31).

3. Means testing is a system whereby the state decides if your income and capital are low enough to qualify for a benefit.

4. Halvorsen et al. (2017) include in these, 'medical assistance and rehabilitation, education and vocational training, assistive technology, personal assistance, and others which all mean to improve the independence and social participation of persons with disabilities' [unpaged].

5. A main difference with respect to disability rights, law and provisions is the 'flexicurity' model in Denmark, 'an integrated strategy for enhancing both flexibility and security in the labour market'. A component that is often considered the cornerstone of the flexicurity model is that employers enjoy extensive freedom to dismiss employees (Arnardóttir et al., 2018, p. 152). This results in higher levels of unemployment among Danish people than in neighbouring Sweden, for example (Liisberg, 2011).

6. In part, this is because there are lower rates and less discussion in the public discourse, also may be an issue of not being the data – municipalities responsible for assessments do not record/share numbers/rate of benefits according to this report: https://www.gov.scot/binaries/content/documents/govscot/publications/foi-eir-release/2018/07/foi-18-01623/documents/foi-18-01632-international-comparison-disability-benefits-report-pdf/foi-18-01632-international-comparison-disability-benefits-report-pdf/govscot%3Adocument/FOI-18-01632%2B-%2BInternational%2BComparison%2Bof%2BDisability%2BBenefits%2B-%2BReport.pdf

7. From https://ec.europa.eu/eurostat/statistics-explained/index.php?title=Glossary:Activity_limitation

Activity limitation is a dimension of health/disability capturing long-standing limitation in performing usual activities (due to health problems). Indicators based on this concept can be used to evaluate the general health status, disability and related inequalities and healthcare needs at the population level.

Exampleof an operational definition used within the European Statistical System:

One question instrument – the Global Activity Limitation Instrument (GALI) - assessing the presence of long-standing activity limitation: "For at least the past 6 months, to what extent have you been limited because of a health problem in activities people usually do? Would you say you have been ..." severely limited/limited but not severely or/not limited at all? The question was developed by the Euro-REVES project. It is used in European Health Interview Survey (EHIS) (HS3 variable) and EU Statistics on Income and Living Conditions (EU-SILC). (PH030 variable)

8. Thirty lived in an inner London borough and 15 were in a coastal town in the South East of England, both areas of social deprivation and high rates of child poverty of over 40% (endchildpoverty.org.uk). In both study areas, around half the mothers were originally from the United Kingdom and were British citizens. In the inner London borough, the British mothers (18/30) included white British, Black British and British Asian mothers, while a third (10/30) had migrated from outside the European Union (West and North Africa). In the coastal area, all the British mothers (8/15) were white. In the total sample, parents in 7 of the 45 families were migrants from mainland Europe. Reflecting wider evidence about poverty and food poverty, lone-parent families were overrepresented (O'Connell et al., 2019).

9. There are challenges in using income as a measure of living standards for people living with disability and long-term health conditions, in part because of the 'extra costs' associated with some conditions (El Dessouky & McCurdy, 2023). However, in order to provide a *rough* comparison of adequacy of income across the two countries, we have given weekly/monthly household income compared to available reference budgets for the closest matching household types. While methodologies differ, reference budgets are a way calculating the expenditure necessary to meet basic needs and, in some cases, customary norms (Padley & Hirsch, 2017)

REFERENCES

Arnardóttir, O. M., Hotvedt, M. J., Nousiainen, K., & Ventegodt, M. (2018). Nordic disability employment laws and policies in a human rights perspective. In R. Halvorsen & B. Hvinden (Eds.), *Youth, diversity and employment* (pp. 150–177). Edward Elgar Publishing. https://doi.org/10.4337/9781783476008.00012

Attree, P. (2005). Low-income mothers, nutrition and health: A systematic review of qualitative evidence. *Maternal and Child Nutrition*, *1*, 227–240.

Bambra, C., & Eikemo, T. A. (2009). Welfare state regimes, unemployment and health: A comparative study of the relationship between unemployment and self-reported health in 23 European countries. *Journal of Epidemiology & Community Health*, *63*, 92–98.

Bonke, J., Anders, E., & Wiese, C. (2016). *Minimumsbudget for forbrugsudgifter - hvad er det mindste, man kan leve for?* Syddansk Universitetsforlag.

Bowen, S., Elliott, S., & Brenton, J. (2014). The joy of cooking? *Contexts*, *13*(3), 20–25.

Boyle, N. B., & Power, M. (2021). Proxy longitudinal indicators of household food insecurity in the UK [version 1; peer review: 1 approved]. *Emerald Open Research*, *3*, 16. https://doi.org/10.35241/emeraldopenres.14311.1

Brannen, J. (2005). *Introduction to a Workshop on Comparative Biographical Research*, 24–25 November, Thomas Coram Research Unit, Institute of Education, University of London. http://eprints.ncrm.ac.uk/10/1/JuliaBrannen-Introduction.pdf

Brannen, J., & Nilsen, A. (2011). Comparative biographies in case-based cross-national research: Methodological considerations. *Sociology*, *45*(4), 603–619.

Brannen, J., & Wilson, G. (Eds.). (1987/2023), *Give and take in families: Studies in resource distribution*. Unwin Hyman.

Brinkmann, S., & Kvale, S. (2018). *Doing interviews*. SAGE.

Bull, R., Miles, C., Newbury, E., Nichols, A., Weekes, T., & Wyld, G. (2023, June). *Hunger in the UK*. https://www.trusselltrust.org/wp-content/uploads/sites/2/2023/08/2023-The-Trussell-Trust-Hunger-in-the-UK-report-web-updated-10Aug23.pdf

CFS. (2009). Reform of the committee on world food security: Final version. *Committee on World Food Security, Thirty-fifth Session*. https://www.fao.org/fileadmin/templates/cfs/Docs0910/ReformDoc/CFS_2009_2_Rev_2_E_K7197.pdf

Clapp, J., Moseley, W., Burlingame, B., & Termine, P. (2022). Viewpoint: The case for a six-dimensional food security framework. *Food Policy, 106*. https://doi.org/10.1016/j.foodpol.2021.102164

Coleman-Jensen, A., & Nord, M. (2013). Food insecurity among households with working age adults with disabilities. In C. Penderson (Ed.), *Food insecurity among disabled adult households* (pp. 1–60). Nova Science Publishers, Inc.

Crow, L. (1996). Including all our lives: Renewing the social model of disability. In J. Morris (Ed.), *Encounters with strangers: Feminism and disability*. Women's Press.

Davis, O., & Geiger, B. (2017). Did food insecurity rise across Europe after the 2008 crisis? An analysis across welfare regimes. *Social Policy and Society, 16*(3), 343–360.

DeVault, M. (1991). *Feeding the family: The social organization of caring as gendered work*. University of Chicago Press.

Ditlevsen, K., Halkier, B., & Holm, L. (2023). Pathways of less healthy diets. An investigation of the everyday food practices of men and women in low income households. *Critical Public Health, 33*(3), 318–331. https://doi.org/10.1080/09581596.2022.2101917

Ditlevsen, K., Holm, L., & Halkier, B. (forthcoming). There is always food in the freezer. *Negotiations of Respectability, Health and Food Among Women in Disadvantaged Conditions.*

Dowler, E. (2002). Food and poverty in Britain: Rights and responsibilities. *Social Policy and Administration, 36*(6), 698–717.

Dowler, E. A., & O'Connor, D. (2012). Rights based approaches to addressing food poverty and food insecurity in Ireland and UK. *Social Science & Medicine, 74*(1), 44–51.

Dowler, E., Turner, S., & with Dobson, B. (2001). *Poverty bites: Food, health and poor families*. Child Poverty Action Group.

Edmiston, D., Robertshaw, D., Young, D., Ingold, J., Gibbons, A., Summers, K., Scullion, L., Geiger, B. B., & de Vries, R. (2022). Mediating the claim? How 'local ecosystems of support' shape the operation and experience of UK social security. *Social Policy and Administration, 56*(5), 775–790. https://doi.org/10.1111/spol.12803

Ejrnæs, M., Larsen, J., & Müller, M. (2020). Parents on low benefits – Coping with poverty. *Journal of Poverty, 24*(7), 610–626. https://doi.org/10.1080/10875549.2020.1740376

El Dessouky, O., & McCurdy, C. (2023). *Costly differences: Living standards for working-age people with disabilities*. Resolution Foundation. https://www.resolutionfoundation.org/app/uploads/2023/01/Costly-differences.pdf

Esping-Andersen, G. (1990). *The three worlds of welfare capitalism*. Polity Press.

Esping-Andersen, G. (2002). Towards the good society, once again? In G. Esping-Andersen (Ed.), *Why we need a new welfare state*. Oxford University Press.

Falster, E., & Ringø, P. (2023). Is something rotten in the state of Denmark? Austerity measures from a child and youth perspective. *Disability & Society*. https://doi.org/10.1080/09687599.2023.2279489

FAO. (1996). *Rome declaration on world food security and world food summit plan of action*. https://www.fao.org/4/w3548e/w3548e00.htm

Fielding-Singh, P., & Cooper, M. (2023). The emotional management of motherhood: Foodwork, maternal guilt, and emotion work. *Journal of Marriage and Family, 85*(2), 436–457.

Firth, J., Gangwisch, J. E., Borsini, A., Wootton, R. E., & Mayer, E. A. (2020). Food and mood: How do diet and nutrition affect mental wellbeing? *BMJ, 369*, m2382. https://doi.org/10.1136/bmj.m2382

Goode, J., Callendar, C., & Lister, R. (1998). *Purse or wallet? Gender inequalities within families on benefits*. Policy Studies Institute.

Hadfield-Spoor, M., Avendan, M., & Loopstra, R. (2022). Food insecurity among disabled adults. *The European Journal of Public Health, 32*(4), 593–599.

Halvorsen, R., Hvinden, B., Beadle Brown, J., Biggeri, M., Tøssebro, J., & Waldschmidt, A. (Eds.). (2018). *Understanding the lived experiences of persons with disabilities in nine countries: Active citizenship and disability in Europe* (Vol. 2). Routledge.

Halvorsen, R., Hvinden, B., Bickenbach, J., Ferri, D., & Marta Guillén Rodriguez, A. (Eds.). (2017). *The changing disability policy system: Active citizenship and disability in Europe* (Vol. 1). Routledge.

Hanmer, J., & Hearn, J. (1999). Social relations of welfare. In F. Williams, J. Popay, & A. Oakley (Eds.), *Welfare research: A critical review*. UCL Press.

Hirsch, D. (2015). *A minimum income standard for the UK in 2015: Full report*. https://www.jrf.org.uk/work/a-minimum-income-standard-for-the-uk-in-2015

Holm, L., MariannePipping, E., Sara, H., & Thomas Bøker, L. (2015). Who is cooking dinner? *Food, Culture and Society*, *18*(4), 589–610. https://doi.org/10.1080/15528014.2015.1088191

Hvinden, B. (2016). *Final report summary – DISCIT (Making persons with disabilities full citizens – New knowledge for an inclusive and sustainable European Social Model)*. https://cordis.europa.eu/result/rcn/185124_en.html [Norway].

Knight, A., O'Connell, R., & Brannen, J. (2020). Families living in hard times. In C. Cameron & P. Moss (Eds.), *Transformation in early childhood in England: Towards a democratic revolution*. UCL Press.

Koutoukidis, D., & Jebb, S. (2019). Public health nutrition in the UK. *Medicine*, *47*(3), 199–203. https://doi.org/10.1016/j.mpmed.2018.12.006

Lambie-Mumford, H. (2017). *Hungry Britain: The rise of food charity*. Policy Press.

Liisberg, M. (2011). *Disability and employment: A contemporary disability human rights approach applied to Danish, Swedish and EU law and policy* [PhD thesis]. Maastrict University.

Loopstra, R., Reeves, A., McKee, M., & Stuckler, D. (2016). Food insecurity and social protection in Europe: Quasi-natural experiment of Europe's great recessions 2004–2012, *Preventive Medicine*, *89*, 44–50.

Loopstra, R., Reeves, A., & Tarasuk, V. (2019). The rise of hunger among low-income households: An analysis of the risks of food insecurity between 2004 and 2016 in a population-based study of UK adults. *Journal of Epidemiology & Community Health*, *73*, 668–673.

Loopstra, R., Reeves, A., Taylor-Robinson, D., Barr, B., McKee, M., & Stuckler, D. (2015). Austerity, sanctions, and the rise of food banks in the UK. *British Medical Journal*, *350*, h1775.

Mitra, S. (2006). Disability and social safety nets in developing countries. *International Journal of Disability*, *2*(1), 43–88.

Narotzky, S., & Besnier, N. (2014). Crisis, value, and hope: Rethinking the economy. An introduction to Supplement 9. *Current Anthropology*, *55*(S9), S4–S16.

Nørup, I. (2020). Social marginalization and chronic illness: A critical analysis of the role of labour-market exclusion. *Acta Sociologica*, *63*(2), 173–190. https://doi.org/10.1177/0001699318821429

Nørup, I., & Jacobsen, B. (2022). Not seeing the elephant in the room: How policy discourses shape frontline work with child poverty. *Social Policy and Administration*, *56*(4), 580–594. https://doi.org/10.1111/spol.12784

O'Connell, R., & Brannen, J. (2019). Food poverty and the families the state has turned its back on: The case of the UK. In H. Gaisbauer, G. Schweiger, & C. Sedmak (Eds.), *Absolute poverty in Europe: Interdisciplinary perspectives on a hidden phenomenon* (pp. 183–211). Policy Press.

O'Connell, R., & Brannen, J. (2021). *Families and food in hard times: European comparative research*. UCL Press.

O'Connell, R., Brannen, J., & Knight, A. (2019). *Living hand to mouth: Children and food in low-income families*. Child Poverty Action Group.

Owens, J. (2015, March). Exploring the critiques of the social model of disability: The transformative possibility of Arendt's notion of power. *Sociology of Health & Illness*, *37*(3), 385–403.

Padley, M., & Hirsch, D. (2017). *A minimum income standard for the UK*. JRF.

Ridge, T. (2009). *Living with poverty A review of the literature on children's and families' experiences of poverty* Department for Work and Pensions, Research Report No 594. DWP.

Saleem, S. (2020). *Replication data for: Disability data* (V2) [Harvard Dataverse]. https://doi.org/10.7910/DVN/AGS7HX

Schwartz, N., Buliung, R., & Wilson, K. (2019). Disability and food access and insecurity: A scoping review of the literature. *Health & Place*, *57*, 107–121.

Scott, G., A. McKay, C. Sawers, and R. Harris. (1999). *What can we afford? A woman's role*. Scottish Poverty Information Unit.

Sen, A. (1981). *Poverty and famines: An essay on entitlement and deprivation*. Oxford University Press.

Snape, D., Otley, M., & Kumar, M. (1999). *Relying on the state, relying on each other*. DSS.

Spicker, P. (2003). Distinguishing disability and incapacity. *International Social Security Review*, *56*, 31–43. https://doi.org/10.1111/1468-246X.00156

Sung, S., & Bennett, F. (2007). Dealing with money in low- to moderate-income couples: Insights from individual interviews. In K. Clarke, T. Malby, & P. Kennett (Eds.), *Social policy review 19: Analysis and debate in social policy*. The Policy Press.

Thomas, G. (2021). Dis-mantling stigma: Parenting disabled children in an age of 'neoliberal-ableism.' *The Sociological Review*, *69*(2), 451–467.

Thomson, R. (2009). *Unfolding lives: Youth, gender, change*. Policy Press.

Toft, U., Kristoffersen, L. H., Lau, C., Borch-Johnsen, K., & Jørgensen, T. (2007). The dietary quality score: Validation and association with cardiovascular risk factors: The Inter99 study. *European Journal of Clinical Nutrition*, *61*, 270–278. https://doi.org/10.1038/sj.ejcn.1602503

Vereecken, C., De Henauw, S., & Maes, L. (2005). Adolescents' food habits: Results of the health behaviour in school-aged children survey. *British Journal of Nutrition*, *94*, 423–431.

Vereecken, C., Pedersen, T., Ojala, K., Krølner, R., Ahluwalia, N., Giacchi, M., & Kelly, C. (2015). Fruit and vegetable consumption trends among adolescents from 2002 to 2010 in 33 countries. *The European Journal of Public Health*, *25*(2), 16–19.

Vitus, K., Tørslev, M. K., Ditlevsen, K., & Nielsen, A. L. (2018). Body weight management and dilemmas of health responsibility for vulnerable groups in the changing Danish welfare state: A comparative case analysis. *Critical Public Health*, *28*(1), 22–34. https://doi.org/10.1080/09581596.2017.1286294

Warde, A. (2016). *The practice of eating*. Polity.

Whitehead, A. (1984). *I'm hungry mum: The politics of domestic budgeting*. Routledge.

WHO. (2011). *World report on disability 2011*. World Health Organization.

WHO. (2019). Factsheet: Disability. https://www.who.int/europe/news-room/fact-sheets/item/disability

EXPLORING THE INDIVIDUAL-LEVEL FACTORS INFLUENCING TRUST IN CONSUMER RIGHTS PROTECTION: A CROSS-NATIONAL STUDY IN EUROPE

Andreea Ioana Alecu

Oslo Metropolitan University, Norway

ABSTRACT

Trustworthy institutions are often seen as a way of maintaining high levels of collaboration in society. Yet, what characterizes individuals who trust that authorities will safeguard their consumer rights remains under-explored. This study addresses this gap by examining cross-national variations in trust that authorities protect consumer rights. In doing so, it explores whether and how one's in-market experiences and perception (experiencing problems or detriment and issues with product safety), knowledge of consumer rights, and one's socioeconomic resources are related to having confidence that public authorities protect one's consumer rights. In doing so, it partly accounts for national-level institutional and policy variation, by employing country and year fixed effects. The study employs multilevel hierarchical models on four rounds of surveys covering 30 European countries in the 2014–2020 period. The results support the hypothesis that trust is malleable, as negative experiences and market perceptions correlate with trust. Trust levels vary across groups with different access to socioeconomic resources. Knowledge of consumer rights does significantly correlate with the outcome, with a few exceptions. In sum, the study suggests a link between trust in public authorities and markets, which may lead to virtuous or vicious spirals of trust.

Consumers and Consumption in Comparison
Comparative Social Research, Volume 37, 67–91

ISSN: 0195-6310/doi:10.1108/S0195-631020240000037004

Keywords: Consumer rights; societal trust; market transactions; consumer policy; public confidence

INTRODUCTION

Trustworthy institutions are often seen as a way of maintaining high levels of interpersonal trust and collaboration in society. High and stable levels of trust in a society are generally considered positive, not least because of their associations with many outcomes ranging from individual well-being to economic growth (Knack & Keefer, 1997; Lopez-de-Silanes et al., 1997; Zak & Knack, 2001). Trust is seen as a prerequisite for market exchange as it reduces complexity (Burt & Knez, 1995; Granovetter, 1985). Although the scholarship on various forms of trust has flourished in the last decades, there are few studies exploring the characteristics of consumers who trust authorities to protect their consumer rights.

For citizens to be willing to hand over resources and tasks to public institutions, it is argued that citizens need to perceive these institutions as fair, impartial, and efficient (Kumlin & Rothstein, 2003; Rothstein & Stolle, 2003). Nevertheless, most studies focus on the citizens' interaction with public institutions such as education, healthcare, police, and the judiciary. Yet, markets and the authorities regulating markets have received limited attention. Unlike interactions with the police, or healthcare which occur relatively seldom, people engage in market transactions at least daily. Hence, citizens become consumers, and these interactions may both inform them both about how well markets function and shape their opinions of how effective institutions regulating markets are. Institutions here refers to public authorities making up the political system (Rothstein, 1998), and especially those charged with implementing policy addressing consumers. Yet, direct interactions with consumer authorities occur seldom for most consumers, and consumer politics has not been highly salient in the EU in the last decade. The few studies on the topic highlight large variations in trust in markets between countries (Berg, 2022; Nessel, 2022; Repo & Timonen, 2017). However, individual-level predictors of confidence that public authorities protect consumer rights remain unclear and are under-explored.

This study aims to address this gap by investigating individual-level mechanisms that can foster or hinder trust formation, such as having negative experiences (experiencing problems or detriment, and issues with product safety) and knowledge of consumer rights in a comparative perspective. More specifically, I estimate multilevel hierarchical models on four rounds of surveys covering 30 European countries in the 2014–2020 period. All the countries' studies are either members of the European Union, or the European Economic Area, and have similar overall consumer regulation measures. Yet, the implementation and enactment of these regulations varies substantially between these countries (Berg, 2022; Nessel, 2022). Thus, the analyses presented here account for some of the between-country differences by employing country fixed effects.

UNDERSTANDINGS OF CROSS-NATIONAL DIFFERENCES IN TRUST IN MARKETS AND CONSUMER AUTHORITIES

Activities and legislation initiated by the European Union serve as potent catalysts in enhancing consumer conditions at the domestic level (Nessel, 2019). Nevertheless, the responsibility of enforcing consumer rights primarily rests with national authorities, albeit with assistance from consumer organizations (Austgulen, 2020; Berg, 2022). The European Commission has established directives outlining basic consumer protection standards for Europe (Nessel, 2019), and these have been reinforced in the European Commission's New Consumer Agenda (European Commission, 2020). Member states have different consumer policy preferences which at times present obstacles to harmonizing legislation and implementing uniform measures to enhance consumer conditions. Countries also differ in the ways in which such bodies are organized, the budgets such organizations have, their legal capabilities, as well as on whether civil society organizations exist and are active in protecting consumer rights (Austgulen, 2020; Nessel, 2019, 2022; Repo & Timonen, 2017). Additional sources of differences between countries may be related to consumer law at the national and transnational level (Micklitz, 2003; Weatherill, 2013).

Differences in resource availability, allocation, and commitment to consumer protection among Member States make legislation uniformity challenging, especially as countries with more resources and higher protection standards resist measures aimed at lowering standards (Austgulen, 2020) and market regulations differ across countries (Kjærnes et al., 2007). As such, several models of classifying consumer policy regimes have been developed (Austgulen, 2020; Nessel, 2019, 2022; Repo & Timonen, 2017). For instance, Repo and Timonen (2017) suggest the existence of five European political regimes, with different economies and institutional settings.

Following this, several studies started to explore macro-level differences in terms of consumer trust in markets at the EU level. Trust, although a complicated theoretical construct, remains high on policy makers' agenda (European Commission, 2020). At its core, confidence in institutions informs of how well institutions are functioning, as well as of their effectiveness and impartiality (Norris, 1999; Rothstein & Stolle, 2008; Van der Meer, 2010). Berg (2022) illustrated this point by showing that fair and effective authorities enhance trust in markets.

Nessel (2022) uses aggregate data from the 28 European Union member states to show how political structures – at the aggregate level – are related to trust in markets. Nessel (2022) builds on an economic sociology framework and draws attention to the importance of political structures as trust fostering mechanisms. Through his analyses, he shows that levels of trust in markets varied considerably across EU member states, using European Consumer Scoreboards data from 2016 as a case. His analyses suggest that this divergence in trust levels can be – at least partly – explained by varying levels of political embeddedness (Nessel, 2022). Using consumer policy as a measurement of political embeddedness, the article posits that institutional or political trust is a crucial factor influencing consumer trust in markets rather than just trust in personal relationships (Nessel, 2022).

Similar findings are echoed by Berg (2022), who also finds that fair and effective consumer authorities are robust predictors of better performing markets (measured by safe consumer conditions). Her analyses account for individual-level factors, such as age, gender, education, and one's financial situation. Differing somewhat from Nessel (2022), Berg (2022) argues in her study that "that people's assessments of their consumer authorities are based on their individual experiences in the marketplace" (Berg, 2022, p. 555), drawing focus on the importance of individual-level factors. Moreover, Berg (2022) finds that enforcement of consumer rights by fair and effective authorities promotes supplier reliability and consumer safety. Her study shows that safe conditions result in positive consumer experiences, fostering trust. Berg (2022) emphasizes that excessive trust could lead to complacency among consumers, resulting in unreflective choices, thus raising important policy questions regarding level of risk consumer authorities should aim to eliminate and how to encourage consumers to make informed, reflective choices. A similar point is also raised by Nessel (2022), who encourages future research to examine more closely the potentially negative consequences of excessive trust.

The present study shifts focus to confidence in consumer authorities rather than confidence in markets. Understanding who trusts consumer authorities is important. National consumer authorities are responsible for deciding whether and how markets are to be regulated, as well as, enacting, and following up legislation passed at the European Union level. Furthermore, if political structures are of importance to how markets are perceived and whether they are trusted by consumers, it is important to further explore what factors may influence trust in consumer authorities.

I argue that confidence in markets can also be seen as a predictor, not only a result of trusting consumer authorities, as consumers get the chance to evaluate the functioning of consumers authorities through their repeated interactions in the markets. As such, market experiences (such as experiencing problems, unsafe products) may shape whether consumers trust authorities to protect their rights.

In other words, I argue that there is a mutual interconnectedness between trust in consumer authorities and trust in markets, at least at a theoretical level. Trust in markets and in consumer authorities are arguably in a mutually re-enforcing relationship, creating either a virtuous or a vicious spiral. In a virtuous spiral, high trust in consumer authorities, stemming perhaps from their fairness and effectiveness, can lead to increased trust in markets. This, in turn, can further enhance trust in the authorities, forming a positive feedback loop. The authorities' enforcement of consumer rights fosters supplier reliability and safe consumer conditions, which then reinforces consumer trust in the market and its regulatory bodies. However, the opposite can also occur, resulting in a vicious spiral. If consumer authorities are perceived as unfair or ineffective, this can lead to reduced trust in markets. This diminished trust in markets can further erode confidence in the consumer authorities, creating a negative feedback loop.

Nevertheless, the relationship between confidence in markets and institutions remains under-explored. The current studies lack the empirical design, and data to assess whether confidence in political institutions *is solely a predictor* of confidence in markets, or whether those with high levels of trust in markets also have more trust in political institutions. This limitation also affects the present study. Nevertheless, comparative studies of individual markets, such as Kjærnes et al. (2007) who focus on trust in food, point out the interdependence between these two concepts (i.e., trust in consumer authorities and trust in markets) and the potential pitfalls in disentangling this causal nexus. Kjærnes et al. (2007) also highlight how trust is shaped by factors regulated at different levels of government nationally and factors regulated supra-nationally, yet that for consumers these two types of trust might intertwine, and they use their own experiences as a heuristic mechanism to disentangle these complex processes.

TRUST AT THE INDIVIDUAL LEVEL: SOCIAL POSITION, CULTURE, AND EXPERIENCE

While national-level factors play a crucial role in understanding trust in consumer authorities, it's equally important to explore individual-level predictors of institutional trust in a comparative perspective. Yet, this relationship has received limited attention within the consumption literature. This section delves into the broader institutional trust scholarship, discussing several approaches to understanding individual-level predictors of confidence in consumer protection institutions. These approaches focus on the roles of culture and personality, personal experiences, and social networks, along with one's social position.

Uslaner (2002, 2003, pp. 171–190) has focused on the importance of cultural norms developed via interactions as trust fostering. Uslaner's approach entails that the levels of trust are relatively stable, as they are influenced by cultural norms transmitted through socialization processes (Uslaner, 2002). From this perspective, variations in trust are explained more by latent individual features like optimism and other socialization-transmitted norms, or culture, rather than by their interactions with institutions, markets, or other people. Hence, trust can be seen as a largely stable attitude formed in childhood that rarely changes. One implication of this perspective is that while large cross-national differences in trust are expected, personal experiences and one's background might have a minimal impact on trust levels when accounting for between-country variations. Hence, following this perspective, an empirical expectation is that there is *no association between consumers' experiences or perceptions of markets and trust that authorities safeguard consumer rights.*

More recent studies introduce the concept of trust as a malleable quality, showing that it can be shaped by personal experiences and interactions with others, even into adulthood (Glanville, 2016; Glanville et al., 2013; Glanville & Paxton, 2007). Large variations in trust levels across nations are not exclusive to consumer politics. Indeed, numerous studies highlight significant differences among European countries in both other forms of institutional trust and interpersonal trust (Delhey & Newton, 2004, 2005; Rothstein & Stolle, 2008). While most of these studies focus on interpersonal trust, and trust in other types of public institutions, the concept of trust's adaptability extends beyond these specific domains. As such, a second empirical expectation is that *one's experiences and perceptions of markets are associated with confidence that authorities protect consumer rights.*

In this study, I will focus on the role of two factors: perceptions of product safety and experiencing problems. These factors serve as proxies for consumers' in-market experiences. When consumers encounter, or think that products are harmful or hazardous, this may undermine the consumer's confidence in the efficacy of the regulatory mechanisms and institutions that are supposed to protect them. Product safety is an area of vital importance for European and national regulators (European Commission, 2020; Kjærnes et al., 2007). Perceptions of product safety are likely influenced by the information they receive from their social networks, and media. Isolated, information from the media and social networks are correlated to several forms of trust (Alecu et al., 2022; Grönlund & Setälä, 2012). As such, perception of product safety is a boarder indicator of both experiences and perceptions of market safety.

Experiencing problems, such as faulty products, or other problems which give a consumers' legitimate reason to complain, may also be linked with trusting consumer authorities. This experience is not always a direct result of sellers/providers intentionally delivering subpar or faulty goods and services (Donoghue et al., 2016; Raval, 2020). Often, it is a complex interplay of various factors, unforeseen manufacturing defects, or even misuse by consumers themselves (Donoghue et al., 2016; Raval, 2020). Regardless of the cause, I argue that when consumers encounter such problems, they may reconsider how they view consumer authorities. On the one hand, experiencing a problem, taking action, and having a rapid redress may contribute to a higher level of trust in authorities. However, I argue that not taking action may be more detrimental to trust in consumer authorities than taking action after encountering a problem. Consumer authorities are seen in this perspective as the guardians of consumer interests, tasked with ensuring fair trade practices and holding sellers/providers accountable. By taking action when experiencing a problem, the consumers the consumers get a chance to experience whether the how consumer protection functions. However, by not taking action, consumers might have either given up hope of redress, have been previously dissatisfied by the available redress mechanisms, or the outcome of their previous redress attempt (Alecu & Dulsrud, 2022). Raval (2020) has shown that in the United States, there are also considerable inequities between those who take action and those who do not after experiencing problems. The analyses will explore whether the strength of these associations varies between countries.

One's knowledge of consumer rights may influence both trust level and mitigate the role of experiences, as consumers more aptly retrieve information or solve problems. For instance, Donoghue et al. (2016) show in their study that South African consumers who had some knowledge of consumer rights were also better equipped to take private and public action. Furthermore, knowledge of consumer rights is linked with complaint behavior through several mechanisms, such as a better understanding of procedural fairness, blame attrition, and expectations of recovery (Choi & Mattila, 2008; Harris et al., 2006; Raval, 2020; Stø, 1989). Yet, whether knowledge of consumer rights is linked with one's level of trust in consumer authorities remains an empirical question, which will be explored in the analyses. A caveat is that knowledge of consumer rights is likely endogenous to one's trust in consumer authorities – as consumer authorities within the EU often work to broaden consumer's knowledge of their rights, as reiterated in the European Commission's New Consumer Agenda.

A third important set of factors is linked to one's social position or socioeconomic resources. One's social position is a correlate of access to social capital which in turn is related to various forms of trust (Brehm & Rahn, 1997; Li et al., 2005; Putnam, 2016), such as interpersonal trust (Freitag & Traunmüller, 2009; Hofstra et al., 2017; Putnam, 1995) and trust in institution (Charron & Rothstein, 2016; Glanville et al., 2013; Smith, 1997). Yet, this link is mediated by the quality of the institutions, both when it comes to generalized trust (Rothstein, 2011) and trust in markets (Berg, 2022; Nessel, 2022). In terms of the mechanisms linking education with trust, it has been suggested that education may make people better informed and improves skills for handling information which should increase their trust (Keefer & Knack, 2005, pp. 701–725).

While education has been the focus of many studies on various forms of trust, I argue that in relationship to confidence in consumer authorities, financial security is also highly relevant. Consumer's financial stability may enable them to take risks with new products or services, knowing that they have the means to absorb potential financial losses. Financially stable consumers may have better access to legal resources and be more capable of asserting their rights when they feel these have been violated. Conversely, consumers with less financial resources may not afford to trust consumer authorities to the same extent. This argument is not new (see, for instance, Offe, 1999s contribution regarding interpersonal trust), yet it has not been studied in relationship to confidence in consumer authorities. A similar association can be expected in relationship to one's occupational position. Individuals in upper class positions generally have larger social networks (Alecu et al., 2022; Li et al., 2008), yet the strength of these associations varies between countries (Otero et al., 2022, 2023). Thus, a third empirical expectation is that individuals with more socioeconomic resources are also more inclined to trust that consumer authorities protect their rights. Higher socioeconomic status (SES) may translate in consumers being more trustful toward institutions, as their networks may help them recuperate potential financial losses.

DATA AND METHODS

The data for this study are sourced from the European Commission's Consumer Conditions Survey (European Commission, n.d.). This survey analyzes consumption habits, experiences, and attitudes in the EU Member States, Iceland, and Norway. A sample of 1,000 respondents is drawn from each country, except for Malta, Luxembourg, Cyprus, and Iceland, where a sample of 500 is drawn (overview of countries in Supplementary Table A2). The survey covers topics such as: consumer trust, knowledge of selected consumer rights, consumer experiences and use of online shopping, product safety, experiencing problems, and taking action, as well as items regarding having experienced dishonest and illegal commercial practices by retailers and market players.

The data were first published in 2008 and have been conducted biennially since then. To better align with EU policy developments, the questionnaire has been revised and changed in this period leading to some overtime comparability issues. To bypass as many of these issues as possible, this study focuses on the period from 2014 to 2020 and only employs variables which have not changed over time. In total, this study includes data from four rounds (2014, 2016, 2018, and 2020) and incorporates 112,359 consumer responses across 30 countries.

Variables

The dependent variable is measured with the following item: "You trust public authorities to protect your rights as a consumer." Respondents answered on a four-point scale, ranging from strongly agree to strongly disagree. For the purposes of the main analyses, this variable was recoded so that consumers who answer that they agree or strongly agree are coded as trusting public authorities, while those who answer that they disagree or strongly disagree are coded as distrusting them. The analyses control for four types of variables which may influence consumer trust: trust in markets, in-market experiences, and market perceptions, knowledge of selected consumer rights, and sociodemographic factors. Except for education and one's self-reported financial situation, all these variables are available for all countries and in the 2014–2020 period. The variables vary over time and between countries. However, an important caveat is that new samples are drawn for each round of data collection. As such, using more stringent (although more precise) individual-level fixed effects is not possible.

Consumer trust in markets is captured by the following item "In general, retailers and service providers respect your rights as a consumer", coded 0 (indicating distrust) if consumers answered disagree or strongly disagree, and 1 (indicating trust) if they agreed or strongly agreed with the statement.

Consumer experiences are proxied by a variable that captures whether individuals have encountered problems when buying products and whether they have taken any action to address these issues. Specifically, respondents are classified as having either (1) experienced problems and taken action, (2) experienced problems but not taken any action, or (3) not experienced any problems. Additionally, the consumer's opinion regarding the prevalence of safe nonfood items in their country is also included as a proxy for consumer experiences. Yet, this item does not necessarily reflect the consumers' own experiences, as it likely captures influences from their families, friends and acquaintances, hence being a measure of perception, as well as experiences. Respondents are asked to indicate whether (1) they consider essentially all non-food products as safe, (2) believe a small number of non-food products are unsafe, (3) believe a significant number of non-food products are unsafe, or (4) think it depends on the specific product. Prior to answering the questions, respondents are informed that unsafe products are defined as those that do not comply with safety standards. Nevertheless, both variables can be argued to be a proxy for the respondent's perception of how well consumer policy is implemented in their respective country.

Consumer knowledge is assessed by the number of correct answers to three scenario questions. These questions test knowledge of consumer rights regarding unsolicited goods, the right to repair or to get a replacement product, and the "cooling-off period" or "cancelation period" when making distance purchases. It is important to note that the consumer rights directive (Directive 2011/83/EU, 2011) encompasses more rights than these three specific scenarios. Although one can argue about the appropriateness of these rights as indicators of consumer knowledge, they are the only ones that have been consistently measured across EU and EEA countries. These questions provide valuable and informative data regarding consumer knowledge, although they have important limitations.

In terms of sociodemographic factors, this study accounts for the respondents' gender, their age, as well as their self-reported occupational category. The occupational category distinguishes between those who report that they are: (1) self-employed, (2) managers, (3) white-collar workers, (4) blue-collar workers, (5) students, (6) not in employment, (7) seeking a job, and (8) retired. As a measure of social class position, or status, this measure is rather crude. Nevertheless, I argue that this measure can be used as a proxy for socioeconomic resources, and that the distinction captured by the variable map relatively close to more classical measures of class, such as a compressed version of the Erikson-Goldthorpe scheme (Erikson et al., 1979).

The respondent's highest level of completed education and self-reported financial situation are not available for the 2014 data collection wave. Additional analyses were estimated for the 2016–2020 waves to account for these variables. Education differentiates between those with a low level of education – Low (ISCED 0-1-2); medium (ISCED 3-4) and high (ISCED 5-6-7-8). The financial situation is assessed using the following variable "Thinking about your household's financial situation would you say that making ends meet every month is . . .?" which differentiates between those who answer (0) Very difficult or fairly difficult, and those who answer (1) Fairly easy, or very easy.

Estimation Strategy

The data is at the individual level and modelled to reflect that individuals are nested in countries over time. The analysis in this study utilizes hierarchical logistic models, which incorporate fixed effects at the country and year level. Country fixed effects are employed to control for all time-invariant country differences, ensuring that any observed effects are not driven solely by country-specific factors. The fixed effects on years have a similar function and capture unobserved time-varying factors that may be specific to each country at the collection of the data. In this way, the country year coefficient captures a policy change that occurred at a specific time point in only one of the countries

(Gelman & Hill, 2007). Nevertheless, with the exception of the remainder of the variables in the models, which vary between countries and over time, it cannot be excluded that other factors may influence the estimates presented here. To test the robustness of the estimates, random effects models (random intercept, random slope) were additionally estimated. These estimations yielded substantially similar results and for parsimony the fixed effects estimates are presented as the main results.

The results are presented on an absolute scale – as average marginal effects (AMEs) bounded by their 95% confidence intervals for ease of interpretation. Unlike relative measures, such as odds ratios, AME are somewhat easier to interpret and can be compared across models and samples (Long & Freese, 2006; Mood, 2010). Interaction effects are presented as conditional marginal effects to better illustrate changes from the baseline level within each country.

RESULTS

Descriptive Findings

Descriptive analyses are presented with median (inter-quantile range) and proportions for all variables used in the regression analyses in Supplementary Table A1. Overall, descriptive findings indicate only minor age and occupational differences between those who trust public institutions to protect their rights and those who do not. There are no apparent differences in terms of gender, or age, or occupational group. However, a higher share of respondents with better financial situations trust that authorities protect their consumer rights. There are also some differences in the levels of confidence that authorities protect consumer rights in terms of product safety, and experiencing problems, but not in relationship to knowledge of consumer rights. A large share of consumers who trust that sellers respect consumer rights also trust that public authorities do so.

Differences in Trust Across European Countries

The average level of trust in public authorities has been relatively stable in these 30 European countries. However, as shown in Fig. 1, there are large variations between the different countries. To ease interpretation, I will employ a geographical grouping of the countries: differentiating between North, East, South, and West. Consumers in Eastern European countries report somewhat lower levels of trust that authorities safeguard their consumer rights, although trust levels have increased in this group from 2014 to 2020. There are considerable differences within this group – as trust levels in Hungary are on par with those in Northern and Western Europe, while trust levels in Croatia and other countries are lower. In Southern European countries, trust levels have increased since 2014, yet consumers still report slightly lower levels of trust in public authorities than in Western European countries. Consumers in Western and Northern European countries report the highest levels of trust in public authorities. Apart from Iceland where trust levels have increased considerably, the

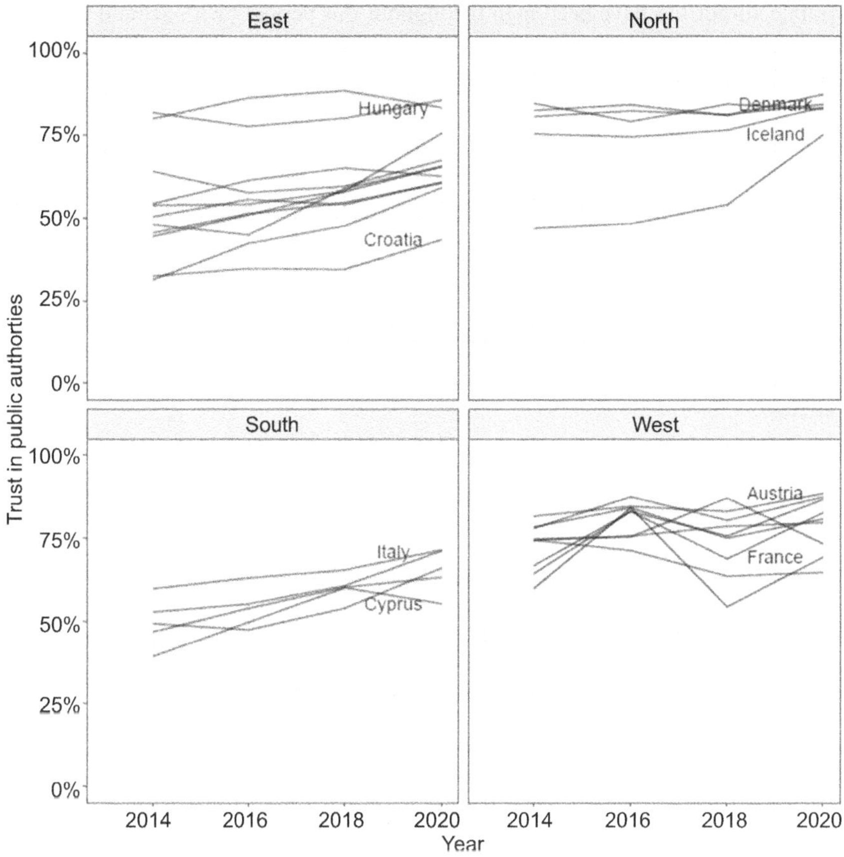

Fig. 1. Differences in Trust Level Across the 30 Countries.

remainder of the Northern European countries have relatively stable and high levels of trust. Among the Western European countries, there is some variation, which can also be driven by measurement error, as there are large changes in trust each time this item was measured in the Consumer Conditions Survey.

Perhaps the most important finding from this figure is that there are important and large cross-national variations in trust level. The trust trajectories of countries also vary in this 6-year period. While levels of trust have remained stable or only increased slightly in Northern and Western European countries, the levels of confidence in public authorities have increased rather substantially in some Eastern and Southern European countries. For instance, in Croatia in 2014, around 32% of the respondents reported that they had confidence in public authorities to protect their rights, while in 2020, 43% reported the same. Another example is Spain, where the levels of confidence have increased from around 46% to around 63% in 2020. In Denmark and Austria, the levels of confidence in public authorities have been high throughout this period – with around 80% who answer that they trust authorities to protect their consumer rights. These findings further motivate the need to explore how the importance of correlates of trust varies across the countries studied.

THE ROLE OF INDIVIDUAL-LEVEL FACTORS ON TRUST LEVELS

Fig. 2 presents the AMEs for three models: a bivariate model controlling only for trust in markets, an adjusted model controlling for all covariates except education and financial situation for the 2016–2020 period, and a model controlling for all covariates for the 2016–2020 period. All the models include country year fixed effects.

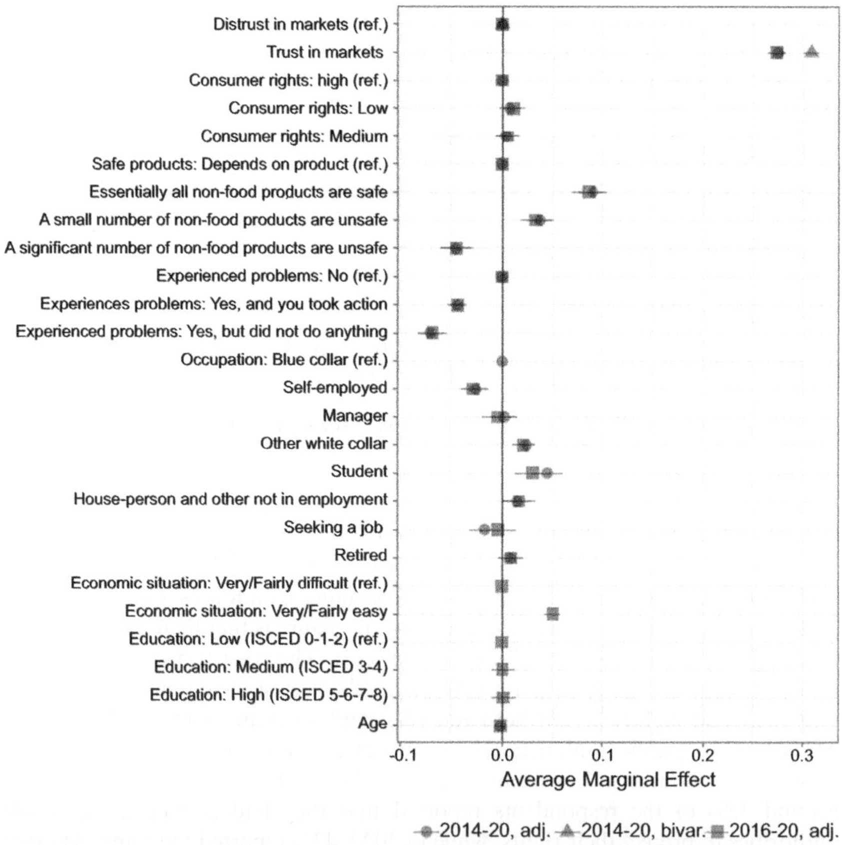

Fig. 2. Individual-Level Predictors of Trust. *Notes:* Average marginal effects from logistic regressions (country year fixed effects).

As shown in Fig. 2, consumers who trust sellers are around 30 percentage points (pp) more likely to trust that public authorities safeguard their consumer rights. As such, trust in markets is the strongest predictor of whether citizens trust public authorities to protect their consumer rights. The AME for this variable is very high and reduces with only around 3 pp, when additional variables were introduced in the model.

The models presented here offer support to the hypothesis that past experiences are linked to one's level of trust that authorities protect consumer rights. Individuals who had experienced problems and took action, as well as those who experienced problems but did not take action, were less likely to trust that authorities protect their rights, compared to those who did not experience problems. The estimations also indicate that not taking action after experiencing problems is linked to a slightly higher decrease in trust (7 pp) compared with those who took actions. Those who took action after experiencing problems were around 4.3 pp ($p < 0.001$) less likely to trust that authorities are protecting consumer rights. This difference is statistically significant.

Furthermore, the respondents' view of the safety of nonfood products is also related to trust that public authorities safeguard their consumer rights. Hence offering support to the hypothesis that not only personal experiences are of importance but also experiences or beliefs that can be informed by others. The results show that believing that "essentially all non-food products are safe", is positively correlated (around 8.9 pp increase, $p < 0.001$) to trust in authorities to respect consumer rights, compared to believing that product safety depends on the product. In contrast, the belief that "a significant number of non-food products are unsafe" was associated with a 4.5 pp ($p < 0.001$) reduction in trust. The difference between answering "a small number of non-food products are unsafe" and "it depends on the product" in relationship to trust that authorities protect consumer rights is statistically significant, yet modest (AME $\approx$0.33–0.37, $p < 0.001$).

There is little support in the models for the hypothesis that knowledge of consumer rights is associated with trusting authorities to protect consumer rights. It is not only that these results are not statistically significant, but the coefficients for these associations are also very close to zero. In sum, this indicates that one's knowledge of consumer rights is not a correlate of trust in consumer authorities.

In terms of occupation, these models indicate small differences in trust levels toward the authorities' commitment to protecting consumer rights. Blue-collar workers are chosen as the reference category. Being self-employed is associated with a lower likelihood of trusting that authorities protect consumer rights (AME ≈ -0.027, $p < 0.001$). Having a white-collar position is associated with a small increase in trust that authorities respect consumer rights compared to being in a blue-collar position. The difference between managers and blue-collar workers is not statistically significant. The managerial group is relatively small, and this nonsignificant finding may be due to lack of statistical power. Nevertheless, student have higher levels of trust that authorities protect consumer rights ($\approx$4 pp, $p < 0.001$), compared to blue-collar workers. Lastly, the difference between those not in employment, seeking a job, or retired and blue-collar workers is either not statistically significant or is of such low magnitude that they can be considered negligible in these estimations. It is important to note that these results are also controlled for educational attainment and the respondents' assessment of their households' financial situation in the models covering 2016, 2018, and 2020. As such, in these models, the magnitude of the coefficients for occupational groups is slightly reduced compared to the models which also include the 2014 data.

Regarding the level of education, there were no statistically significant differences in trust between persons with different levels of education. Both the medium and high education levels (ISCED 3-4 and 5-6-7-8) had AMEs close to zero ($\approx$0.001 and $\approx$0.002, respectively) and large *p*-values ($\approx$0.930 and $\approx$0.841, respectively) compared to the reference level of low education (ISCED 0-1-2). In additional analyses, the importance of education over time has been estimated[1]. These results show that while the differences are small in the entire period, the nonsignificance of the results is mainly driven by the data from 2018. In both 2016 and 2020, the results indicate that persons with a high level of education have slightly higher levels of trust that public authorities protect consumer rights (Supplementary Fig. A1).

Respondents who reported that their financial situation was very or fairly easy had a $\approx$5 pp increase in the probability of trusting that authorities protect consumer rights, holding all other variables constant. The magnitude of this difference has remained relatively constant over time (Supplementary Fig. A2). Individuals who perceive their economic situation as easier are more likely to trust that authorities are protecting consumer rights. These findings suggest that one's financial situation is a more robust predictor of trusting authorities to protect consumer rights, while education does not have an equally important role in this context. Furthermore, in additional estimates, the interaction between one's financial situation and knowledge of consumer rights, or experiencing problems respectively, is not statistically significant.

CROSS-NATIONAL DIFFERENCES IN THE IMPORTANCE OF EXPERIENCES

Cross-national variations in trust have been of paramount importance in studies of trust in markets and consumer protection (Repo & Timonen, 2017). As previously discussed, in relationship to consumers' trust in markets, the extant literature has proposed different groupings of countries, or regimes. As the focus of this study is on the individual characteristics, and especially on the role of experiences and perceptions of markets, the remainder of the analyses will explore cross-national differences in terms of these factors.

Fig. 3 illustrates how the importance of experiencing problems varies between the countries included in the study. The figure includes only the countries where at least one of the interaction terms was statistically significant. This interaction is not statistically significant in 9 out of 30 countries[2]. Both in terms of magnitude and statistical significance, the results indicate that not taking action when

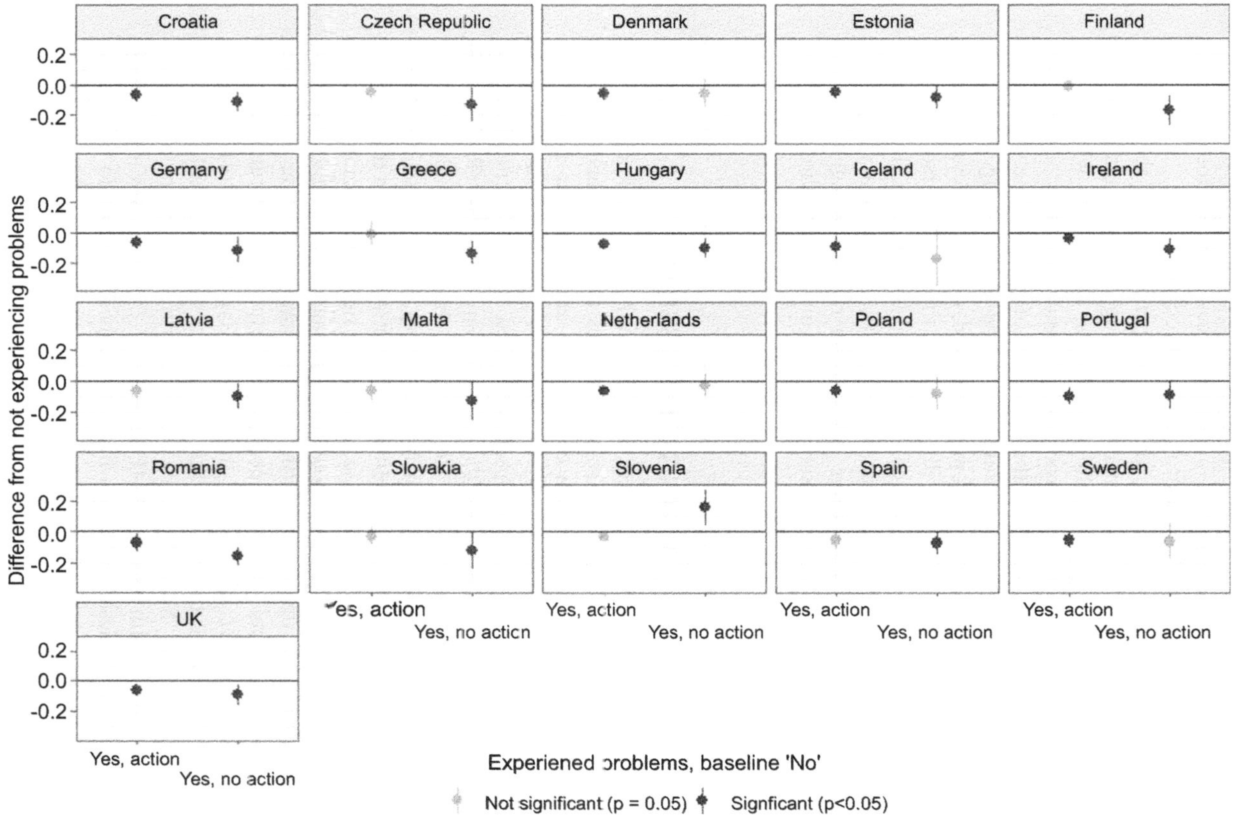

Fig. 3. Conditional Marginal Effects of Experiencing Problems of the Interaction Between Experiencing Problems and Country.
Notes: Adjusted results based on adjusted model for 2014–2020.

experiencing problems is linked to a larger decrease in trusting that authorities protect consumer rights. Furthermore, this pattern seems especially clear for countries in Eastern and Southern Europe. In Denmark, Malta, the Netherlands, and Sweden, there are no differences in trust between who did not experience problem and those who experienced problems and took no action.

Similar analyses were carried out for the role perceptions of the safety of non-food products and the role of consumer knowledge. These results show that consumers in Greece, Luxembourg, Bulgaria, Malta, and Cyprus who felt that "only a small number of non-food products are unsafe", or that "a significant number of products are unsafe", have the same level of trust as those who believe that "essentially all non-food products are safe" (Supplementary Fig. A3). In the remainder of the countries, there is an important and statistical decrease in trust between these groups. These findings illustrate that the role of personal experiences is, to a certain extent, mitigated by national-level factors. In terms of knowledge of consumer rights, only consumers in France, Hungary, Slovakia, and Norway who had high knowledge of consumer rights had higher levels of trust in the authorities to protect consumer rights, contrasted to those who had low knowledge of consumer rights.

CONCLUDING DISCUSSION

Having confidence in public authorities has been high on the political agenda. Yet, what characterizes people who trust authorities to protect their consumer rights has seldom been explored in a comparative and over time perspective. Theoretically, this study builds on broader theories of institutional trust. The most dominant perspectives within this field suggest that confidence in public authorities is indicative of whether they are fair and effective (Rothstein & Uslaner, 2005; Van der Meer, 2010). Furthermore, the present study builds on extant comparative studies of trust in markets (Berg, 2022; Nessel, 2022) and proposes a mutually reinforcing relationship between confidence in markets and confidence in public institutions to protect consumer rights. Theorizing these two phenomena as interconnected, and potentially mutually reinforcing, can allow future scholarship to investigate further what characterizes the potentially virtuous or vicious spirals that may emerge. The study findings underline the strong predictive power of trust in markets for consumers' trust in public authorities' role in protecting their rights. Consumers who have trust in markets are considerably more likely to believe in authorities' commitment to safeguarding their rights, with a robust AME range of 27–30 pp across various model specifications. Due to design and data limitations, these findings do not conclusively prove a mutually reinforcing causal link between these two phenomena but offer empirical support for this hypothesis.

Empirically, the study employs data from four rounds (2014, 2016, 2018, and 2020) of the European Commission's Consumer Condition Survey, covering 30 EU or EEA countries. Studying trust in a comparative perspective is not without challenges. The first is namely that one can argue that trust is a deeply culturally rooted phenomenon (Yamagishi et al., 1998; Yamagishi & Yamagishi, 1994), and that the factors that may shape trust are deeply embedded in cultural settings, rendering comparisons less fruitful. I argue that understanding what factors correlate with trust cross-nationally has an intrinsic value, by highlighting factors which may shape trust across national borders.

The results showed that one such factor is past experiences. Consumers who encountered problems and either acted or chose inaction had lower trust in authorities' commitment to the protection of consumer rights. Interestingly, inaction following an issue led to slightly higher distrust. These findings underscore the need for consumers to have clear channels for complaints and understanding of redress options. While individual inaction may be tied to personal traits, such as blame attribution (Choi & Mattila, 2008; Harris et al., 2006), the institutional setup within a country also shapes consumer responses to problems. Notably, most countries where this interaction isn't significant are high-income with robust institutions. Overall, these results endorse the hypothesis that experiences, not fixed latent attributes, shape trust.

Respondents' perception of non-food product safety was linked to their trust in authorities. Broad safety was associated with increased trust, whereas concerns with product safety correlated with less trust. Unlike the experiencing problems with products, perceptions of product safety are also shaped by influences from media and social networks. The analyses show that this a robust predictor robust of trust in authorities' protection of consumer rights. The magnitude of this association varies across countries (except for in Greece, Luxembourg, Bulgaria, Malta, and Cyprus). Knowledge of consumer rights did not significantly correlate with trust, except for in France, Hungary, Slovakia, and Norway – where a better knowledge of consumer rights is associated with higher levels of trust. This finding is somewhat counterintuitive given the theoretical expectations. However, estimating this relationship is challenging in the data at hand for two important reasons; the indicators that are included are limited and only cover three consumer rights, and secondly knowledge of consumer rights is endogenous to the efficacy of public authorities and redress pathways.

The findings suggest a positive association between socioeconomic resources and trusting that authorities safeguard consumer rights. Minor variations in trust were seen across occupations, with self-employed individuals showing less trust, while white-collar workers and students exhibited more trust compared to blue-collar workers, a pattern mirrored in studies of other forms of trust (Delhey & Newton, 2003). Respondents with a comfortable financial situation displayed higher confidence in consumer authorities. Nevertheless, the importance of one's level of education varied during this time period, indicating that economic resources may have a stronger impact on this form of trust.

These results are robust across model specifications. This suggests that the findings are not being unduly influenced by the structure of the data or the assumptions of the model. In the fixed effects model, the assumption is that something within each unit (country-year, in this case) may impact or bias the predictor or outcome variables and needs to be controlled for, hence allowing for country-year specific intercepts. Despite these mitigation steps omitted variable bias is still a concern. Furthermore, this study has not investigated the role played by regulatory standardization and harmonization of consumer policy during this period. Yet, it is important that such data are collected and these dimensions, to which also previous research has drawn attention to (Austgulen, 2020; Nessel, 2022) be explored further. Lastly, future research should develop and test more targeted indicators of institutional design that can be measured over time and across countries, so that the institutional mechanisms which lead to different levels of trust in authorities are explored.

To conclude, this study highlighted the interconnectedness of trust in authorities' protection of consumer rights and trust in markets, and both are shaped by individual and country-level factors. People with fewer socioeconomic resources and "bad" experiences have less confidence that authorities safeguard consumer rights. While too high levels of trust may be inherently problematic as they make citizens passive and inattentive to important political discussions (Berg, 2022; Nessel, 2022), these results show those with fewer socioeconomic resources cannot afford to trust that authorities defend their consumer rights.

NOTES

1. Results available upon request.
2. The countries where the interaction terms are not statistically significant are Belgium, France, Italy, Luxembourg, Austria, Bulgaria, Cyprus, Lithuania, and Norway.

REFERENCES

Alecu, A., & Dulsrud, A. (2022). Consumer dissatisfaction, complaints, and experiences in Norwegian e-commerce. https://oda.oslomet.no/oda-xmlui/bitstream/handle/

Alecu, A., Helland, H., Hjellbrekke, Johs., & Jarness, V. (2022). Who you know: The classed structure of social capital. *The British Journal of Sociology*, *73*(3), 505–535. https://doi.org/10.1111/1468-4446.12945

Austgulen, M. H. (2020). Understanding national preferences in EU consumer policy: A regime approach. *Journal of Consumer Policy*, *43*(4), 767–798. https://doi.org/10.1007/s10603-020-09468-8

Berg, L. (2022). The importance of consumer authorities for the production and maintenance of trust and social capital in consumer markets. *Journal of Consumer Policy*, *45*(3), 537–559. https://doi.org/10.1007/s10603-022-09523-6

Brehm, J., & Rahn, W. (1997). Individual-level evidence for the causes and consequences of social capital. *American Journal of Political Science*, 999–1023.

Burt, R. S., & Knez, M. (1995). Kinds of third-party effects on trust. *Rationality and Society*, *7*(3), 255–292.

Charron, N., & Rothstein, B. (2016). Does education lead to higher generalized trust? The importance of quality of government. *International Journal of Educational Development*, *50*, 59–73.

Choi, S., & Mattila, A. S. (2008). Perceived controllability and service expectations: Influences on customer reactions following service failure. *Journal of Business Research*, *61*(1), 24–30.

European Commission. (2020). New consumer agenda. *Strengthening consumer resilience for sustainable recovery*. https://eur-lex.europa.eu/legal-content/EN/TXT/PDF/?uri=CELEX:52020DC0696&from=EN

European Commission. (n.d.). Key consumer data. https://commission.europa.eu/strategy-and-policy/policies/consumers/consumer-protection-policy/key-consumer-data_en

Delhey, J., & Newton, K. (2003). Who trusts?: The origins of social trust in seven societies. *European Societies*, *5*(2), 93137.
Delhey, J., & Newton, K. (2004). *Social trust: Global pattern or nordic exceptionalism?* https://www.tandfonline.com/doi/abs/10.1080/1461669032000072256
Delhey, J., & Newton, K. (2005). Predicting cross-national levels of social trust: global pattern or Nordic exceptionalism? *European Sociological Review*, *21*(4), 311–327.
Directive 2011/83/EU. (2011). http://data.europa.eu/eli/dir/2011/83/oj/eng
Donoghue, S., Van Oordt, C., & Strydom, N. (2016). Consumers' subjective and objective consumerism knowledge and subsequent complaint behaviour concerning consumer electronics: A South African perspective. *International Journal of Consumer Studies*, *40*(4), 385–399.
Erikson, R., Goldthorpe, J. H., & Portocarero, L. (1979). Intergenerational class mobility in three Western European Societies: England, France and Sweden. *British Journal of Sociology*, *30*, 415–441.
Freitag, M., & Traunmüller, R. (2009). Spheres of trust: An empirical analysis of the foundations of particularised and generalised trust. *European Journal of Political Research*, *48*(6), 782803.
Gelman, A., & Hill, J. (2007). *Data analysis using regression and multilevel/hierarchical models*. Cambridge University Press.
Glanville, J. L. (2016). Why does involvement in voluntary associations promote trust? Examining the role of network diversity. *Sociological Inquiry*, *86*(1), 29–50.
Glanville, J. L., Andersson, M. A., & Paxton, P. (2013). Do social connections create trust? An examination using new longitudinal data. *Social Forces*, *92*(2), 545–562.
Glanville, J. L., & Paxton, P. (2007). How do we learn to trust? A confirmatory tetrad analysis of the sources of generalized trust. *Social Psychology Quarterly*, *70*(3), 230–242.
Granovetter, M. (1985). Economic action and social structure: The problem of embeddedness. *American Journal of Sociology*, 481–510.
Grönlund, K., & Setälä, M. (2012). In honest officials we trust: Institutional confidence in europe. *The American Review of Public Administration*, *42*(5), 523–542.
Harris, K. E., Mohr, L. A., & Bernhardt, K. L. (2006). Online service failure, consumer attributions and expectations. *Journal of Services Marketing*, *20*(6), 453–458.
Hofstra, B., Corten, R., van Tubergen, F., & Ellison, N. B. (2017). Sources of segregation in social networks: A novel approach using Facebook. *American Sociological Review*, *82*(3), 625–656.
Keefer, P., & Knack, S. (2005). *Social capital, social norms and the new institutional economics* (pp. 701–725). Springer.
Kjærnes, U., Harvey, M., & Warde, A. (2007). *Explaining Trust in Food* (U. Kjærnes, M. Harvey, & A. Warde, Eds., pp. 185–202). Palgrave Macmillan UK. https://doi.org/10.1057/9780230627611_10
Knack, S., & Keefer, P. (1997). Does social capital have an economic payoff? A cross-country investigation. *The Quarterly Journal of Economics*, 1251–1288.
Kumlin, S., & Rothstein, B. (2003). Investing in social capital: The impact of welfare state institutions *130*. https://www.researchgate.net/profile/Bo-Rothstein/publication/228700418_Investing_in_Social_Capital_The_Impact_of_Welfare_State_Institutions/links/544954a70cf244fe9ea2bf04/Investing-in-Social-Capital-The-Impact-of-Welfare-State-Institutions.pdf
Li, Y., Pickles, A., & Savage, M. (2005). Social capital and social trust in britain. *European Sociological Review*, *21*(2), 109123. https://doi.org/10.1093/esr/jci007
Li, Y., Savage, M., & Warde, A. (2008). Social mobility and social capital in contemporary Britain. *The British Journal of Sociology*, *59*(3), 391411.
Long, S. J., & Freese, J. (2006). *Regression models for categorical dependent variables using stata*. Stata Press.
Lopez-de-Silanes, F., La Porta, R., Shleifer, A., & Vishny, R. (1997). Trust in large organizations. *The American Economic Review*, *87*(2), 333–338.
Micklitz, H.-W. (2003). The necessity of a new concept for the further development of the consumer law in the EU. *German Law Journal*, *4*(10), 1043–1064.
Mood, C. (2010). Logistic regression: Why we cannot do what we think we can do, and what we can do about it. *European Sociological Review*, *26*(1), 67–82. https://doi.org/10.1093/esr/jcp006

Nessel, S. (2019). Consumer policy in 28 EU member states: An empirical assessment in four dimensions. *Journal of Consumer Policy*, *42*(4), 455–482.

Nessel, S. (2022). Political structures and trust in markets: A comparative examination of consumer trust in 28 EU member states and the effects of consumer policy on trust. *Journal of Sociology*, *58*(4), 462–480. https://doi.org/10.1177/14407833211001932

Norris, P. (1999). *Critical citizens: Global support for democratic government*. OUP.

Offe, C. (1999). How can we trust our fellow citizens. *Democracy and Trust*, *52*, 4287.

Otero, G., Volker, B., Rözer, J., & Mollenhorst, G. (2022). The lives of others: Class divisions, network segregation, and attachment to society in Chile. *The British Journal of Sociology*, *73*(4), 754–785. https://doi.org/10.1111/1468-4446.12966

Otero, G., Völker, B., Rözer, J., & Mollenhorst, G. (2023). Differences in access to social capital across societies. *European Sociological Review*, *40*, jcad035. https://academic.oup.com/esr/advance-article-abstract/doi/10.1093/esr/jcad035/7201975

Putnam, R. (1995). Bowling alone: America's declining social capital. *Journal of Democracy*, *6*, 68.

Putnam, R. (2016). *Our kids: The American dream in crisis*. Simon & Schuster.

Raval, D. (2020). Whose voice do we hear in the marketplace? Evidence from consumer complaining behavior. *Marketing Science*, *39*(1), 168–187.

Repo, P., & Timonen, P. (2017). Regime market performance analysis: Informing European consumer policy. *Journal of Consumer Policy*, *40*(1), 125–143. https://doi.org/10.1007/s10603-016-9333-9

Rothstein, B. (1998). Just institutions matter. In *Just Institutions Matter: The Moral and Political Logic of the Universal Welfare State* (pp. 116–143). Cambridge University Press.

Rothstein, B. (2011). *The quality of government: Corruption, social trust, and inequality in international perspective*. University of Chicago Press.

Rothstein, B., & Stolle, D. (2003). Social capital, impartiality and the welfare state: An institutional approach. In *Generating social capital: Civil society and institutions in comparative perspective* (pp. 191–210). Palgrave.

Rothstein, B., & Stolle, D. (2008). The state and social capital: An institutional theory of generalized trust. *Comparative Politics*, *40*, 441–459.

Rothstein, B., & Uslaner, E. M. (2005). All for all: Equality, corruption, and social trust. *World Politics*, *58*(01), 41–72.

Smith, T. W. (1997). Factors relating to misanthropy in contemporary American society. *Social Science Research*, *26*(2), 170–196.

Stø, E. (1989). Når forbrukerne klager. In B. Eli et al. (Eds.), *Forbruksforskning i går, idag og i morgen*. Statens institutt for forbruksforskning.

Uslaner, E. M. (2002). *The moral foundations of trust*. Cambridge University Press.

Uslaner, E. M. (2003). Trust, democracy and governance: Can government policies influence generalized trust? In *Generating social capital: Civil society and institutions in comparative perspective* (pp. 171–190). Palgrave.

Van der Meer, T. (2010). In what we trust? A multi-level study into trust in parliament as an evaluation of state characteristics. *International Review of Administrative Sciences*, *76*(3), 517–536.

Weatherill, S. (2013). *EU consumer law and policy*. Edward Elgar Publishing.

Yamagishi, T., Cook, K. S., & Watabe, M. (1998). Uncertainty, trust, and commitment formation in the United States and Japan. *American Journal of Sociology*, *104*(1), 165–194.

Yamagishi, T., & Yamagishi, M. (1994). Trust and commitment in the United States and Japan. *Motivation and Emotion*, *18*(2), 129–166.

Zak, P. J., & Knack, S. (2001). Trust and growth. *The Economic Journal*, *111*(470), 295–321.

SUPPLEMENTARY MATERIAL

DESCRIPTIVE STATISTICS

Table A1. Descriptive Measures of Predictors.

Characteristic	Distrust, N = 35,959	Trust, N = 72,615
Age	51.48 (16.24)	49.28 (17.07)
Gender		
Male	47%	47%
Female	53%	53%
Occupation		
Self-employed	8.8%	7.9%
Manager	7.6%	7.9%
Other white collar	25%	29%
Blue collar	15%	15%
Student	3.3%	5.5%
House-person and other not in employment	6.1%	5.5%
Seeking a job	5.0%	3.6%
Retired	30%	25%
Unknown	*147*	*270*
Safe Products		
Essentially all non-food products are safe	12%	24%
A small number of non-food products are unsafe	52%	55%
A significant number of non-food products are unsafe	31%	16%
It depends on the product	5.1%	4.6%
Unknown	*1,163*	*2,167*
Experienced Any Problem When Buying or Using Products		
Yes, and you took action to solve the problem	17%	14%
Yes, but you did not do anything	7.4%	4.5%
No	76%	82%
Unknown	*234*	*444*
Knowledge of Consumer Rights		
Low knowledge	59%	58%
Medium	31%	32%
High knowledge	9.4%	10%
Trust Sellers to Respect Rights		
Distrust	42%	14%
Trust	58%	86%
Unknown	*1,355*	*1,784*
Financial: Making Ends Meet		
Very/Fairly difficult	45%	30%
Very/Fairly easy	55%	70%
Unknown[a]	*10,846*	*17,759*

(Continued)

Table A1. *(Continued)*

Characteristic	Distrust, N = 35,959	Trust, N = 72,615
Level of Education		
Low (ISCED 0-1-2)	12%	10%
Medium (ISCED 3-4)	47%	45%
High (ISCED 5-6-7-8)	42%	44%
Unknown[a]	*10,577*	*17,316*

[a]Large share of missing as the question was not asked in 2014.

Table A2. Overview of the Included Countries and Number of Respondents Per Country (for the 2014–2020 Period).

Country Marker	Freq.
Belgium	4,011
Denmark	4,005
Germany	4,01
Greece	4,008
Spain	4,014
Finland	4,015
France	4,013
Ireland	4,011
Italy	4,011
Luxembourg	2,002
Netherlands	4,009
Austria	4,014
Portugal	4,009
Sweden	4,001
UK	4,014
Bulgaria	4,008
Cyprus	2,000
Czech Republic	4,002
Estonia	4,005
Hungary	4,006
Latvia	4,023
Lithuania	4,012
Malta	2,063
Poland	4,011
Romania	4,016
Slovakia	4,026
Slovenia	4,023
Iceland	2,004
Croatia	4,007
Norway	4,006
Total	112,359

ADDITIONAL ESTIMATIONS

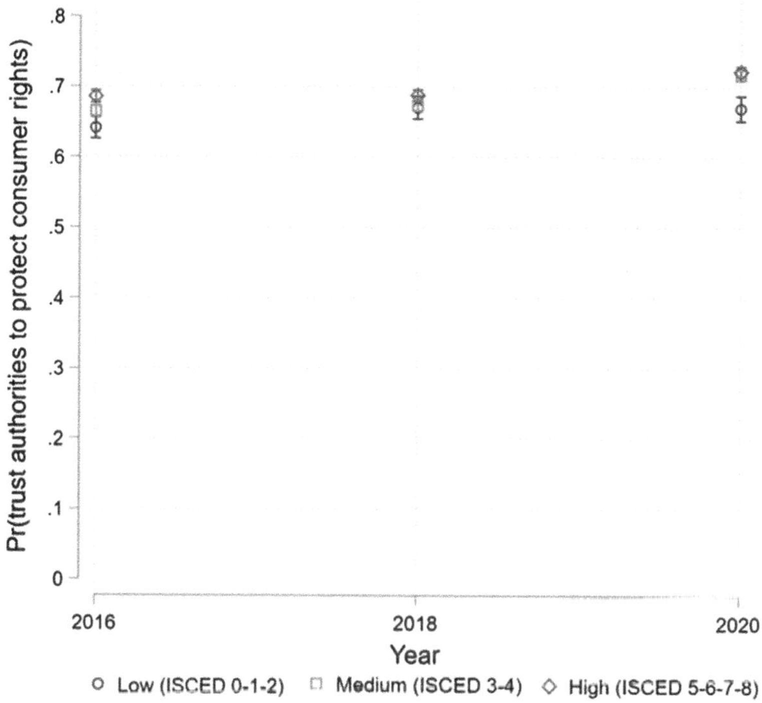

Fig. A1. Interaction Between Education Level and Year. *Notes:* Adjusted Model.

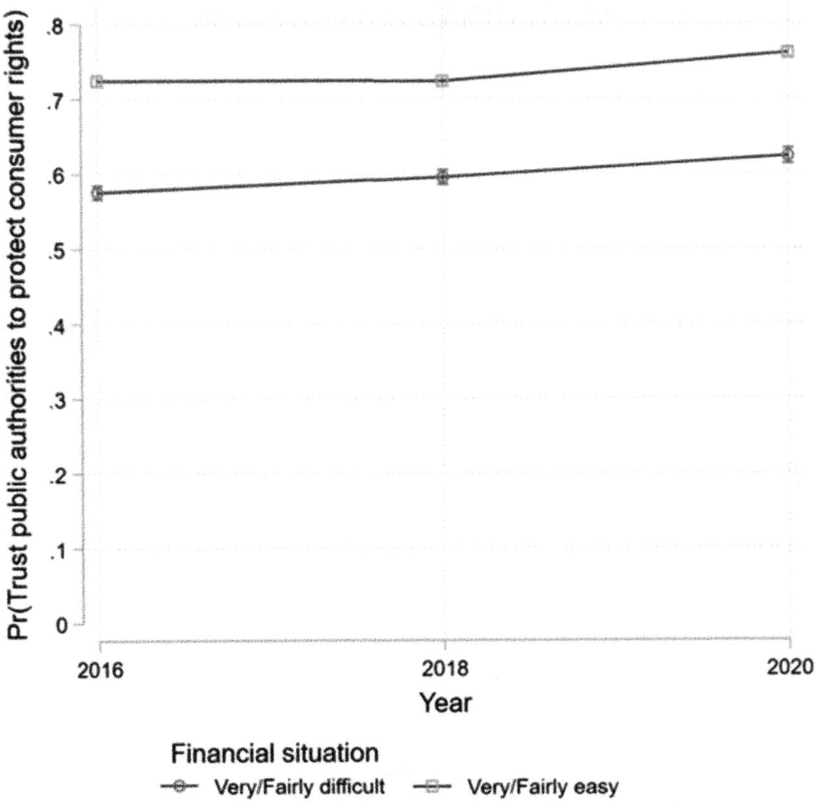

Fig. A2. Interaction Between Education Level and Year. *Notes:* Adjusted Model.

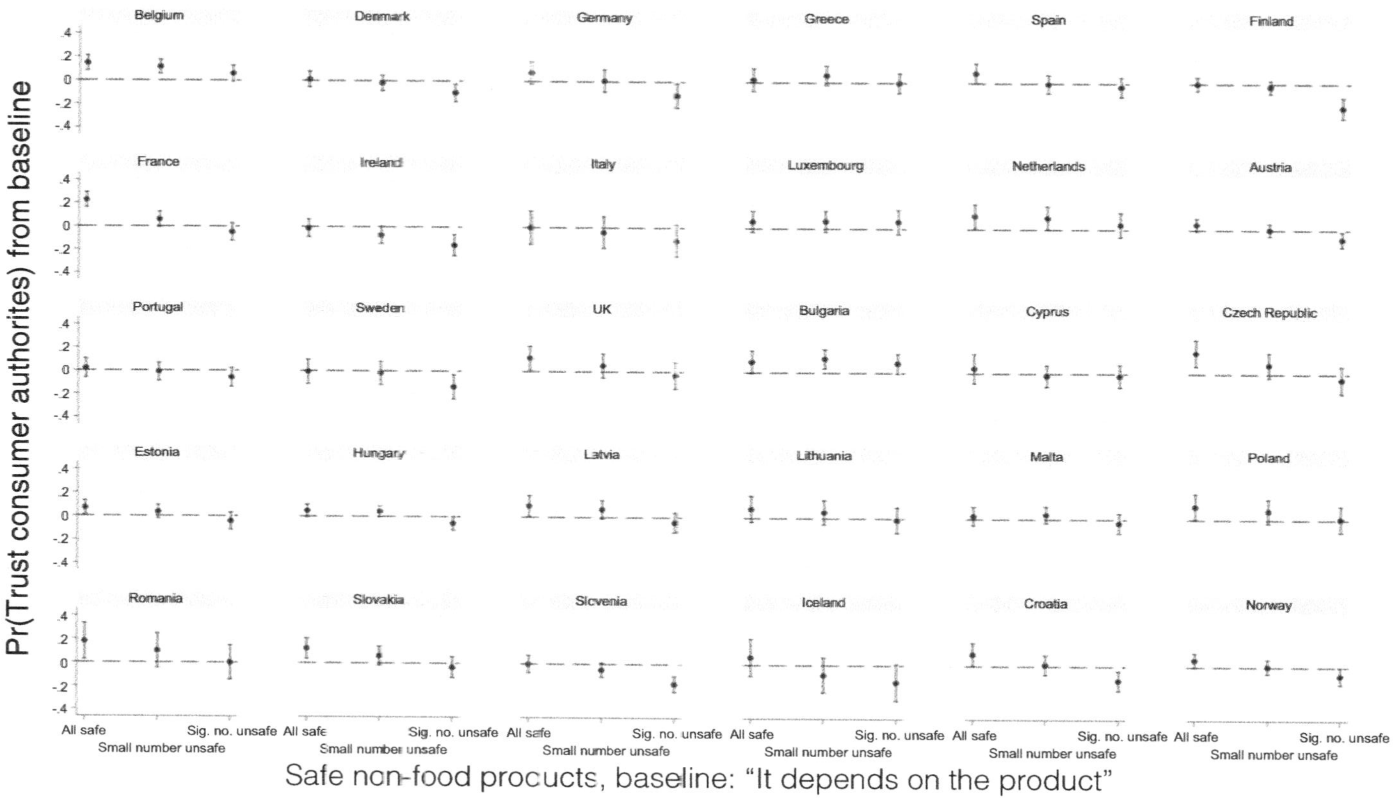

Fig. A3. Conditional Marginal Effects Interaction Between Safe Non-food Products the Interaction and Country in Relationship to Trust That Consumer Authorities Protect Consumer Rights. *Notes:* Adjusted Results, Based on Model FE 2014–2020.

NEO-MATERIALIST MOVEMENT ORGANISATIONS' SCALING THROUGH STRATEGIES AND CONSUMER COLLECTIVE ACTION: COMPARING THREE EUROPEAN FOOD MOVEMENT SCENES

Stefan Wahlen[a], Francesca Forno[b] and Mikko Laamanen[c]

[a]*Justus Liebig University Giessen, Germany*
[b]*University of Trento, Italy*
[c]*Oslo Metropolitan University, Norway*

ABSTRACT

The article examines the experiences of local activists involved in the food movement scene in Germany, Italy and the United Kingdom, with the objective of comparing strategies in localising food movement politics and seeking scale for collective action through institutions. Specifically, it delves into the grassroots-driven, bottom-up development of food policies by neo-materialist movement organisations (NMMOs) asking why food has become a central focus, what these organisations do and who participates, and how and why strategies for working with local institutions are implemented. Success in food movements, as in other social change efforts, often depends on experimenting with different approaches to generating interest and expanding the movement among consumers. At the same time, activists emphasise the need to change the food system, typically by promoting the benefits of local produce and fostering connections between producers and consumers. These connections serve as a vital resource for collective action, as food allows movements to easily mobilise and engage with consumers' values and beliefs. Through a

Consumers and Consumption in Comparison
Comparative Social Research, Volume 37, 93–113

Published under exclusive licence by Emerald Publishing Limited
ISSN: 0195-6310/doi:10.1108/S0195-631020240000037005

comparative analysis of local food activism across Bristol, Cologne and Rome, the study elucidates that while each context grapples with distinct challenges, such as reconciling administrative tensions in Rome or negotiating financial constraints and bureaucratic intricacies in Bristol and Cologne, all underscore the pivotal role of collaborative engagement with local authorities as a catalyst for effecting change in food systems and beyond.

Keywords: Neo-materialist movement organisation; consumption; collective action; comparative analysis; qualitative; local food policy

INTRODUCTION: FOOD AND COLLECTIVE ACTION

Contemporary societies grapple with multifaceted challenges spanning environmental, economic and social domains. The globalised food system, characterised by industrialised production, profoundly shapes current food consumption. In Europe, standardised products stemming from such an industrialised food system are widespread. While the advantages of standardised mass production are evident, they also contribute to environmental degradation, economic crises and persistent societal inequalities. Industrialised production in the Global North is intricately linked to exploitation and poverty in peripheral regions (Davidson, 2018; Wallerstein, 2004). Notably, the standardisation of food products may not necessarily contribute to well-being; instead, increased quantities of ultra-processed food may have adverse effects on both individual and planetary health (Bartolini, 2021). The current modes of food production and consumption pose threats to health and the environment, underscoring the imperative for alternative approaches to address societal challenges.

Since the late 1990s, recurring crises have given rise to pockets of localised and sustainable food production and consumption. These initiatives have primarily gained traction among the middle and upper class, as well as more educated consumers who possess both time and financial resources (Goodman, 2004; Veen & D'Amico, 2019; Forno et al., 2022; Zwart & Mathijs, 2020). The aftermath of the global pandemic and the inflation-induced cost of living crisis has heightened the significance of these niches. However, they also reveal the vulnerability of lifestyle-based, alternative food systems within the middle class, which can easily transition towards less sustainable options.

Over the years, movements advocating for change in food production and consumption have presented compelling arguments, including the advantages of localising food systems, showcasing the availability of quality food and addressing issues of food security or poverty. These developments underscore the growing opposition to globalised and industrial food production, shifting economic competition and ecological destruction from the local to the global level. This opposition manifests through various means, from individual lifestyle choices, like vegetarianism and veganism, to community-level initiatives, such as community-supported agriculture and other forms of localised procurement (Taylor et al., 2020). Despite their merit, these individual or small-group efforts have, over time and as indicated above, demonstrated limitations in engaging only specific segments of the population without fundamentally altering the broader food system.

In recent decades, social movement actors and organisations have adapted their strategies to address challenges in the food system and beyond. Many movements now scrutinise prevailing models of production and consumption across diverse aspects of daily life, with food being a prominent focus (Laamanen et al., 2023; Schlosberg & Craven, 2019). An escalating interest and mobilisation capacity surround the realm of food, recognised alongside energy and mobility as a pivotal category where consumers can significantly contribute to sustainability transformations (Forno et al., 2022; Fuchs et al., 2021). Food mobilisations highlight the challenges associated with a global and industrialised food system, seeking to redirect attention towards local and material aspects of sustainability. This shift entails collective engagement with the tangible, real-world impacts of sustainable practices: for reforms to be viable, they must be grasped and made 'real' to the wide population towards a positive difference in their daily life. Thus, food system reforms must transcend individual interests, be connected to local markets and gain leverage in policy, above all at the municipal level. We call the strategy aiming at this 'scaling through.'

This article theorises and explains how movement organisations have recognised municipal authorities and public policy institutions as occupying a central role in the amplification of local transformations that movement groups advocate. Following this, the article compares strategies in localising movement politics and seeking scale for collective action though institutions in three local food scenes. Localising efforts can lead to transformations that address specific needs and challenges related to sustainability within local, municipal institutional frameworks. Food policies are often of national concern and limited in municipalities; yet delving into these dynamics, we compare mobilisation and collection actions in three food movement scenes, Bristol (United Kingdom), Cologne (Germany) and Rome (Italy). Through in-depth interviews with leaders of key organisations and document analysis on approaches to institutionalise food mobilisation, we explore and compare actions that have contributed to diverse experiences and practices in food consumption, particularly countering the distortive impacts of recurring crises. Our comparative analysis contributes to a better understanding of current forms of consumer collective action and provides novel insights into the shifting landscape of politicising the everyday.

CONCEPTUAL FRAMEWORK: CONSUMER MOBILISATION AND SCALE OF CHANGE

In their work, Forno and Graziano (2014) conceptualised consumer movement communities as grassroots collective efforts to establish alternative, productive and sustainable networks of production and exchange. These grassroots initiatives, called sustainable community movement organisations (SCMOs), act on the market with the aim of creating new economic and cultural spaces for civic learning and consumer activism. They mobilise citizens primarily – though not exclusively – through their purchasing power. SCMOs' build alternative markets based on knowledge exchange, solidarity and mutual trust (Forno & Graziano, 2014). The working principles of SCMOs arise from the challenges faced by contemporary social movements as they deal with (1) institutions less capable or willing to mediate new demands for social justice and (2) the difficulties of creating and maintaining solidaristic and cooperative bonds in a highly individualised contemporary society (Forno & Graziano, 2014). This shift opened strategic opportunities for community-based movements in the everyday life, provision of human needs in just and sustainable manners, addressing rising inequalities and disruptions caused by neoliberalist capitalism (Harvey, 2007; Trentmann, 2009). Focus points have been the illustrations of the faults in the system (as part of the Global Justice Movement and highlighting the wrongdoings of global enterprises; Forno & Graziano, 2014) as well as the adjustments individuals make in the face of economic insecurity, political fragmentation and continuing crises.

Overall, SCMOs highlight the limited autonomy and collective power of the rational consumer – the citizen consumer. Building on this, Laamanen et al. (2023, p. 858) propose a focus on 'experimental local initiatives that mobilise in inclusive, reflexive moral practice with a particular focus on material dimensions of collective action' in what they call neo-materialist movement organisations (NMMOs). NMMOs differ from traditional materialist movements, such as the labour movement, that prioritised production over consumption, linking sustainable consumption to employment (e.g. fair work) rather than environmental impact or social justice. NMMOs address a 'blind spot' of SCMOs (and other identity-based movements) that have redirected their attention from the state towards the market; SCMOs engage in experimentation with local sustainable production and consumption following the tradition of consumer identity mobilisation of the so-called new social movements (see, e.g. Haenfler et al., 2012; Kozinets & Handelman, 2004). Identity-based mobilisation, nevertheless, tends to limit impact to immediate spaces with little reverberations in the broader societal structures (Blühdorn, 2023; Laamanen et al., 2023). The local traits of SCMOs are visible as individuals participating movement practices exhibit personal commitments to, e.g. choosing a slower, simpler life, communal living or adopting a vegan lifestyle. These practices deepen participants' identification with the movement, that is, *scale deep* to destabilise neoliberal socialisation and amplify alternative lifestyle practices. SCMOs supplement *scaling deep* for personal transformation with *scaling up* for the creation of critical mass and visibility in protest (e.g. boycotts) and replication of initiatives across different locations or *scaling out*.

Laamanen et al. (2023) discuss how these scaling strategies (see Table 1) are similarly present in NMMOs; here these strategies mobilise individuals around the *material* nature and consequences of sustainable consumption. Yet, Laamanen et al. (2022) underscore how radical change also requires the aggregation of shared interests among various stakeholders and thus, recalibration of the SCMO focus from an 'ethical' 'responsibilised' consumerism (the consumer citizen) to active citizenship – calling on the *citizen consumer*. In the face of worsening climate and environmental conditions, increasing economic insecurity and injustice, declining

Table 1. Different Scaling Strategies in NMMOs (Laamanen et al., 2023).

Strategy	Definition
Scaling deep	Individuals changing practices through political and communal expressions in private lives and communities, seen in lifestyle movements like alternative economy communities and ecovillages.
Scaling up	Amplifying demand and pressure sectoral/corporate change, influencing image and regulation through public demonstrations, boycotts, cultural jamming, and naming and shaming.
Scaling out	Multi-cause networks to 'take back the economy', establishing alternative, sustainable networks through open participation and replication in areas like finance, commons assemblies, and community-supported agriculture.
Scaling through	Consider government as a possible path for change, aiming to cooperate or infiltrate institutions, bypassing market provision for social provision, directing action towards post-capitalism in projects like new municipalism and radical municipalism.

quality of democratic participation and violent global politics, individual practices are increasingly seen as insufficient to promote systemic change that is rapid, profound and broad enough to achieve urgent goals. Thus, beyond individual actions, NMMOs aim to utilise citizenship in action with a *scaling through* strategy. This scaling strategy is a more recent direction, previously absent or rarely deployed in the politics of SCMOs, lifestyle movements or many new social movements.[1] A scaling through strategy aligns with recent citizen platforms and participatory mechanisms, like new municipalism and political populism. Scaling through considers new conceptions of the consumer-citizen, also viewing the state as caring, responsible, solidaristic and activist (Cooper, 2020).

Our empirical work explores the implications of NMMO scaling through strategies in consumer collective action, redefining social change after economic, environmental and social disruptions. The central question driving our efforts in this research is: *How do scaling through strategies of neo-materialist movement organisations manifest in localised consumer collective action?*

METHOD: COMPARING THREE FOOD MOVEMENTS

Empirically, we aim to compare scaling through strategies of three food movement scenes across Europe. We would like to know how *scaling through*, as an NMMO collective action strategy, aims to influence governing institutions. Food movements combine social aspects of food (in)security and (in)justice with environmental degradation and pollution through industrial food production. Thus, taking food movements as demonstrative actors engaging in strategic and localised social change, we compare scaling through strategies across three food movement scenes in three European territories.

The sampling of our cases utilises several categories (Patton, 2002). Firstly, we select cases where food movement organisations and/or alternative/sustainable food movement scenes are emerging in a bottom-up approach and with a strategic approach to co-create local policy, influence legislation and/or promote participatory processes. Thus, insular food movement groups without a policy orientation are excluded as are municipality-driven top-down initiatives where food movement groups and organisations can be participants. Secondly, we selected scenes that illustrate different European sociopolitical and economic realities (North/South, EU/post-Brexit). Our sample (Table 2) consists of food movement scenes in Bristol (UK), Cologne (Germany) and Rome (Italy). Thirdly, we utilise a snowballing approach moving from the 'core' of these locations and the most representative organisations towards more 'singular' participant organisations. For instance, in Bristol, the two organisations interviewed were networking organisations whose most important role was to connect and establish dialogue with other actors in the field. In Cologne, the organisation in focus took a lead in establishing a local food policy council, over time taking an exemplary role for comparable initiatives across Germany. In Italy, we started with the organisation that initiated the process of building Rome's food policy by lobbying the municipal administration through the construction of a coalition of local civil society associations.

In each scene, we interviewed community movement leaders; leaders are important informants given their position, access and expertise, making them to be able to explore the strategic processes in their organisations. Thus, our sampling of informants rests on information-rich, 'extreme' cases (Patton, 2002). We interviewed five leaders in Rome, two in Bristol and three in Cologne. The composition of the final informant sample pertains to the dynamics of scene

Table 2. Informants of the Study.

Organisation (Acronym)	Informant Position and Experience	Date, Length of Interview (minutes)
Terra ONLUS (TO, Rome)	Director of terra and journalist, initiator of the process	30.06.23/65
Res Roma (RR, Rome)	Economists, active in solidarity economy initiatives	04.07.23/55
Fair Trade Organisation (FTO, Rome)	Coordinator of a working group in the process towards the Roma Food Policy	21.07.23/68
Cattive Ragazze (CR, Rome)	Coordinator of a working group in the process towards the Roma Food Policy	01.08.23/88
Slow Food Roma (SFR, Rome)	Anthropologist, coordinator	01.08.23/78
Feeding Bristol (FB, Bristol)	Director, organisation focussed on food justice and inequalities, active also in food production	18.07.23/66
Bristol Food Network (BFN, Bristol)	Director, networking organisational cooperation and consumer skills development	08.09.23/56
Food Policy Council Cologne (FPCC, Cologne)	Chairperson, two executive directors	27.09.23/93

maturity/professionalisation and personal availability. For instance, during the recruitment of informants in the Bristol food scene, request to different constituent groups of the network would be forwarded to an informant already interviewed (i.e. illustrating centralisation). Alternatively, movement scenes can be overwhelmed by external requests (such as those from academia or media) and decline these due to limited time, personnel or general informant fatigue.

The use of a semi-structured interview guide (see Appendix) with a potential of deviation and further prompting allows for depth but also relative standardisation and comparison across the three cases. All interviews are transcribed *verbatim*, shared amongst the researcher team and analysed collectively for illustration of the scaling strategies *in situ* and lessons learnt. Beyond semi-structured qualitative interviews with these key activists, we also collected documentation of the food activism strategies (resolutions, manifestos, reports, etc.) as well as already published articles elaborating the community efforts within the food movement spaces. Our analytic approach is to compare narratives of local food activism and policy development, e.g. how the food movements started and where they are going, tracking the journey of the food movements participant NMMOs and their strategies and repertoire through the institutions. Our methodological approach can thus be described here as deductive, in qualitatively testing existing theorisation (particularly the NMMO scaling hypothesis of Laamanen et al., 2023). The accuracy of analysis and representation is secured with the participants reading through the final manuscript with particular focus on their input ('member check', Patton, 2002).

RESULTS: MOBILISING CONSUMERS INTO FOOD ACTION AND DEVELOPING FOOD POLICY

This results section concentrates on the arrangement of local food actions and how movements mobilise consumers in three municipal food scenes. We acknowledge that food can also be a starting point to address other issues intricately connected to food actions. The three food movement scenes exhibit both similarities and differences in the way they attempt to implement food policies; however, importantly, they build upon and capitalise on expertise in food-related issues. In the following, we first explore how the food scenes came into being, that is, what were the initial issues taken up by individual organisations and how the movement space established itself. We then take up participation and how multiple dynamics came to change the focus from scaling deep to scaling through, which is also the argument we pick up in the discussion.

Setting the Scenes

The three food movement scenes set up a variety of projects in their respective municipalities, focusing on different aspects of food consumption and production. In Cologne, these activities ranged from the creation of local food supply chains, food education and public catering in schools to urban agriculture and an edible city. A way to directly mobilise consumers in Cologne is the open cooking pot, which is a regular event that promotes exchange on regional food supply and healthy eating. Under the umbrella of an edible living environment, several neighbourhoods (*Stadtquartier*) set up community gardens and public green spaces as social meeting places. In a mutual symbiosis, gardens benefit from social organisations and these use gardens as spaces for their work, for encounters and intercultural exchange. Embedded in the Edible Living Environment-project, the aspect of community gardening has been explored in greater depth, emphasising the social importance of edible urban green spaces. The project focused on two different forms of *community gardens* and beneficiaries: neighbourhood gardens in the residential environment where residents with fewer opportunities had the possibility to participate, and company gardens at business premises. To build continuation and 'sustainable' structures, the project primarily addressed housing associations, social space coordinators, citizens' associations and company management (e.g. HR managers) rather than individual consumers.

Mobilising in Bristol started with the organic boom in the mid-noughties which led to significant changes on how food was grown. Around 2014, the Feeding Britain policy report pointed to issues of food insecurity and hunger. Regionally, Feeding Bristol took this as its political focus: it emphasises food insecurity and food inequality with focus on active citizen participation and choice. With this they distinguish *a food pantry* from that of a food bank model: a food pantry gives the users a choice and includes a financial transaction that subsequently adds dignity for the users and allows subsidising the produce entering the system from the local producers. As the director of the charity explains, they are seeing a movement to try to engage the local food growing system and set up positive connections with the user contexts and food cultures:

> The idea was that Feeding Bristol would be focused around addressing issues of Food insecurity in young, vulnerable children that are eligible for preschool meal vouchers over school holidays when they had no access to support for food and food insecurity. (FB, Bristol)

This informant was also actively involved with The Bristol Food Producers Organisation, which focused on supporting local growers by collaborating with the council to identify and allocate suitable land for fair and inclusive community use. The food producers' organisation prioritised access for various groups, including refugees, asylum seekers, and skilled farmers entering the country, to foster a more inclusive and supportive farming community. Feeding Bristol leads work on the food justice, the food inequality angle, alongside the work they do around food production in the city. Over time and particularly amplified by the pandemic, the focus extended to include the wider food insecurity in the population given 'number of issues that people were maybe a little bit blind to beforehand' (FB, Bristol). Particularly,

> ...much more evident over lockdown experiences of people of colour, people from minority ethnic backgrounds, and their ability to get a hold of culturally appropriate food and the kind of issues they face from food insecurity perspective people who are disabled ... Those that are homeless, those that are refugees, there's a whole host of different factors around food

> insecurity that maybe we're not being addressed or supported properly during the lockdown or had been properly addressed in the past. (FB, Bristol)

Feeding Bristol engages with over 90 stakeholders in the city, collaborating with organisations addressing poverty and related issues, not limited to food. They actively involve communities in the formulation of strategies and action plans, seeking diverse perspectives. The organisation focuses on raising awareness locally, providing feedback to the Feeding Britain network at the national level, and supporting networking efforts to share best practices and address specific area-related challenges. Additionally, Feeding Bristol facilitates conversations and endeavours to secure funding for local organisations involved in addressing food issues.

As in Cologne and Bristol, several initiatives have spread in Rome over the past decades to reclaim the importance of food for citizens and producers, and in so doing reactivating more general discussions on sustainability and social justice. These initiatives include urban and peri-urban multifunctional agricultural projects, solidarity purchasing groups, and farmers' markets. In Rome, grassroots organisations supporting food policy processes include organisations that over the years have tended to mobilise through political consumerism and sustainable lifestyles (cf. SCMOs). As a member of one historical fair trade organisations elaborates on the role of food in mobilising consumers:

> Food is quite a simple thing, it engages you, and in fact it's led us to expand our network, because for example you go to the school canteen where you know it's already a kind of community incubator because there's the child, there's the mother, there's the grandmother who maybe accompanies the child to school, so you already have all the generations. And it is easy to explain what would change if school canteens served healthy, nutritious products that come from local producers, therefore with less impact on the environment. All these issues, which are easily connected to food, make it very easy to make connections with larger social and environmental issues, whereas if we go to other levels, talking about economics or trade itself, it is more difficult to explain. When instead we use food as a means of communication, everything becomes easier, because food itself, if you like, is simpler. Then, when analysing the entire food chain, the various complexities emerge. Let's say we start from a simple, understandable topic. (FTO, Rome)

Or put differently:

> The interest in food lies in the fact that through food we can actually address a whole range of important political and social issues concerning social and environmental justice. In other words, food represents a vector … Family participation in school canteens is an important channel for participation. It is a way to create food education projects, but above all, for us, it has been a way to nurture parental participation in school that otherwise does not exist. (CR, Rome)

However, over time, the activists themselves have come to recognise how mobilising individual consumers has altered their message. Although food is a topic that all the activists interviewed agree is appealing because it relates to everyday life, conscious consumption can be practised without feeling part of a movement. It can be an individual effort motivated by self-regulatory reasons. Yet, despite the movement's ability to engage a growing segment of the population in food-related issues, these activities have often developed in a fragmented way with limited coordination between them, thus limiting their ability to reach a critical mass. Being involved in consumer actions has also been criticised by one of our Italian respondents:

> You can garden, you can choose to go to the market instead of going to the supermarket … You can also exercise that kind of activity individually, you can testify, for example, that you bought the head of salad and not the bagged salad. This is an element of incredible strength, but it is also an element of incredible weakness of this form of activism. Because in recent years it has turned this into *individual* battles. (TO, Rome, emphasis added)

The activists themselves feel that this strategy has achieved little over time.

> What have we done over the years? Many initiatives … We did a lot of urban agriculture projects, from self-building to courses for horticulturists and farmers … before there was this idea of self-determination, which was also very political in its own way, but it also presupposed the idea that there was an autonomy from politics. Today, instead, we say that you can change the world if you change the choices of politics. (TO, Rome)

Similarly, turning away from an individual consumer focus, the food policy council in Cologne aims at 'developing a sustainable, fair, effective and ecological food system in the city.' They therefore promote an active dialogue between politics, administration, producers, distributors and consumers in order to strengthen the structures of a regional food supply in the long term and sustainably. They developed a food strategy for the city of Cologne that allows all citizens in the city to eat a healthy and regional diet while at the same time preserving rural agriculture in the surrounding area. Specific projects are being initiated in close cooperation with the city administration and state ministries. The ultimate aim is for Cologne to become *a model region for a local food policy focussed on sustainability and regionality*, from whose experience other cities in the state and federal government can benefit.

Rome is among the Italian cities that have signed the 'Milan Pact' (MUFFP) in 2015 as did the city of Cologne (in 2015) and Bristol (in 2018). The Milan Pact is an important legacy of Expo 2015, which advocates a systemic and integrated approach to address the social, environmental and economic challenges of agriculture and food. However, it was in Rome only ratified in April 2021 by the municipal assembly in form of a resolution committing the city to adopt a food policy for the Italian capital (Marino & Mazzocchi, 2022). What differentiates the case of Rome from other contexts is that the municipal resolution was the result of the collaboration of more than 50 civil society organisations united in a Food Policy Promoting Committee (CPFP). This coalition formulated an initial food policy proposal in 2019 (Terra! Onlus, Lands Onlus, 2019). Similar things happened in the Bristol Food Network, which:

> …began as a grassroots organisation and actually that started in way back in the 1990s … the founding directors of Bristol Food Network … have been very embedded in community grassroots activity for a long time … so those food activists work to start things like some

> farmers markets in Bristol, some of which are still going through relationships that some of those people had with the public health team. There was some sort of engagement with the local authority then, and some funding to start a project called Food Links, which was around farmers markets. (BFN, Bristol)

Ultimately, a Bristol Food Policy Council was formed: our informant considers that the Food Policy Council was important for organisational seeding that still continues, even though the council itself dissolved some years ago. Generally, in the food movement scene, organisational boundaries and structures are in flux, and change over time; so also, do the activists involved in food actions. In Cologne, developing the food policy strategy was a longer process. Along the way, as our informant highlights:

> ...you somehow start out with a totally diffuse group of incredibly committed people who are somehow passionate about the cause. And then that develops further and further. And then you have progress and then it consolidates in a certain way. And I think this avant-garde, which simply wants a lot and pushes very quickly that gets lost to a certain extent once you've achieved something. With every further step that you take, where it somehow settles down a little, you lose those people a little. They look for something else where they can keep pushing. (FPCC, Cologne)

Overall, there are various similarities in the food mobilisations that can be detected in the three food scenes. All were turning away from consumers, and the focal points also show differences in terms of whom to include along the process. These dynamics and changes are what we turn to next.

Participation and Practices: Multiple Changes, Multiple Dynamics in Food Politics

Individual activism has several limitations, as it can lead to fragmented efforts and often falls short in addressing complex systemic issues related to food (in) security or sustainability. Our informants in the three contexts are very aware of this and also reflect upon this action's economic and class-based limits. In the case of the director of Feeding Bristol who was also the former managing director of a CSA as well as a founder and board member of a producers organisation (and thus has substantial experience in the broad food movement field), he states:

> I was getting very frustrated with going to the same areas to have the same conversations with the people you know, or the same demographic. It was very white. It was very middle class. It was very hipster ... And the people that were coming, say you'd be sitting at a table and you'd be like "oh, it's you again. It's you again. It's you again. It's you again." Great. We're just going to have the same conversation with the same people about the things that need to change. (FB, Bristol)

While individual activism (of scaling deep in food choice and community participation) can be a powerful means of expressing personal values and taking initiative, our informants argue that collective engagement, including political advocacy and community involvement, is necessary to achieve meaningful and lasting change in the food system. This is particularly linked to the crises that can affect the ability to engage in individual consumer activism. The cost of living crisis, combined with the lingering effects of the pandemic, has hit those in privileged positions hard:

> ...people's disposable income [are] being squeezed to the point where even people who were middle class customers of things like veg box schemes pre-COVID are now stopping buying from them ... So, a lot of the veg box schemes and farms that run them have really faced significant crises to keep going. (BFN, Bristol)

In Bristol, an important shift in food activism took place during the pandemic:

> There was a huge amount of active activism in Bristol around emergency food provision in COVID for vulnerable people. Actually, one of my colleagues, set up an organisation called National Food Service. And that was all about *emergency food provision*. And there were other organisations, there was an organisation that formed that's now since dissolved called Bristol Food Union that, that kind of came out in the pandemic. And that was partly about providing work and income for people in hospitality who suddenly had to close their businesses and getting those skills and kitchens to produce food again for vulnerable people. (BFN, Bristol, emphasis added)

In Rome, the issue of food has become increasingly important due to the significant increase in poverty. This has become a pressing social concern that requires new policy approaches. The development of local food policy in Rome has effectively brought together various emerging fronts and stakeholders. This collaborative effort involves parent committees advocating for school canteen improvements, researchers investigating food-related matters, and activists dedicated to various food-related causes. These diverse groups have fostered a constructive dialogue with city authorities, working collectively towards shared objectives. This collaborative effort has helped to establish a unified approach in Rome's food policy landscape, highlighting the importance of cooperation and shared objectives in shaping policies that address various aspects of food and nutrition in the city. As one interviewee noted:

> Undoubtedly the most important function of the path towards a food policy is the attempt to create a common space ... We entered the process to see if it is possible to create a systemic action on the issue of food. But Rome is a complex city, I mean really complex, so we have tried to create a space where we can discuss these issues in the city. But it's not that it's our space. I always say that it is not that the food policy for us will be the place where we think to build something. It will be a place, a political arena, of conflict and exchange, from which we can try to push and affect processes. But it is not that it will be the place of transformation, that is, it will be the place where we can somehow better understand the governance of food in the city. We have focused on this, so we don't do the usual little things like the marketplace. I mean, let's try to get into the system, let's confront the big retailers and so on. We try to have our say. We try to see if we can find a space both for projects and activities and to discuss serious problems like school canteens, like access to land for farmers. (RR, Rome)

Although it seems that informants in Cologne were less focused on the crisis and its direct impact on their activities, activists in this scene still made heightened efforts towards inclusivity. For instance, the establishment of the Cologne Food Policy Council was approached in an inclusive manner. The process started by bringing together a variety of initiatives that were working on food in 2015. A meeting at the City Hall convened more than 100 individuals, serving also as a vision workshop to set the cornerstone of what developed into a local food policy strategy. Subsequently, the core group distilled the workshop's most significant aspects identified by both citizens and activists. This draft was then disseminated to a broader audience through a virtual platform, inviting further contributions. Ultimately, the core group finalised a local food strategy, which was accepted and ratified by the City Council in 2019 as a guiding principle for the Food Policy Council.

The development of Rome's food policy has involved increased participation. However, activists in Rome have encountered challenges in maintaining an open public discussion space. This highlights the difficulties in ensuring an inclusive and transparent debate, despite efforts to involve various stakeholders. Preserving this discussion space is a crucial aspect of the food policy development process in Rome. Currently, this process focuses on governance with three main themes being emphasised. Firstly, there is an acknowledgement of the pivotal role cities play in food consumption, necessitating a radical shift in urban policies to effect meaningful changes in food policies. Secondly, there is recognition of the complexity of the food system, advocating for multilevel policies involving local, regional, national, and international authorities. Finally, it is important to involve all stakeholders in the dialogue to find solutions, ensuring that diverse perspectives and interests are taken into account when shaping food policies. This inclusivity in the dialogue is considered essential for effective policy development and implementation.

However, collaboration with the municipality presents challenges even when there is good liaison with some municipal departments, as in the case of the environmental department in Cologne. Communication between departments can prove challenging when talking about responsibilities relating to school gardens:

> Part of this relates to schools and school gardens. We wanted to create a school garden action plan. Our goal: a school garden for every school in Cologne, we formulated it so simply. A school garden is now something, so garden and green would now be the responsibility of the green space office, like green cuttings, trees. But of course, there is the school development office, which is in charge of the schools. We leave pedagogy out of it, that's a state matter. But of course, there is also the building, a property office and everything to do with educational measures or environmental education is then back in the environmental office. Yes, now try to organise a school garden project. Until they've finished their ping-pong, three quarters of a year have already passed. (FPCC, Cologne)

There is also a debate about resource availability and resource allocation. Small-scale projects serve as valuable examples to attract partners and demonstrate what's achievable. The previous mainstay of participation from middle-class individuals is challenged as these are increasingly facing financial constraints due to rising costs of living prompting them to reassess their level of engagement. Consequently, there are observable changes in the typical participant profiles within the alternative/sustainable food scene, particularly among middle-class consumers. There is a growing push for diversity and inclusivity within food movement scenes, aiming to incorporate a broader spectrum of voices and perspectives. This shift towards greater inclusivity seeks better to reflect the diversity of society as a whole.

Overall, the accounts illustrate the multifaceted nature of food activism and policy development. These encompass efforts to foster inclusivity, collaboration and impactful initiatives at the local level while dealing with challenges related to representation, economic constraints and bureaucratic hurdles. Across these different geographies, advancing a change agenda seems to point to a direction where 'we've found it's been easier to actually work "business to business" with the public sector to support local producers. Whereas trying to increase support for consumers can be a bit complex' (BFN, Bristol). This suggests that the movements have moved from focussing on the consumer as target for mobilisation to addressing institutional avenues more specifically.

Food Politics: Calling Back the Citizen by Scaling Through Institutions

When movement organisations utilise institutional avenues for growth and/or legitimacy, they engage in what Laamanen et al. (2023) consider scaling through strategies: this approach is a way to establish (support for more) social provision. This strategy has its roots in the failure of markets where the power in the system is with the supermarkets and their price point, as one of our Bristol informants puts it. The food system is broken and 'not fit for purpose' (FB, Bristol), it is 'going to break us apart at some point soon' (FPCC, Cologne) by leading to 'discrimination and almost oppression' (FB, Bristol).

Indeed, 'many people and organisations now recognise that the current pattern of food capitalism in Britain needs an overhaul and reorientation. A new more devolved regionalism is overdue to rebuild connection and engagement between the people and their food.' (Lang, 2020), a more universal problem to which various national and local governments need to react. Institutionalising change can be viewed as a means of scaling through institutions, facilitating collaboration with and through local governments to promote change. This comes not always without its problems as 'what [we] activists in an ideal scenario might want to change and system that might not always fit with what the council necessarily wants or is able to achieve' (BFN, Bristol).

In this context, it is illustrative to consider what one of our interviewees from Rome shared about the inherent tension in the administration regarding food policy. In particular, about a struggle to balance different priorities and interests, especially with regard to promoting sustainable and ethical food choices.

> Ensuring convenience in decision-making for the administration is crucial, which is why we advocate for it continuously. However, it's evident that if the goal is to promote the transition away from animal protein in school canteens, reviving the meat centre presents a conflicting stance. Despite this, we firmly believe that embracing a bold shift towards protein transition is not only ethically sound but also holds significant political potential. Persisting with the focus on the meat centre lacks coherence, but we understand the pressures faced by the administration, including vested interests from entrepreneurs and business entities. (SFR, Rome)

Indeed, there are clear limits to the extent to which a local authority can act. Firstly, this has to do with financial resources allocable to food activities. To do more needs with grant or public sector funding which is difficult '...in the context of austerity over the last decade, 15 years and the fact that local authorities just have no money.' (FB, Bristol)

Secondly, the bureaucratic and complex structure of a local authority means that they may mediate food related actions through food movement organisations. The local council can be:

> ...an absolute beast of an organisation. You know, the city council and public health team are massive and most of the time they don't have a clue what's going on in the other part of what they're doing. You know, they're, even within the teams they've got, they don't know what's going on. (FB, Bristol)

While sometimes feeling that they operate as a 'switchboard' for the different teams of the council, this can allow for food movement actors a strategic opportunity to navigate discussion and decision-making. When it comes to increasing access to land through allocation procedures, both in Bristol and Cologne, the food movement actors work to coordinate the allocation process.

Thirdly, the food movements have professionalised to provide what the municipalities are missing: 'Quite frankly, they don't have expertise in this area either at all. It would take many years to get that level of expertise within their organisation' (FB, Bristol). At the same time, the movement organisations are struggling with their grassroots identity: 'when I talk to the head of department at the environmental agency, I'm no longer grassroots' (FPCC, Cologne). They continue:

> ...maybe we don't need this representation in the grassroots ... maybe we don't need that as legitimation, if we say: this is the food strategy, we somehow have a common problem here and we are legitimised by the fact that we are taking care of this problem, tackling it, all together. (FPCC, Cologne)

Thus, the experience in Cologne heavily illustrates how the Food Policy Council wants to represent and give representation to the 'common man' without alienating them with too strong alignment to a grassroots identity. It means for activists to strike a balance between involving citizens on the one hand and to find a way to engage with public authorities.

These limitations offer strategic openings to the food movement actors to strengthen their work in connection to the loci of power in local authorities. Food movement activists in Rome target the municipality due to the key role it plays in decisions relevant and related to their agenda. This encompasses a wide range of issues, with respondents highlighting concerns such as the management of tenders for school catering services, in particular school meals:

> The municipality plays a crucial role because it has a number of tools, from legislation to authorisations, that are needed to implement ideas and projects on the ground. Take, for example, tenders for school catering services. Although there may be bottom-up initiatives, to achieve real change towards a more sustainable catering service, the involvement of municipal authorities and institutions is necessary. (FTO, Rome)

Focus on school meals was also the origin of Feeding Bristol also where the organisation would be focused around addressing issues of food insecurity in young, vulnerable children that are eligible for preschool meal vouchers over school holidays, a focus aligned to the mayor's platform of 'no child should go to school hungry.'

For the food movement actors, the best scaling through initiatives are such that allow for movement autonomy, that is, bottom-up processes that include a variety of stakeholders, such as the local authority. Here, the council can curate a right kind of environment for a long-term strategic change that gives the movement autonomy as compared to a situation where the food policy projects would be housed in the local authority. For example, in Rome, the municipality influences the urban landscape by determining the locations of neighbourhood markets, which can directly impact citizens' ability to make sustainable and local purchases. The city can also negotiate agreements with supermarkets to reduce the use of plastic, contributing to environmental sustainability efforts. Furthermore, as one of our informants in Rome reported: 'The City of Rome manages two large agricultural enterprises, and the decisions made regarding their role can significantly influence food supply and sustainability within the city' (TO, Rome). Similarly in Cologne, where the food policy council is an independent organisation, financially supported by the municipality. Here as well, they contribute to the transformation of the food system on the one hand, but also assist in processes that do not fall under the mandate of the municipal administration.

Bristol illustrates a similar experience in the origins of the food movement in establishing farmers' markets in collaboration with the city, then the food policy council with public health and sustainability team members sitting in boards and steering groups of food movement organisations. In Bristol, the food policy has been very much driven into the council strategic plans by the networked sustainable food scene.

> We have very good advocacy from public health and the sustainable city team at the council. We worked with them to develop this idea for Bristol Good Food 2030, which was essentially about developing a kind of set of plans for action for Bristol's food system for the rest of the decade. (BFN, Bristol)

The city council, which certainly has a reputation of being progressive and active, and a plan for a fair, healthy, sustainable city by 2050, was developed by the mayor's office. This document aligns climate and ecological emergency strategies. However, a focus on food was missing:

> But what we felt was needed and we then kind of worked with the council to develop the concept of Good Food 2030 … to kind of really draw out and build on the food aspects that were in those plans … [the city] kind of provided a starting point, but then we wanted to build that into a more comprehensive plan … they've been really quite involved and quite supportive of food systems governance … So, they've really been involved all along. (BFN, Bristol)

The experience in Cologne points to how the networking practices of the local food policy council is not a task that can be taken up by an administration. This is rather consistent through our data where the role of the food movement is not to follow authoritative top-down agenda, but to assist the local authority in a bottom-up approach. The political approach in Cologne aims to create consensus, representation, communication and involvement; the more a variety of actors are involved, the more they also take ownership of the change agenda:

> Food policy councils exist to see where there is common ground. So how can we get everyone round the table to solve a common problem that we have? … These are basically all tasks that you can't do on your own. (FPCC, Cologne)

This is also confirmed by the Feeding Bristol:

> I think the bottom up approach is incredibly important because it gets people involved in those processes. I think the way that we try to work around the food equality action plan strategy the key thing was right, we want people to be, feel they're part of this journey. (FB, Bristol)

Yet, extensive networking of different municipal and non-municipal actors can lead to other challenges, such as those experienced in Cologne in the work of creating procurement criteria for day care centres:

> Now we want to ensure politically that this is rolled out here in Cologne not just as a model in our 50 day-care centres, but across the city. It didn't go any further than that. Then, when the city of Cologne adopted the food strategy, it also decided to carry out a regional study which has not yet been published TODAY. It was completed last year but has not yet been published. Because if you now derive recommendations for action from it, which you have done, this again affects many different branches of the administration. And accordingly, you can't publish them as long as you haven't clarified with these other branches in advance like: by the way, here is a recommendation for action that applies to your branch and so on. (FPCC, Cologne, emphasis added)

In the best case, the relationship develops to become a 'realistic partnership' with municipal institutions and where the food movement organisations will be able to go to them and say:

> …"these are the things that we need to do. These are things that we need to change. These are the kind of policies we need to look at" and then they can go "Okay, how do we look at these policies?" How do we look at housing and transport and other areas of the city so that they can benefit food and access to food. Look at access to land in the city and what we're in control of and what can we realistically work on to do that. (FB, Bristol)

From the experiences of our informants, the relationships with institutions and positions of authority that can promote a change agenda need to be based on transparent realism across all aspects that influence inequality and injustice in connection to and also beyond food.

DISCUSSION: CALLING BACK THE CITIZEN AND INSTITUTIONS IN FOOD POLICY

In this article, we attempt to capture the experiences of local activists' working in the local food movement scene in Bristol, Cologne and Rome, with the goal of comparing strategies for localising and scaling collective action. We compared on bottom-up food policy development by NMMOs considering (1) how food become a central focus, (2) what do they do and who participates and (3) why and how do strategies to collaborate with local institutions manifest? Success of food movements, as with other movements seeking social change, often rests on trialling a variety of approaches to attract interest and grow the movement over time. Activists turn towards consumers claiming that the food system needs to be changed: in municipal terms, this typically happens through highlighting the benefits of local produce and local connection between the producers and consumers. These ties are a fundamental resource for municipal collective action. Food allows movements to mobilise and engage easily speaking to consumers' values and beliefs. The main compelling reason in food mobilisations is the attempt to bypass (supra-)nationally regulated market systems and establish support for more localised social provision.

In the food movement scenes we compared, we saw a variety of initiatives, from urban gardening to food pantries, community supported agriculture schemes or food education programs. Yet, as we highlight through our analysis of the three food movements, the focus on individual collective action (Micheletti, 2003) runs the risk of endorsing political and ideological approaches that circumvent the fundamental objective of addressing market regulation problems through institutional interventions (Jacobsen & Dulsrud, 2007). Globalisation, coupled with economic, environmental and social crises, seems to have increasingly shifted the action of movements towards the local dimension. At the same time, social movements have become more professionalised and adept at exposing the shortcomings of existing markets and experimenting with potential solutions.

There is a growing awareness among individuals and organisations that the current model of the industrialised food system requires significant restructuring and reorientation. Many advocate for a transition towards local food systems that re-establish connections between producers and consumers in a perspective of food sovereignty. Dynamic changes in the environments of food movements can lead to disruptions in usership and increase the need to adjust strategies. Municipalities play a central role in this process, as they have the power to use various tools – from legislative authority to resource (e.g. money and land) granting authorisations – that are essential to turning ideas and initiatives into concrete results. Through years of experimenting with organised small-scale distribution methods, such as sustainable land-use initiatives, food movement organisations have come to regard municipalities as fundamental allies and interlocutors to carry out their projects. However, municipalities may lack the necessary expertise and persuasive arguments to effectively encourage citizens to adopt more sustainable lifestyles and consumption. This can create favourable conditions for activists and administrators to intervene.

Contrary to radically transformative social movements that avoid cooperation with local authorities, this article argues for a current tendency to draw on institutional (local) powers, make claims to political institutions and even 'infiltrate' institutional positions (e.g. as experts). The localisation of food politics can be achieved through scaling via institutions, which 'recognises (local) government as an appropriate path through which to achieve change' (Laamanen et al., 2023, p. 866). Due to the increasing implementation of public management through austerity measures, food movement organisations have the potential to serve as hubs for expertise in alternative food practices. They can respond to tenders and build networks of different actors. Food movement organisations, as NMMOs, enable collaboration between movement organisations and city administration, and their movement entrepreneur leaders.

Comparing the experiences of local food activism in Rome, Bristol and Cologne illustrates that each context faces unique challenges. For example, Rome must address tensions within the administration, while Bristol and Cologne must navigate financial constraints and bureaucratic complexities. However, all three contexts emphasise the importance of collaborating with local authorities to drive change. While Rome directly targets the municipality to implement sustainable initiatives, Bristol and Cologne adopt more collaborative and strategic approaches. All aim to integrate food policy into broader city strategies and emphasise bottom-up engagement to address common challenges. Despite differences in focus and approach, all informants highlight the significance of advocacy, community engagement and pragmatic partnerships in effecting transformative change within food systems.

In summary, it is increasingly recognised by activists that local authorities play a central role in shaping food and sustainability policies – policies that have a direct impact on the daily lives of citizens. This shift in perspective highlights the importance of political engagement and recognises that policy choices can significantly shape the world. This is in contrast to previous ideas of self-determination, which often implied a level of independence from political influence by movement organisations. However, some activists argue that involving the municipality in promoting food can also be risky, moving the focus from good, clean, and fair food for every citizen (again) towards elitist, gourmet aspects of local food, such as with local culinary excellence. Activists are concerned that administrative involvement may not fully consider the food needs and rights of all individuals regardless of their resources or social positions.

NOTE

1. Lifestyle movements (Haenfler et al., 2012) do often not directly engage confrontation in the political arena, while some new social movements (such as the feminist, civil rights or pride movement) do; yet, materialist dimensions of the everyday life may remain a peripheral strategic issue for the latter movements.

REFERENCES

Bartolini, S. (2021). *Ecologia della Felicità. Perché Vivere Meglio Aiuta il Pianeta*. Aboca Edizioni.

Blühdorn, I. (2023). Recreational experientialism at 'the abyss': Rethinking the sustainability crisis and experimental politics. *Sustainability: Science, Practice and Policy*, *19*(1), 46–60. https://doi.org/10.1080/15487733.2022.2155439

Cooper, D. (2020). Towards an adventurous institutional politics: The prefigurative 'as if' and the reposing of what's real. *The Sociological Review*, *68*(5), 893–916. https://doi.org/10.1177/0038026120915148

Davidson, D. (2018). Metabolism. In M. Boström & D. J. Davidson (Eds.), *Environment and society: Concepts and challenges* (pp. 47–70). Palgrave MacMillan.

Forno, F., & Graziano, P. (2014). Sustainable community movement organisations. *Journal of Consumer Culture, 14*(2), 139–157. https://doi.org/10.1177/1469540514526225

Forno, F., Laamanen, M., & Wahlen, S. (2022). (Un-)sustainable transformations: Everyday food practices in Italy during COVID-19. *Sustainability: Science, Practice and Policy, 18*(1), 201–214. https://doi.org/10.1080/15487733.2022.2037341

Fuchs, D., Sahakian, M., Gumbert, T., Di Giulio, A., Maniates, M., Lorek, S., & Graf, A. (2021). *Consumption corridors: Living a good life within sustainable limits*. Routledge.

Goodman, D. (2004). Rural Europe redux: Reflections on alternative agro-food networks and paradigm change. *Sociologia Ruralis, 44*(1), 3–16. https://doi.org/10.1111/j.1467-9523.2004.00258.x

Haenfler, R. J., Johnson, B., & Jones, E. (2012). Lifestyle movements: Exploring the intersection of lifestyle and social movements. *Social Movement Studies, 11*(1), 1–20. https://doi.org/10.1080/14742837.2012.640535

Harvey, D. (2007). Neoliberalism as creative destruction. *The Annals of the American Academy of Political and Social Science, 610*(1), 21–44. https://doi.org/10.1177/0002716206296780

Jacobsen, E., & Dulsrud, A. (2007). Will consumers save the world? The framing of political consumerism. *Journal of Agricultural and Environmental Ethics, 20*, 469–482. https://doi.org/10.1007/s10806-007-9043-z

Kozinets, R., & Handelman, J. (2004). Adversaries of consumption: Consumer movements, activism, and ideology. *Journal of Consumer Research, 31*(3), 691–704. https://doi.org/10.1086/425104

Laamanen, M., Forno, F., & Wahlen, S. (2023). Neo-materialist movement organisations and the matter of scale: Scaling through institutions as prefigurative politics? *Journal of Marketing Management, 39*(9–10), 857–878. https://doi.org/10.1080/0267257X.2022.2045342

Lang, T. (2020). *Feeding Britain. Our food problems and how to fix them*. Pelican.

Marino, D., & Mazzocchi, G. (2022). L'evoluzione della Food Policy a Roma: Quali scenari?. *RE|Cibo, 1*, 55–72. https://doi.org/10.13135/3034-834X/7400

Micheletti, M. (2003). *Political virtue and shopping: Individuals, consumerism and collective action*. Palgrave Macmillan.

Patton, M. Q. (2002). *Qualitative research and evaluation methods* (3rd ed.). Sage.

Schlosberg, D., & Craven, L. (2019). *Sustainable materialism. Environmental movements and the politics of everyday life*. Oxford University Press.

Taylor, P. J., O'Brien, G., & O'Keefe, P. (2020). *Cities demanding the Earth. A new understanding of the climate emergency*. Bristol University Press.

Terra! Onlus, Lands Onlus. (2019). *Una Food Policy per Roma. Perché alla Capitale d'Italia serve una Politica del Cibo*. https://www.politichelocalicibo.it/wp-content/uploads/2019/10/Una-Food-Policy-per-Roma.pdf

Trentmann, F. (2009). Disruption is normal: Blackouts, breakdowns and the elasticity of everyday life. In E. Shove, F. Trentmann, & R. Wilk (Eds.), *Time, consumption and everyday life: Practice, materiality and culture* (pp. 67–84). Berg.

Veen, E. J., & D'Amico, S. (2019). Practices of food provisioning in alternative food networks: How different practitioners engage in different practices, depending on their emotional energy. *International Journal of Sociology of Agriculture and Food, 25*(1), 1–20. https://doi.org/10.48416/ijsaf.v25i1.20

Wallerstein, I. (2004). *World-systems analysis: An introduction*. Duke University Press.

Zwart, T. A., & Mathijs, E. (2020). Exploring emergent practices in alternative food networks: Voedselteams in Belgium. *Journal of Rural Studies, 80*, 586–594. https://doi.org/10.1016/j.jrurstud.2020.10.049

APPENDIX: INTERVIEW GUIDE

Category	Questions
Introduction and warm-up:	• Who are you? • What is your background? • What does your organisation do? • How long have you been working for your organisation? • Which other organisations/associations/movements are you part of?
Food action	• I know your organisation is involved in the food actions. Which type of action are you involved in?? • What are the food actions that are going on in Rome/Cologne/Bristol? • Food actions are today very common; would you be able to date when they have started to spread? Who were the first movers to raise the issue? • How many networks and movement organisations mobilise around food issues in Rome/Cologna/Bristol? • Are there any efforts towards the constitution of a local food policy? • If yes, what role have bottom-up organisations played in pushing towards this end?
Participation and practices	• Could you tell me about changes in participation related to food issues over the years? • Thinking of individuals, who participates in the activities? Why (particular profile, beliefs, values…)? Could you see any changes? • How do you/other actors get people involved locally? • Have the focus themes and practices changed over the years, how? • What are the 'dominant ideas' at present? • What is the role of other national and international networks? Is there a difference in the actions between your local and other settings?
Scaling through	• What is the role of the municipality in changing food systems/food movements? How has this changed over the years? What kind of practices/ structures can the municipality help create (e.g. food policy council, loose CSA networks, etc.)? • What advantages do you see in targeting (again) the municipality/state (although at the local level) and what are the obstacles? • What are the specific practices that you need/use in collaboration with municipalities/the state?

CONDITIONS FOR SUSTAINABLE FOOD CONSUMPTION: A COMPARATIVE STUDY OF EUROPEANS' VALUATIONS OF CHICKEN MEAT

Gunnar Vittersø[a], Mattia Andreola[b], Unni Kjærnes[a], Sabina Kuraj[a], Alexander Schjøll[a] and Hanne Torjusen[a]

[a]*Oslo Metropolitan University, Norway*
[b]*University of Trento, Italy*

ABSTRACT

Presently, we are witnessing an increased public attention directed towards the negative impacts on climate and environment from food production and consumption. Policies aimed at changing consumption patterns are focused on voluntary measures, such as information and labelling schemes for consumers to make conscious choices in the market. However, such measures have proven to be of highly variable importance and only a small proportion of consumers consciously choose so-called ethical products when buying food. By a comparison of Europeans' valuations of chicken meat, we discuss the dynamics between individual processes and the social and contextual conditions for consumption changes. This study is based on national representative surveys carried out in seven European countries, and concerns peoples' valuations of indirect quality factors related to origin, animal welfare and their relation to producer, brand and production methods (organic, breed). Overall, the engagement varies considerably across Europe as well as in the sociodemographic patterns. We ascribe this variation mainly to cultural, social and institutional differences. This chapter concludes that despite European harmonization of regulations and integrated markets, the consumer role is

Consumers and Consumption in Comparison
Comparative Social Research, Volume 37, 115–138

Published under exclusive licence by Emerald Publishing Limited
ISSN: 0195-6310/doi:10.1108/S0195-631020240000037006

shaped quite differently depending on cultural and social structures as well as institutional configurations and trust. These contextual conditions need to be considered when formulating policies on food consumption and food system transitions.

Keywords: Food production; consumer consciousness; ethical consumption; environmental policy; food systems

INTRODUCTION

In light of political goals to reduce greenhouse gas (GHG) emissions and stimulate more sustainable consumption patterns, there is increased public attention to the role of consumers as agents of change and how so-called ethical or political consumption can play a role in this transition (Evans et al., 2017; Kjærnes et al., 2022). Several international agreements, such as the Paris agreement on climate change, the Kunming-Montreal Global Biodiversity Framework and the UN Sustainable Development Goals (SDGs), all point to the need to change production *and* consumption patterns. Strict policies aiming to kerb GHG emissions by taxation of foods with a high carbon footprint may prove quite effective (Lykkeskov & Gjerris, 2017). Yet, with considerable political and public opposition to strict regulations, policies based on individual voluntary solutions are often preferred. Consumer-oriented environmental policy, not least in the European Union, seeks to encourage individuals acting as consumers to make conscious choices in the market. Labelling schemes and information measures aimed at consumers are key policy instruments to achieve these goals (Gorton et al., 2021). They are all based on the idea of ethical or political consumers who, by 'voting with their wallet', can contribute to significant changes in production and consumption patterns (Jacobsen, 2017; Micheletti, 2010; Micheletti & Stolle, 2012; Morgan, 2010; Seyfang, 2005). This type of 'soft' measure has proven to be of limited and highly variable importance in the European market, where it turns out that only a small proportion of consumers consciously choose so-called ethical products (Grunert et al., 2014).

However, there is insufficient empirical knowledge about the conditions that promote or hinder more ethical or sustainable consumption as part of everyday practices. We address this by looking at the food quality aspects that people appreciate, particularly aspects that are not directly perceptible, but rather linked to how the food has been produced and sourced, such as organic food or animal welfare issues, in this chapter defined as indirect quality aspects. A comparative survey across seven European countries seeks to improve the understanding of such processes. Using chicken meat as a concrete case, this chapter will take a closer look at what factors are important when purchasing food.

We ask how and why interest in environmentally sustainable purchases varies in the population of different countries and regions in Europe. A European comparison allows us to discuss the dynamics between individual opinions on consumption change and the structural and contextual conditions for such changes.

Sustainable Food Consumption and the Consumer

The neoliberal notion of individualism and the long liberal tradition that celebrates the free market have framed choices as an expression of free will based on self-determination, and thus ascribing responsibility for actions solely to individuals (Giesler & Veresiu, 2014; Lemke, 2001). However, it is argued that individual explanatory models overlook the normative and habitual structures in which consumption practices form (Warde, 2016), as well as the specific institutional and political systems that shape these structures (Dubuisson-Quellier, 2022; Johnston & Goodman, 2015; Smith & Jehlička, 2007). Dubuisson-Quellier (2022), for instance, states that specific market technologies frame different groups of consumers and argues against the use of a generalized ideal-typical consumer model detached from its social foundations (see also Boström & Klintman, 2009; Jacobsen & Dulsrud, 2007; Terragni et al., 2009). Comparative studies have found important differences in food consumption that are attributed to institutional factors related to markets and regulations (Kjærnes et al., 2013, 2022; Veisser et al., 2008), as well as cultural conditions and features of civil society in different European countries. These differences are among others formed by local geographical, cultural, economic and political conditions (Amilien, 2011; Amilien et al., 2022; Barjolle & Sylvander, 2000; Boström & Klintman, 2009; Halkier et al., 2007; Holm & Gronow, 2019; Kjærnes et al., 2013; Mann, 2019).

In the Nordic countries, Niva et al. (2019) point out that: 'consumers' and citizens' mobilization in sustainable consumption takes shape in the context of societal, economic and political developments on local, national and international level' and that 'specific national configurations of discourses, markets and policies significantly affect what people think and do as food consumers' (Niva et al., 2019, p. 189). Factors, such as inequality in the social model itself (Esping-Andersen, 1990), governance traditions and not least food culture have an impact on the engagement with food issues in the population (Thøgersen, 2010). While the food sector in the North of Europe is characterized by a greater sense of trust and consensus among actors, South and East European countries have lower trust, hence food quality and safety being of major concern in the population.

In this chapter, we use such social and contextual factors as an interpretative framework for analyzing variations in public opinions on the importance of environmental and ethical concerns when purchasing chicken. Chicken is an everyday food item to most Europeans, but also contested in terms of safety, animal welfare and environmental issues. Moreover, in the last 50 years, the consumption of chicken meat has increased almost threefold. Today, chicken meat is the second most consumed type of meat in the European Union with an average of 25.6 kg per capita versus the 31.1 kg of pig meat consumed per capita (Bellini, 2021). Almost 80% of European consumers state that they eat chicken once a week or more often (Vittersø et al., 2022). Chicken represents a mundane product perceived by many as relatively affordable and probably less subject to social distinction compared to for instance beef. In this context, chicken is particularly suitable as a proxy for food in general.

First, we explore to what extent Europeans are concerned about a range of qualities related to the origin of the product, production methods and animal welfare, the breed of the chicken, labels and brands. We have called these *indirect quality aspects.*

Second, we search for social variations, and ask what are the sociodemographic and socio-economic characteristics common to those who seek out indirect quality aspects and to what extent may such characteristics explain variations in the focus on these aspects? In accordance with an individual perspective on sustainable transitions, many studies focus on who the 'sustainable consumers' are, especially in terms of socio-economic background. Those characterized as ethical consumers, similar to those emphasizing indirect aspects of food and engage in sustainable food practices, are often portrayed as well-educated upper middle-class women (Schjøll & Thorjussen, 2019; Starr, 2009; Wier et al., 2008). To what extent do our data confirm such an image?

Third, we ask how trust in information from food system actors may affect the valuation of indirect food quality aspects, as indicated by several previous comparative and national studies on trust in food (see, e.g. Berg, 2014; de Jonge et al., 2008; Kjærnes et al., 2013, 2022; Murphy et al., 2021; Wu et al., 2021). Trust in food system actors affects how people orient themselves in the food market. Chicken has been subject to significant critique and distrust due to the industrialized farming practices that characterize modern broiler production. High trust may imply trust in product labels that describe some quality aspects (origin, organic, animal welfare, etc.) and brands. To the contrary, generalized trust in the food system may mean that they, as consumers, do not take labels or other indirect quality aspects into consideration when buying food, because they trust that the food products in themselves are safe and live up to high quality standards. High distrust may lead to very specific purchase strategies within or outside conventional markets – or apathy and non-involvement. We anticipate that the different ways in which trust is important for purchases and engagement, both generally and in the market, depend on broader contextual political and cultural factors.

Fourth, to what extent is emphasis on indirect food qualities part of a broader engagement in sustainable food practices? Grunert et al. (2014) have found considerable country differences, where a general concern for sustainability issues does not necessarily translate into behaviour and the authors relate this to contextual factors on the country level. Other studies find that 'ethical consumption' often is ideologically motivated (e.g. engagement in environmental organizations or specific political party preferences) and connected to certain 'lifestyles' (e.g. engaged in other sustainability practices, dietary choices or cooking skills) (see, e.g. Boström & Klintman, 2009; Holt, 1993; Niva et al., 2014, 2019; Schjøll & Thorjussen, 2019; Terragni et al., 2009; Torjusen et al., 1999; Torjusen & Vittersø, 2023, ch. 7). Thus, we investigate possible links between emphasis on indirect quality aspects of chicken and engagement in food sustainability practices more generally.

In the following, we first present the data and the analytical design followed by a presentation and discussion of the results. The results are discussed in relation to previous comparative research on sustainable food consumption and trust in food emphasizing a European configuration of citizens' engagement. The conclusion points to a complex dynamic between individual engagement and structural factors, in terms of social structures as well as institutional trust within the country context. Despite European harmonization and market globalization, European countries have characteristically different institutional configurations and interrelationships with people as consumers and the role of food in everyday life.

DATA

Data were collected in an online survey using a web panel in June 2019 in seven European countries: France, Germany, Italy, Norway, Poland, Spain and the United Kingdom. The survey was conducted as part of the EU Horizon 2020 project Organic-PLUS[1] and the countries represented 70% of all EU inhabitants (including the United Kingdom) at the time of the data collection. Norway was included as the only country outside the European Union. Kantar Norway was responsible for data collection in all seven European countries of study, and the survey population was sampled from Kantar's web panels in each country.

Researchers from Consumption Research Norway (SIFO) were drafting the questionnaire and researchers from the countries of the study contributed to adapt the questionnaire to each national context. The questionnaire was then translated into the official language in each country, and back translated into English to secure the reliability of the translations. More about the data collection can be found in Vittersø et al. (2019).

The sample (Table 1) is representative for gender, age and the number of people living in the household. When it comes to education and income, the sample is skewed towards the higher levels. This is a general problem with public opinion surveys and should be noticed here because people with high income and

Table 1. Sociodemographic and Socio-economic Characteristics of Survey Respondents by Country.

Variable	Country							Grand Total	*N*
	Norway	France	UK	Spain	Poland	Italy	Germany		
Women	50	51	52	53	53	53	52	51.8	8,156
Age Groups									
Under 30	20	17	18	13	20	13	16	16.8	2,364
30–44	25	25	26	25	28	25	22	25.1	3,538
45–59	26	25	26	29	24	28	29	26.6	3,743
60+	29	32	31	33	27	4	32	31.4	4,422
Education									
Primary school	3	2	1	3	2	3	3	2.3	355

(Continued)

Table 1. *(Continued)*

Variable	Country							Grand Total	*N*
	Norway	France	UK	Spain	Poland	Italy	Germany		
Secondary school	16	22	34	23	44	35	22	28.3	4,398
Vocational college	16	28	25	26	9	31	47	26.2	4,077
University degree (bachelor)	34	31	27	33	12	18	12	23.7	3,680
University degree (master or higher)	30	16	13	13	31	13	13	18.2	2,829
Other	0	1	1	2	1	1	3	1.4	220
Income									
Low income	23	54	56	35	8	42	48	38.3	5,356
Middle income	55	39	31	56	50	32	40	43.1	6,023
High income	23	8	13	9	43	26	12	18.6	2,608
People Living in the Household									
1	25	23	19	9	9	9	28	16.5	2,264
2	42	36	35	34	29	30	39	33.9	4,644
3	14	18	20	25	27	28	17	22.4	3,070
4	14	17	17	23	21	26	12	19.4	2,657
5+	6	5	8	8	13	7	5	7.7	1,056
N	1,655	2,034	2,059	1,935	1,876	1,933	2,018		13,510

Notes: Percent (N = 13,510).

education traditionally may be more interested in environmental issues and have greater capacity to pay the price for expensive food (Martin & Schouten, 2012).

RESEARCH DESIGN

The Dependent Variable

As part of the Organic-PLUS project, the questionnaire was developed to capture European citizens' views on phasing out contentious inputs in organic agriculture (Vittersø et al., 2019). In addition, we collected data on people's perception of, and commitment to, sustainable food consumption. The respondents were asked several questions about frequencies of eating different food products, food practices and purchasing habits, use of food labels, trust in food system actors and quality aspects they consider when purchasing food, including 'chicken meat'. As basis for the dependent variable, we used this question: 'When buying chicken (in any form), which of the following factors are important to you?' Respondents were asked to rate from 1 'not at all important' to 5 'very important' for the following factors for chicken meat:

- Specific brand;
- Specific breeds of chicken;

- Price;
- Animal welfare/free range production;
- Organic production;
- Taste;
- My knowledge of the producer;
- Produced in (name of home country [Italy, Germany, Poland, the United Kingdom, Norway, Spain and France]);
- Produced in my local area;
- Best before date.

As shown in Table 2, the factor analysis revealed two dimensions. One dimension contains the *direct* (search and experience) quality aspects, and includes *price*, *taste* and *best before date*. The other dimension includes the seven ***indirect*** quality aspects. These aspects are often referred to as *credence qualities*, especially in marketing research; however, the aspects included in this study comprise a broader range of quality issues that are not only reduced to the credence value of the product. We have, thus, introduced *indirect quality* as a more general term. The factor analysis formed the basis for creating one indicator on indirect quality aspects for chicken utilized as dependent variable in analyses of the research questions. An additive index was constructed to form a general measure of the extent to which respondents emphasized indirect aspects of food quality. A reliability test was carried out, calculating the Cronbach's Alpha parameter to measure the internal consistency of the battery of Likert questions, giving a result of 0.86.

Following the strategy also adopted in Niva et al. (2014), the individual items were recoded, leaving the most extreme response categories isolated (1 'not at all important' and 5 'very important') and combining the three central response

Table 2. Structural Matrix of a Factorial Analysis of Quality Aspects Considered When Buying Chicken Meat.

Quality Aspect	Component	
	1	2
Specific brand	0.683	
Specific breeds of chicken	0.745	
Price		0.711
Animal welfare	0.710	0.330
Organic production	0.773	
Taste	0.326	0.717
My knowledge of the producer	0.775	
Produced in the (name of the country)	0.681	0.324
Produced in my local area	0.785	0.300
Best before date	0.370	0.718

categories (2, 3 and 4). This was done to obtain a normal distribution, thus allowing the application of common regression techniques, such as multiple linear regression (MLR). A Kolmogorov-Smirnov normality test confirms the normal distribution of the dependent variable under investigation (results not shown). From a purely logical point of view, it seemed reasonable to allocate the index scores by distinguishing between those who are not at all interested in the parameters, those who have a degree of interest greater than one but less than the maximum and those who have the maximum interest. Fig. 2 shows the distribution for each country. We use the indicator for emphasis on indirect quality aspects to answer our first research question.

Independent Variables

The remaining three research questions were studied using MLR, where various types of independent variables were introduced in a stepwise procedure reflecting each of these questions. Thus, five sociodemographic and socio-economic variables, a variable on trust in food system actors, and a variable on sustainability practices were included in the analyses.

The sociodemographic and socio-economic variables are the following: gender, age, education, income and number of household members. Gender was coded as a binary variable where the constant is male. Age was classified into four categories at 15-year intervals (the first category includes all individuals younger than 30 years and the last includes all respondents over 60 years). Regarding education, it was measured with a five-category variable, where the categories were (1) primary school only or no education, (2) secondary school, (3) vocational college, (4) a bachelor's degree and (5) a master's or higher university degree. Income, originally classified into 12 categories (adapted to each country), was remodelled into three ordinal categories: low income, middle income and high income. The number of household members is coded from a minimum of 1 to a maximum of 25.

A trust index was constructed based on a question concerning truth-telling of various food system actors. The question was retrieved from the comparative European research study *Trust in Food* only modified by specifying 'organic' chicken (Kjærnes et al., 2013): 'Imagining that there is a food scandal concerning salmonella in organic chicken. Do you think that the following would tell the whole truth, only tell part of the truth, or would give misleading information?', with the following options to be rated on a scale 1–3 (Give misleading information, Parts of the truth or Whole truth): 'press, television and radio', 'the processing industry', 'supermarket chains', 'farmers or farmer organizations', 'consumer organizations', 'politicians', 'public food authorities', 'organic food labelling bodies' and 'independent food experts (e.g. academic/researchers)'. The index was constructed as an average of all the ratings in each country. All the institutions/actors are treated equally, meaning that the index is not weighed. In theory a country could have a high trust index if just one actor/institution has a high trust, and all others have medium trust.

Table 3. Imagining That There Is a Food Scandal Concerning Salmonella in Organic Chicken.

Institution	Norway	France	UK	Spain	Poland	Italy	Germany
Press, television and radio	2.07	1.79	1.85	1.72	1.80	1.79	1.81
The processing industry	1.86	1.56	1.69	1.56	1.69	1.62	1.54
Supermarket chains	1.89	1.65	1.81	1.63	1.57	1.74	1.75
Farmers or farmer organizations	2.06	1.96	2.01	1.93	1.88	1.95	1.92
Consumer organizations	2.39	2.29	2.15	2.17	2.10	2.20	2.18
Politicians	1.73	1.46	1.59	1.42	1.42	1.49	1.53
Public food authorities	2.33	2.03	2.16	1.88	1.96	2.06	2.02
Organic food labelling bodies	2.23	1.96	2.04	1.94	2.06	1.95	1.91
Independent food experts (e.g. academic/ researchers)	2.44	2.09	2.22	2.23	2.18	2.20	2.16
Trust index	2.10	1.87	1.95	1.83	1.85	1.89	1.88

Notes: Do you think that the following would tell you the whole truth, only tell part of the truth or would give misleading information? (From Vittersø et al., 2019).

As demonstrated in Table 3, country responses reflect very similar relative ratings of the various types of actors/institutions while levels vary consistently between the countries. This justify using a non-weighted index since the relative valuation of the institutions across countries is almost the same.

Regarding sustainable food practices, we asked a battery of questions previously used by Niva et al. (2014) and Tobler et al. (2011). Respondents were asked 'Are you doing or planning to do the following things to reduce your environmental impact?', with the following sub questions: 'buy regional (local) food', 'avoid food products that were imported by airplane', 'consume only seasonal fruit and vegetables', 'buy organic food' and 'consume meat at most twice a week or a little at a time'. Four answering alternatives were given to the respondents: 'I am doing this already'; 'I would like to do this and I already know how to start'; 'I would like to do this, but I do not know how'; 'I am not doing this'. Based on these statements an index of engagement in sustainability practices was constructed where the highest score was given to the respondents answering 'I am doing this already' and the lowest score were given to 'Not doing this'. These questions, initially included in a larger battery, were selected by performing a factor analysis to ensure that they all identified the same dimension. Subsequently, a one-dimensional index was created to measure the level of engagement of the respondents' food-related sustainability practices. A high score on the index, thus, means high level of engagement.

Analysis

The effects of the independent variables on the indirect quality index were explored by means of MLR, using SPSS statistical software. We used stepwise regression. In the first model, we examined the effects of sociodemographic and socio-economic variables (gender, age, education, income and number of household members). In model 2, the trust index variable was included as an explanatory variable followed by the sustainability practice variable in model 3 as illustrated in Fig. 1. Analyses were made separately for each study country to allow for different country dynamics between the various elements.

The first model was included to analyze the importance of social and demographic status (e.g. gender, education and income) for emphasis on indirect qualities. As discussed previously, the literature is somewhat divided regarding engagement in sustainability as a marker of socio-economic and/or -demographic status. The purpose of model 2 was to investigate how trust in the food system effect interest in indirect food qualities. Based on previous research we anticipated differences between countries on the importance of trust. The introduction of sustainability practices in model 3 opened the possibility to investigate the relationship between a more general engagement in food and sustainability issues and emphasis on indirect qualities. In addition, it allowed us to examine if the associations found in model 1 and 2 changes when introducing sustainability practices into the analysis. Fig. 1 indicates associations rather than causal links, all within a specific country context. The order of the MLR of variations in emphasis on indirect qualities has the following logic:

There were considerable variations in response patterns across Europe. Regressions were therefore run country by country (Table 4). An aggregate model was also used, with the respondents' country of residence as a variable, to test the effects of the previous models and to see how much is determined by the contextual (policies,

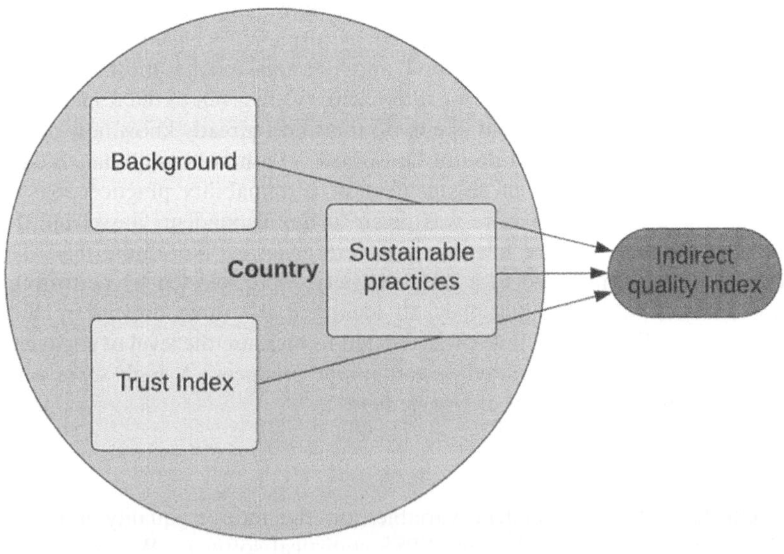

Fig. 1. Influences on Public Opinions on the Importance of Indirect Qualities.
Notes: An analytical model.

Table 4. Regression Table on Social Variations in the Importance Given to Indirect Quality Aspects When Purchasing Chicken.

		Country						
Model	Variable	Norway	France	UK	Spain	Poland	Italy	Germany
1	Constant	**11.547**	**13.687**	**13.014**	**14.093**	**13.675**	**15.573**	**13.168**
	Gender	**0.855**	**0.448**	0.042	0.189	**0.985**	0.257	0.287
	Education	0.063	-0.056	**0.35**	**-0.111**	0.079	-0.095	0.081
	Income	0.118	**0.526**	**0.609**	-0.066	**-0.465**	-0.151	0.185
	Age group	0.01	**0.193**	**-0.432**	**0.443**	**0.315**	**0.283**	0.151
	No. in the house.	-0.045	0.113	0.051	**0.201**	**0.144**	**0.146**	**0.207**
Adjusted R^2		0.024	0.023	0.09	0.027	0.053	0.013	0.013
2	(Constant)	**11.351**	**11.912**	**11.821**	**13.518**	**12.468**	**13.878**	**12.401**
	Gender	**0.845**	**0.376**	0.076	0.177	**0.946**	**0.292**	0.27
	Education	0.061	-0.066	**0.347**	-0.104	0.082	-0.083	0.079
	Income	0.118	**0.498**	**0.577**	-0.066	**-0.467**	-0.162	0.17
	Age group	0.009	**0.178**	**-0.434**	**0.441**	**0.307**	**0.283**	**0.156**
	No. in the house.	-0.045	0.088	0.054	**0.198**	**0.14**	**0.136**	**0.212**
	Trust index	0.012	**0.123**	**0.073**	0.035	**0.077**	**0.096**	**0.047**
Adjusted R^2		0.023	0.048	0.099	0.028	0.062	0.029	0.016
3	(Constant)	**7.557**	**9.171**	**7.708**	**9.594**	**9.124**	**10.591**	**9.359**
	Gender	**0.541**	0.156	-0.04	-0.003	**0.565**	0.102	0.035
	Education	-0.043	**-0.151**	**0.161**	-0.082	0.077	-0.094	-0.027
	Income	**0.299**	**0.332**	**0.288**	-0.123	**-0.511**	**-0.202**	-0.037
	Age group	-0.014	-0.009	**-0.333**	**0.332**	0.124	0.099	-0.03
	No. in the house.	-0.067	0.113	0.084	**0.237**	**0.092**	0.089	**0.224**
	Trust index	0.004	**0.067**	0.008	-0.019	**0.039**	**0.066**	-0.016
	Sust pract. index	**0.436**	**0.378**	**0.522**	**0.411**	**0.418**	**0.348**	**0.430**
Adjusted R^2		0.229	0.18	0.339	0.179	0.218	0.13	0.225
N		**1,269**	**1,574**	**1,533**	**1,632**	**1,619**	**1,675**	**1,571**

Notes: Linear regression. Statistical significance (<0.05 *p*-value) in **bold**.

markets and cultural) elements of individual countries. Detailed results of this analysis are not shown, but comments will be added where relevant.

RESULTS AND DISCUSSION

Our *first* question was how respondents across Europe view various indirect quality aspects when purchasing chicken. All the seven indirect quality factors were considered of less importance than the direct qualities, such as taste, best before date and price (see Vittersø et al., 2022). However, Fig. 2 shows marked differences between the indirect quality factors on average and between countries. According to the average percentage values among the seven factors, the characteristic considered

Fig. 2. Views on the Importance of Various Indirect Quality Aspects by Country (N = 13,421). *Notes:* Percent.

most important is the origin being one's own country, considered very important by more than 4 out of 10 respondents (44%). Following this, animal welfare also appears clearly relevant, indicated as very important by almost the same number of respondents (39%). The chicken being produced locally is seen as an essential factor by almost 3 out of 10 respondents (29%). One out of four respondents emphasized organic production (25%) and knowledge of the producer (24%), respectively, as very important factors. On the other hand, aspects such as branding and the use of specific breeds seem secondary, indicated as very important by less than one in five respondents (18% and 19%, respectively).

Overall, we observe that the Norwegian respondents are the most disinterested in all these characteristics. The exception is the chicken being produced in their own country, rated as very important by more respondents in Norway than in the United Kingdom. French and British respondents seem to primarily emphasize country of origin and animal welfare. Italian respondents, on the other hand, are the most interested in all these indirect factors, apart from the use of specific breeds.

Regarding animal welfare, the figure obtained from this survey (39% of participants said they were very interested) does not differ too much from the results of the various Eurobarometer surveys (47% in 2016, latest survey on the subject which also presents data for the United Kingdom). Previously Italians have been among the European populations least interested in this aspect; however, figures from the Eurobarometer 2023 may indicate increased concern about animal welfare among Italians (European Commission, 2023). In our survey, the Spanish are the next most interested, after the Italians, in knowing the producer. Poles, on their part, emerge as the second population after Italians most interested in organic production. Finally, Germans appear as least distinctive, with ratings of these indirect quality aspects quite close to the average for all seven countries.

The study has found that engagement in indirect qualities as a reference for the respondents appears to be moderate. If at all important, there seems to be some consensus that the country of production of chicken is most decisive, people generally preferring chicken produced in their own country. This is in line with earlier studies (see, e.g. Fuentes et al., 2023; Harju et al., 2024; Nagy et al., 2023; Thøgersen et al., 2019). People know how the system in their own country operates, while imports involve a series of unknown actors whose standards may be more uncertain. For instance, in Norway domestic chicken is viewed as safer due to less instances of foodborne diseases associated with chicken meat than in many other European countries.

Least importance is placed on brands and breeds. Conventional production of chicken is based on a few varieties of breeds in most European countries and consumers are mainly unfamiliar with the different breeds used for poultry meat (Escobedo del Bosque et al., 2021). The production process is highly standardized and with relatively little differentiation in the supermarkets. This may explain why respondents regard brands and breeds of less importance when buying chicken meat. Relatively high importance is given to organic production and animal welfare. In the overall sample, respectively 25 and 39% state that this is very important. This is in accordance with earlier studies. When asked, people tend to emphasize aspects such as organic production and animal welfare to a greater extent than sales data suggests (Thøgersen, 2009, chap. 11, 2010). This seemingly lack of consistency between valuation and purchases may either be that people answer in accordance with what they view as socially acceptable or desirable, or that sales data do not reflect the actual demand for organic and animal welfare products. Little availability and too little information are often mentioned as important barriers towards buying these products (Grunert et al., 2014; Vittersø et al., 2019).

Our *second* research question concerns to what extent sociodemographic and socio-economic factors matter for whether people emphasize indirect aspects when purchasing chicken. The findings for the first regression model (Table 4), including a range of demographic and social background variables, indicate that generally such factors matter to some, but not to a very large extent. Yet, patterns vary considerably across the seven European countries. Socio-economic distinctions, income and education are most pronounced in France and the United Kingdom. This is of some importance in Poland, too, but then with a negative impact of income, meaning that lower level income groups emphasize indirect quality more. Income matters more than education. In the overall data set, the influence of educational level is not significant (data not shown). On the country level, education is significant only in the United Kingdom. Sociodemographic background is least important in Germany and Norway, but the two countries differ in that while gender is more important in Norway, household type is decisive in Germany. In South and Eastern Europe, what seems more important is the type of household and age, perhaps indicating that this is a matter of family type and phase of life. While the constant for age is positive in these countries, indicating that interest in indirect qualities increases with age, this is more common among younger age groups in the United Kingdom. However, taken together, in all seven countries these sociodemographic and socio-economic variables explain less than 1% of the variation in the dependent variable (adjusted R^2). Thus, the direct effects of distinctive social background factors seem weak and highly heterogeneous across Europe.

Often, engagement in food and sustainability issues has been associated with personal resources. The conventional picture of those who take ethical (organic or animal welfare) and/or food system aspects (local or national origin or knowing the producer) into consideration when buying food, is one of well-educated women, often young or middle-aged (Schjøll & Thorjussen, 2019; Starr, 2009; Wier et al., 2008). Instead, our study finds variations across Europe in the socio-economic patterns of engagement. At one end, there is a highly socially homogeneous pattern in Norway, while the United Kingdom, at the other end, is strongly differentiated when it comes to socio-economic background. While, as discussed above, for the countries between these two, demographic influences, age and household type, seem to matter more.

Research question *three* concerns how trust in food system actors may affect the valuation of indirect food quality aspects. In model 2, the effect of trust is statistically significant when controlled for social background factors in all but two countries, Norway and Spain. The coefficients are positive; as the respondent's level of trust increases, so does the importance attributed to indirect factors when purchasing chicken. Introducing trust to the model does not seem to change the significance of social background factors, thus suggesting that the importance of trust in this case is not socially divided. Moreover, despite significant effects, adding the trust index does not increase the explanatory power of the model to any large extent, with some exception for France and Italy, where the adjusted R^2 is doubled by adding trust.

A previous study of trust in food safety found that highly diverse opinions across Europe could be linked to specific configurations and interrelationships between the various institutions and elements of the food system (Kjærnes et al., 2013). This involved market structures, regulatory arrangements, civil society and public discourse, as well as household structures and food cultures. In broad terms, the study identified three basically different configurations that tended to dominate in different regions of Europe (to some extent also in accordance with different types of welfare states (the classical reference is Esping-Andersen, 1990). These different configurations imply different types of trust formation.

In the North, in Scandinavia, highly concentrated and standardized markets are found (Alfnes et al., 2019), closely associated with 'behind the scenes' political traditions, and a homogeneous consumer culture (Kjærnes et al., 2022). The highly generalized system trust is reflected in low involvement and activism among people as consumers as well as a consensual public discourse, with widespread beliefs that institutional actors together ensure that conditions for, for example farm animals are acceptable, often with public authorities taking a leading role. In Norway, the food market involves neither much product differentiation nor alternatives to standardized supermarket distribution. Consumers in the mainstream Norwegian food market therefore have limited possibilities to take distinctive quality aspects into consideration in their food practices. In Norway we find relatively low engagement and little social differentiation (Kjærnes et al., 2022). The level of trust in information from institutional actors does not matter much for their engagement.

Second, and to the contrary, most typical in the South-European countries, there is highly generalized distrust in institutional actors, who in turn appear distant and disinterested. Despite harmonized European regulations, the implementation of them is here less obvious and frequently met with suspicion. The sale of fresh food from butchers and market stalls is more important. Consumer strategies are often quite laborious, based on personal interrelations and emphasis on direct experience of quality and knowledge of origins, such as the chicken farmer (Halkier et al., 2007; Torjusen et al., 2024).

Emphasis on indirect qualities may thus follow from tradition and general distrust in societal institutions rather than representing modernization and a new trend. This kind of involvement is also associated with a family-oriented food culture (Halkier et al., 2007). The configuration and its implications seem to make sense for the interpretation of our findings especially from the Italian respondents. They are more engaged in a range of indirect quality aspects, in particular origins and familiarity. Age and household type matter for their engagement, as part of a broader set of everyday practices. In a context of generalized distrust, trust is important for their engagement. The association between engagement and trust in the model may suggest that those being engaged are more trusting.

A third type of configuration is, according to Kjærnes et al. (2013), dominated by competitive and differentiated markets, with supermarkets taking a lead position, linked to expressly market promoting, but also controversial, policies and a consumer culture focusing on active market participation. Trust in the various institutional actors is much more contingent upon what they do and say, as reflected even in a more contentious public discourse and collective activism. Contrary to generalized system trust, this more 'reflexive' type of trust/distrust refers to distinctive market strategies (e.g. product labelling), less to what the government does. In Europe and the European Union, both discourse and political strategies have reflected such an understanding, closely linked to market-oriented policies with individual consumer involvement and responsibility for issues such as environmental concerns and farm animal welfare through consumer choice (European Commission, 2023).

Using this as a frame for understanding the United Kingdom findings, it may then come as no surprise that this is where we find the clearest patterns of socio-economic differentiation. However, France, rather than responding similarly to Italy and Spain, also has relatively distinct socio-economic response patterns. The quality of meat is being strongly emphasized, but through (often government supported) labelling schemes (e.g. Label Rouge) rather than personal relationships. Moreover, along with a high-end quality-oriented distribution system, there is a strong, highly price-oriented market – addressing economically different market segments (Kjærnes et al., 2009). This makes the consumer role more similar to that in the United Kingdom (Plessz & Le Pape, 2019).

German respondents take a 'middle position' in this categorization, with emphasis on indirect qualities close to average and with few very distinctive features in the regression analyses. However, as in the South, the German engagement has the same associations with age and household type and trust does matter. Earlier studies have shown that distrust in food institutions is higher, compared to countries in the North and the West. The explanatory power of the regression model (adjusted R^2) is quite good, thus suggesting that the relevance of the model is at the same level as the other countries.

Finally, *the fourth research question* asks to what extent is emphasis on indirect food qualities part of a broader engagement in sustainable food practices? In model 3, by including the sustainability practices, the picture changes considerably. In all countries, emphasizing indirect qualities for chicken appears to be closely associated with a more general pattern of food and household practices related to sustainability, all with levels of significance below 0.1%. There is, furthermore, a substantial increase in the explanatory power of the model, the adjusted R^2. An emphasis on indirect food quality aspects of chicken is strongly connected to sustainability practices, suggesting that this emphasis is an expression also of a broader engagement for sustainable food. This is in line with previous studies that have found a strong association between sustainable eating and purchasing practices and broader environmental concerns (see Niva et al., 2019; Tobler et al., 2011).

Turning to results for individual countries, we observe a highly complex dynamic. The influence of social background variables changes and, for most countries, becomes more significant, but with highly diverse effects (see Table 4). Starting out with Norway, the effect of gender has remained, now joined by income, when controlled for sustainable practices. Thus, taking practices into consideration reveals that engagement in indirect quality is affected by income. In Germany, the effect of social background factors seems independent, not through sustainable practices. The role of household size remains significant. The same goes for the United Kingdom, even though here with socio-economic differentiation being most significant, plus age (negative). Even in Poland, gender (positive) and income (negative) remain significant. However, the effect of age is now non-significant, indicating an indirect effect of age upon giving emphasis to indirect quality, through sustainable practices. In France, however, significance patterns change. While the effect of income remains significant, gender and age now have become non-significant while education has become significant, suggesting a moderating effect of sustainability practices. So, gender and age mainly influence through practices. In Spain, age and household size remain significant, while education is non-significant in this model. In Italy, household composition, gender and age have become non-significant by adding practices to the model. This suggests that opinions on the indirect qualities of chicken is not only embedded in more general sustainable practices but is also associated with life phase and certain types of family life. As in Poland, it is the lower level income groups who emphasize indirect quality in Italy, with practices having a moderating effect.

While somewhat confusing, these dynamics do suggest that many effects of sociodemographic background factors are indirect, framing and shaping people's daily practices and environmental sustainability more specifically. Opinions on the importance of various indirect quality dimensions for chicken seem to develop with reference to – or embedded in – such more general patterns of practices. This influence is to some extent socially differentiated within each country, while the main variations appear when comparing different countries.

It is also worth noticing that trust in information from various institutional actors is variably affected by introducing sustainable practices to the model. In Model 3, the effect of trust on opinions on indirect qualities disappears in the United Kingdom and Germany, while being reduced, but still significant, in Poland. In France and Italy, the effect of trust remains strong and independent of sustainable practices, while in Norway and Spain opinions on indirect factors remain unaffected by trust. In other words, trust seems to be expressed through specific practices in the United Kingdom and Germany, while having an independent effect on the importance attributed to indirect qualities in France and Italy.

Based on the results of the complete regression analysis, we argue that engagement in indirect quality aspects manifest itself differently in countries and regions of Europe. This was also shown in Fig. 2 where we found noteworthy variations between countries in the importance given to indirect quality aspects. For instance, as much as 46% of the Italian respondents answered that it is very important that the food is produced in my local area compared to only 9% among the Norwegians. In the following section, these national and regional variations will be further discussed.

EUROPEAN CONFIGURATIONS

Based on previous comparative studies we have argued that food culture and practices follow some distinct patterns or configurations on a European level. It must be emphasized that these schematic descriptions and country configurations are neither uniform nor static. Importantly, the European countries included in this study have many shared features, for example the increasing role of supermarket distribution and a European regulatory framework. Yet, it does make sense that Norwegians show the least emphasis on indirect food qualities, while respondents in the Mediterranean countries are the most engaged.

The systematic country variations found in this study underlines the importance of the contextual political, structural (market) and cultural differences in Europe. Perceptions of good and proper food are related to the character of the frameworks for food provisioning and purchasing decisions (Dubuisson-Quellier, 2022; Halkier et al., 2007; Kjærnes et al., 2022 and others). The survey here confirms that it is a 'silk-curtain' (Amilien, 2011) dividing the North and South of Europe. However, Poland is, interestingly, more like the Southern European countries than, for instance, Germany as a neighbour country. Germany is probably more regional divided with the Northern regions equal to other North- and Western European countries and the southern regions more similar to the South-European countries. Poland on the other hand, may represent a different type of configuration more generally, associated with other Eastern European countries, where especially strong social bonds combined with informal types of food economies (local barter or self-provision) contribute to preserving cultures and social institutions (Kopczyńska, 2020; Smith & Jehlička, 2007). This might contribute to explain more similarities to the Southern European patterns than to a general applicability of West- and North-European forms of sustainability.

The social dynamics in these configurations are very different. In Continental and South-European countries, emphasis on indirect qualities as well as sustainable food practices seems to be associated with particular types of households and phase of life. Being conscientious about what food to buy and eat emerges as part of establishing a family, often then maintained even later in life. The opposite pattern can be observed in the United Kingdom, where emphasis is more connected to younger generations and highly divided according to socio-economic differentiation. In Norway, the social dynamic is much less distinctive. Yet, overall, economic resources in the household become more significant when the practice level is brought into the model. These varied social dynamics underline the need to also consider cultural features and the wider societal context within which it develops.

It has been suggested that there is a positive relationship between trust in food system actors and emphasizing indirect quality aspects. While not contradicting this, Boström and Klintman (2009) state that 'political consumers are critical in orientation and take a critical – albeit active – stance on mainstream established domestic political institutions'. They have underlined that this active and critical consumer role emerges as part of a broader process of collective mobilization and political discourse. This seems, in our analysis, to capture the role of trust in the third configuration as represented mainly by the United Kingdom. The significance of an active, critical consumer role is illustrated by the Norwegian findings, where high institutional trust occurs together with a passive, accepting consumer role. Rather than addressing consumers, the environmental movement in Norway tends to concentrate on political decision-making. However, and importantly, we have found consumer engagement in indirect qualities within a very different societal configuration, namely the one characterized by generalized institutional distrust. Here, engagement in indirect qualities seems to be part of a wide, culturally defined concept of food quality to be ensured by more specific control of and insight into the production and provisioning of specific food items. In this chapter, our findings from Italy, and to some extent Poland and France, indicate such a dynamic between trust and engagement in indirect qualities, embedded in everyday food practices and family life with influences going both ways between trust and engagement. This also underlines a multidimensionality of trust that our study, building on one question on trust, does not capture. Trust may be specific or highly generalized and build on different social and cultural mechanisms (Kjærnes et al., 2013).

Dubuisson-Quellier (2022) has analyzed how consumption is framed by subtle, differentiating market strategies and technologies applied by retail businesses. Without overlooking social variations in engagement, based on our analyses, it seems rather that these technologies are applied differently in different markets and countries. Competition on price matters everywhere, while the role and expressions of quality are highly varied. Chicken meat has become 'cheap' meat compared to other meat and fish, but may also be sold with references to its local origins, taste, treatment, etc. As for safety, indirect quality aspects may be ensured through standardized regimes or personal interrelationships.

The survey was conducted before the Covid-19 pandemic and war in Ukraine and price will probably have become a much more important issue since then.

CONCLUDING REMARKS

Environment friendly and local food and good animal welfare are 'good causes' that gain wide support and, when asked, many people are concerned. However, the practical implications tend to be limited. Our study shows that when asked about buying chicken, direct factors related to food consumption and eating, such as price, taste and 'best before date', are most important.

Contrary to widespread beliefs, engagement across Europe does not seem to be tied to one specific sociodemographic or -economic group. Instead, patterns vary, with some regional commonalities. Our analyses thus underline the need to compare across different contexts, here represented by different countries, to unravel the dynamics that promote or prevent food-related practices becoming more sustainable. This is in line with sociological theories of eating (Warde, 2016), which sees the choice of food and the emphasis on ethics or sustainability (indirect quality aspects) as part of a complex set of practices, influenced by and formed within broader social and cultural conditions.

Our study shows that while emphasis on indirect qualities in the purchase of chicken is characterized by a broader commitment to sustainability and food consumption, this commitment is expressed or configured differently from country to country and regions in Europe. Moreover, there seem to be a range of different venues or social processes leading to engagement in sustainable practices as concretized here by what people emphasize when purchasing chicken. For example, while such engagement seems to emerge among young, quite resourceful, but also critical, people in the United Kingdom, interest in the ethical and sustainable aspects of chicken production among Norwegians is often not being associated with their own food-related practices, instead referring to the responsibility of producers and public authorities. Yet, in both these countries, animal welfare forms a specific issue. In a country like Italy, engagement in such issues is often embedded in a comprehensive concept of good food quality, often symbolized by a specific – local – sourcing communicated via personal interrelationships (Torjusen et al., 2024). This 'good food' is not just a selling argument but is closely linked to family meals and thus to family patterns.

Our study has an explorative character, referring to previous studies on national differences and regional configurations. Further studies are needed to clarify whether we should develop further types of configurations, for example a typically Eastern European and/or a Continental type (see, e.g. Smith & Jehlička, 2007). More efforts are also needed to develop a theoretical framework for systematic comparative studies to capture how practices change and how they are made to change. We see a need for methodological development, where quantitative and qualitative methods complement each other to build updated insights into the dynamic between people's everyday practices and expectations, on the one hand, and institutional and cultural conditions, on the other. This type of analysis can provide even greater insights into the conditions that promote or hinder more ethical or sustainable consumption as part of everyday practices.

ACKNOWLEDGEMENTS

The comparative survey that this chapter is based on was part of the Organic-PLUS project that received funding from the European Union's Horizon 2020 research and innovation programme under grant agreement No [774340]. The data material has been further analyzed within the FOOdIVERSE project an ERA-NET SUSFOOD2 and CORE Organic Co-fund 2019 with contributions from the Research Council of Norway, grant no. 320943. We would like to thank our co-researchers in different countries in both the Organic-PLUS project and FOOdIVERSE project contributing to the data collection and interpreting of results, respectively.

NOTE

1. European Union's Horizon 2020 research and innovation program under grant agreement No. [774,340].

REFERENCES

Alfnes, F., Schjøll, A., & Dulsrud, A. (2019). *Kartlegging av utviklingen ibutikkstruktur, dagligvare-utvalg og dagligvarepriser* (*Mapping the development in grocery store structure, product range and prices*). Report No. 5 – 2019. Consumption Research Norway, Oslo Metropolitan University. https://hdl.handle.net/20.500.12199/2234

Amilien, V. (2011). From territory to terroir? – The cultural dynamics of local and localized products in Norway. *Sosiologisk Årbok*, *3–4*, 85–106.

Amilien, V., Discetti, R., Lecoeur, J.-L., Roos, G., Tocco, B., Gorton, M., Biasini, B., Menozzi, D., de Labarre, M. D., & Filipović, J. (2022). European food quality schemes in everyday food consumption: An exploration of sayings and doings through pragmatic regimes of engagement. *Journal of Rural Studies*, *95*, 336–349.

Barjolle, D., & Sylvander, B. (2000). *PDO and PGI products: Market, supply chains and institutions. Protected designations of origin and protected geographical indications in Europe: Regulation or policy*. FAIR–CT 95–Final Report. European Commission.

Bellini, S. (2021). The pig sector in the European Union. In L. Iacolina, M. Penrith, S. Bellini, E. Chenais, F. Jori, M. Montoya, K. Ståhl, & D. Gavier-Widén (Eds.), *Understanding and combatting African swine fever - A European perspective*. Wageningen Academic Publishers.

Berg, L. (2014). Consumer markets' trust regimes across Europe. *European Societies*, *16*(4), 480–499. https://doi.org/10.1080/14616696.2014.915418

Boström, M., & Klintman, M. (2009). The green political food consumer – A critical analysis of the research and policies. *Anthropology of Food*, *S5*. https://doi.org/10.4000/aof.6394

de Jonge, J., van Trijp, J. C. M., van der Lans, I. A., Renes, R. J., & Frewer, L. J. (2008). How trust in institutions and organizations builds general consumer confidence in the safety of food: A decomposition of effects. *Appetite*, *51*(2), 311–317. https://doi.org/10.1016/j.appet.2008.03.008

Dubuisson-Quellier, S. (2022). How does affluent consumption come to consumers? A research agenda for exploring the foundations and lock-ins of affluent consumption. *Consumption and Society*, *1*(1), 31–50. https://doi.org/10.1332/UHIW3894

Escobedo del Bosque, C. I., Spiller, A., & Risius, A. (2021). Who wants chicken? Uncovering consumer preferences for produce of alternative chicken product methods. *Sustainability*, *13*(5), 2440. https://doi.org/10.3390/su13052440

Esping-Andersen, G. (1990). *The three worlds of welfare capitalism*. Princeton University Press.

European Commission. (2023). *Attitudes of Europeans towards animal welfare*. Special Eurobarometer 533. European Union. https://doi.org/10.2875/872312

Evans, D., Welch, D., & Swaffield, J. (2017). Constructing and mobilizing 'the consumer': Responsibility, consumption and the politics of sustainability. *Environment and Planning A*, *49*(6), 1396–1412. https://doi.org/10.1177/0308518X17694030

Fuentes, A., Tormo, E., Barat, J. M., & Fernández-Segovia, I. (2023). Importance of the origin, organic production and other extrinsic parameters in fruit and vegetable choices. *Food Science and Technology International*. https://doi.org/10.1177/10820132231206413

Giesler, M., & Veresiu, E. (2014). Creating the responsible consumer: Moralistic governance regimes and consumer subjectivity. *Journal of Consumer Research*, *41*(3), 840–857. https://doi.org/10.1086/677842

Gorton, M., Tocco, B., Yeh, C.-H., & Hartmann, M. (2021). What determines consumers' use of eco-labels? Taking a close look at label trust. *Ecological Economics*, *189*, 107173. https://doi.org/10.1016/j.ecolecon.2021.107173

Grunert, K. G., Hieke, S., & Wills, J. (2014). Sustainability labels on food products: Consumer motivation, understanding and use. *Food Policy*, *44*, 177–189. https://doi.org/10.1016/j.foodpol.2013.12.001

Halkier, B., Holm, L., Domingues, M., Magaudda, P., Nielsen, A., & Terragni, L. (2007). Trusting, complex, quality conscious or unprotected? Constructing the food consumer in different European national contexts. *Journal of Consumer Culture*, *7*(3), 379–402. https://doi.org/10.1177/1469540507081629

Harju, C., Lähtinen, K., Heinola, K., Väre, M., Bonnefous, C., Collin, A., Cozma, V., Kliphuis, S., Parrott, P. A., Rodenburg, T. B., Spinu, M., & Niemi, J. (2024). Consumers' views on egg quality and preferences for responsible production – Results from nine European countries. *British Food Journal*, *126*(2), 623–644. https://doi.org/10.1108/BFJ-03-2023-0183

Holm, L., & Gronow, J. (2019). Introduction. Eating in modern everyday life. In J. Gronow & L. Holm (Eds.), *Everyday eating in Denmark, Finland, Norway and Sweden: A comparative study of meal patterns 1997–2012* (pp. 1–14). Bloomsbury Academic.

Holt, G. C. (1993). *"Ecological eating", food ideology and food choice. An analysis of the changing British diet with reference to the consumption of meat and organically produced food.* Food Policy Research Unit, Department of Biomedical Sciences, University of Bradford.

Jacobsen, E. (2017). Political consumption – Citizenship and consumerism. In I. M. Keller, B. Halkier, T.-A. Wilska, & M. Truninger (Eds.), *Routledge handbook on consumption* (pp. 181–190). Routledge.

Jacobsen, E., & Dulsrud, A. (2007). Will consumers save the world? The framing of political consumerism. *Journal of Agricultural and Environmental Ethics*, *20*, 469–482. https://doi.org/10.1007/s10806-007-9043-z

Johnston, J., & Goodman, M. (2015). Spectacular foodscapes. Food celebrities and the politics of lifestyle mediation in an age of inequality. *Food, Culture and Society*, *18*(2), 205–222. https://doi.org/10.2752/175174415X14180391604369

Kjærnes, U., Bock, B. .B., Higgin, M., & Roex, J. (Eds.). (2009). *Farm animal welfare within the supply chain: Regulation, agriculture, and geography*. Welfare Quality Reports No. 8. Cardiff University. https://www.welfarequalitynetwork.net/en-us/reports/

Kjærnes, U., Borgen, S. O., & Thorjussen, C. B. H. (2022). Behind a fluttering veil of trust: The dynamics of public concerns over farm animal welfare in Norway. *Sociologia Ruralis*, *62*(4), 763–781. https://doi.org/10.1111/soru.12405

Kjærnes, U., Harvey, M., & Warde, A. (2013). *Trust in food - A comparative and institutional analysis*. Palgrave.

Kopczyńska, E. (2020). Are there local versions of sustainability? Food networks in the semi-periphery. *Sustainability*, *12*(7), 2845. https://doi.org/10.3390/su12072845

Lemke, T. (2001). 'The birth of bio-politics': Michel Foucault's lecture at the Collège de France on neo-liberal governmentality. *Economy and Society*, *30*(2), 190–207. https://doi.org/10.1080/03085140120042271

Lykkeskov, A., & Gjerris, M. (2017). The moral justification behind a climate tax on beef in Denmark. *Food Ethics*, *1*(2), 181–191. https://doi.org/10.1007/s41055-017-0017-1

Mann, A. (2019). *Voice and participation in global food politics*. Routledge.

Martin, D., & Schouten, J. (2012). *Sustainable marketing*. Prentice Hall.

Micheletti, M. (2010). *Political virtue and shopping: Individuals, consumerism, and collective action* (2nd ed.). Palgrave.

Micheletti, M., & Stolle, D. (2012). Sustainable citizenship and the new politics of consumption. *The Annals of the American Academy of Political and Social Science*, *644*(1), 88–120. https://doi.org/10.1177/0002716212454836

Morgan, K. (2010). Local and green, global and fair: The ethical foodscape and the politics of care. *Environment and Planning A: Economy and Space*, *42*(8), 1852–1867. https://doi.org/10.1068/a42364

Murphy, B., Benson, T., Lavelle, F., Elliott, C., & Dean, M. (2021). Assessing differences in levels of food trust between European countries. *Food Control*, 107561. https://doi.org/10.1016/j.foodcont.2020.107561

Nagy, L. B., Unger-Plasek, B., Lakner, Z., & Temesi, Á. (2023). Confidence in organic food: A cross-country choice based conjoint analysis of credibility factors. *Humanities and Social Sciences Communications*, *10*, 762. https://doi.org/10.1057/s41599-023-02293-7

Niva, M., Mäkelä, J., Kahma, N., & Kjærnes, U. (2014). Eating sustainably? Practices and background factors of ecological food consumption in four Nordic countries. *Journal of Consumer Policy*, *37*(4), 465–484. https://doi.org/10.1007/s10603-014-9270-4

Niva, M., Mäkelä, J., Kahma, N., & Kjærnes, U. (2019). Eating sustainably. In J. Gronow & L. Holm (Eds.), *Everyday eating in Denmark, Finland, Norway and Sweden. A comparative study of meal patterns 1997–2012* (pp. 173–190). Bloomsbury Academic.

Plessz, M., & Le Pape, M.-C. (2019). The political dimension of consumption work, or political consumption as work: How French households do gatekeeping on the food market. *Food, Culture and Society*, *22*(3), 334–353.

Schjøll, A., & Thorjussen, C. B. H. (2019). *Menneskerettigheter og etisk forbruk*. Report No. 9-2019. Consumption Research Norway, Oslo Metropolitan University. https://hdl.handle.net/20.500.12199/2914

Seyfang, G. (2005). Shopping for sustainability: Can sustainable consumption promote ecological citizenship? *Environmental Politics*, *14*(2), 290–306. https://doi.org/10.1080/09644010500055209

Smith, J., & Jehlička, P. (2007). Stories around food, politics and change in Poland and the Czech Republic. *Transactions of the Institute of British Geographers*, *32*(3), 395–410. https://doi.org/10.1111/j.1475-5661.2007.00258.x

Starr, M. A. (2009). The social economics of ethical consumption: Theoretical considerations and empirical evidence. *The Journal of Socio-Economics*, *38*(6), 916–925. https://doi.org/10.1016/j.socec.2009.07.006

Terragni, L., Torjusen, H., & Vittersø, G. (2009). The dynamics of alternative food consumption: Contexts, opportunities and transformations. *Anthropology of Food*, *S 5*. https://doi.org/10.4000/aof.6400

Thøgersen, J. (2009). Consumer decision-making with regard to organic food products. In T. de N. Vaz & P. Nijkamp (Eds.), *Traditional food production facing sustainability: A European challenge*. Routledge.

Thøgersen, J. (2010). Country differences in sustainable consumption: The case of organic food. *Journal of Macromarketing*, *30*(2), 171–185. https://doi.org/10.1177/0276146710361926

Thøgersen, J., Pedersen, S., & Aschemann-Witzel, J. (2019). The impact of organic certification and country of origin on consumer food choice in developed and emerging economies. *Food Quality and Preference*, *72*, 10–30. https://doi.org/10.1016/j.foodqual.2018.09.003

Tobler, C., Visschers, V. H. M., & Siegrist, M. (2011). Eating green. Consumers' willingness to adopt ecological food consumption behaviors. *Appetite*, *57*(3), 674–682. https://doi.org/10.1016/j.appet.2011.08.010

Torjusen, H., Nyberg, A., & Wandel, M. (1999). *Økologisk produsert mat: Forbrukernes vurderinger og bruksmønster. En spørreundersøkelse fra Stange- og Hamarområdet*. Report no. 5-1999. National Institute of Consumer Research (SIFO). https://hdl.handle.net/20.500.12199/5361

Torjusen, H., G. Vittersø, S. Kuraj, S. O. Borgen, M. Uldahl, R. van Kesteren, A. Evans, M. Kneafsey, U. Schmutz, E. Kopczynska, K. Stępnik, F. Forno, M. Giovannini, B. Mahr and S. Wahlen (2024). *Diversifying sustainable and organic food systems. Report from Focus Groups in five European countries – Diversity in eating practices*. Deliverable D 2.2 from the FOOdIVERSE project. ERA-NET SUSFOOD2 and CORE Organic Co-fund 2019.

Torjusen, H., & Vittersø, G. (2023). Sustainability conventions in a local organic consumer cooperative in Norway: Hope and trouble of participants. In O. Morrow, E. Veen, & S. Wahlen (Eds.), *Community food initiatives. A critical reparative approach*. Routledge.

Veisser, I., Butterworth, A., Block, B., & Roe, E. (2008). European approaches to ensure good animal welfare. *Applied Animal Behaviour Science*, *113*(4), 279–297. https://doi.org/10.1016/j.applanim.2008.01.008

Vittersø, G., Torjusen, H., & Kuraj, S. (2022). *Diversity in food culture and consumption patterns. Survey results from seven European countries*. Report No. 6-2022. Consumption Research Norway, Oslo Metropolitan University. https://hdl.handle.net/11250/3024006

Vittersø, G., Torjusen, H., Thorjussen, C. B. H., Schjøll, A., & Kjærnes, U. (2019). *Report from survey on public opinion regarding contentious inputs*. Deliverable 2.2. Organic-PLUS. Coventry University. https://organicplusnet.files.wordpress.com/2019/11/d2.2-o-survey-on-puplic-opinion-regarding-contentious-inputs.pdf

Warde, A. (2016). *The practice of eating*. Polity Press.
Wier, M., O'Doherty Jensen, K., Andersen, L. M., & Millock, K. (2008). The character of demand in mature organic food markets: Great Britain and Denmark compared. *Food Policy*, *33*(5), 406–421. https://doi.org/10.1016/j.foodpol.2008.01.002
Wu, W., Zhang, A., & van Klinken, R. D. (2021). Consumer trust in food and the food system: A critical review. *Foods*, *10*(10), 2490. https://doi.org/10.3390/foods10102490

COMPARING MALE AND FEMALE WARDROBES: GENDER DYNAMICS IN THE PRACTICE OF DRESSING

Vilde Haugrønning and Ingrid Haugsrud

Oslo Metropolitan University, Norway

ABSTRACT

This chapter explores the influence of gender on clothing consumption and the impact on differences in clothing volumes between men and women. Based on a qualitative and quantitative wardrobe study, we employ Schatzki's (2002) social ontology of practice combined with Butler's (1990) gender performance concept to examine the relationship between gender and clothing consumption in 15 households in Norway. The findings show that women had on average 497 items and the men had 258 items, and the main difference between male and female wardrobes was due to the number of items per occasion. These findings highlights the complexities and tensions faced by women in navigating clothing norms and maintaining a balance in the practice of dressing between appropriate dress, feminine expressions and having an ideal and more sustainable wardrobe. This chapter contributes to a better understanding of the interplay between occasions and gender dynamics that shape clothing consumption patterns. Moreover, it illustrates the potential of 'occasion' as an analytical concept and the implications of gender in clothing consumption, challenging the prevailing studies on clothing and fashion that often overlook the nuanced practices and actions that influence clothing volumes.

Keywords: Occasions; clothing consumption; gender; wardrobe studies; social practices

Consumers and Consumption in Comparison
Comparative Social Research, Volume 37, 139–165

ISSN: 0195-6310/doi:10.1108/S0195-631020240000037007

INTRODUCTION

Clothing is one of the most distinctive ways people do gender in everyday life. Gender scholars argue that clothing and dressing are one of the main and first attributes that people look for in categorising others as belonging to various gender identities (West & Zimmerman, 1987). People dress differently as part of performing gender (Butler, 1990) in accordance with social and cultural expectations of masculine and feminine dressing practices.

During the past century, women's wardrobes have changed more than men's wardrobes in line with growing consumption and increased commercialisation (Ulväng, 2021). This has resulted in a common association between women and high rates of clothing acquisition, positioning clothing and fashion as domains of consumption typically associated with femininity and women. Women are seen as 'the dupes of an exploitative fashion industry, buying and wearing clothes when they are deemed fashionable but discarding them when they are deemed unfashionable' (Banim & Guy, 2001, p. 204). Stereotypical gender roles indicate that men consume fashion more sufficiently, in terms of lower acquisition and turnover, because it is the appropriate masculine way of doing gender and the opposite applies to femininity (Wallaschkowski, 2023). However, when it comes to gender differences in sustainable consumption, men's overall consumption is found to be less sustainable than women's due to increased travel distances and a higher reliance on transportation modes like cars and motorcycles (Bloodhart & Swim, 2020). Because clothing is considered a feminine topic, both in research and daily life (Tseëlon, 2001), there has been few studies on men's clothing consumption and even fewer studies that compares the wardrobes of men and women (Maldini et al., 2023). This reinforces stereotypes about women as high consumers of clothing without necessarily adding any nuance to the social mechanisms that influence these consumption patterns. Simultaneously, men continue to be overlooked as significant consumers of clothing, a phenomenon referred to by Breward (1999) as 'the hidden consumer'.

In studies of consumption and everyday life, wardrobe studies have shown to be a constructive method for investigating the dynamics and complexities of clothing consumption (Fletcher & Klepp, 2017; Maguire & Fahy, 2022; Woodward, 2014). This stands in distinction from studies in sociology and fashion that understand clothing consumption as symbolic, focused on individuals that communicate meaning and identities through clothes (Pilcher, 2011). Wardrobe studies focus on the materiality of clothing and fronts the need to understand clothing as involved in everyday routines, much aligned with a practice theory framework (Reckwitz, 2002; Schatzki, 1996; Warde, 2005). This follows that consumption patterns are not explained as a result of individual behaviour alone, but as interwoven in everyday life as routinised practices, and intimately linked to reproducing what people understand to be normal (Warde, 2005).

This study operates within the space of gender awareness from a feminist empiricism perspective, which may result in the reproduction of stereotypes or victimisation of female consumers (Mittner, 2018; Schuster & Van Dyne, 1985).

However, the intention is to contribute to a better understanding of how gender dynamics influence clothing volumes, as few studies in wardrobe research have explored this topic. Combining Schatzki's (2002, 2001) social ontology of practice with the concept of performing gender (Butler, 1990), this study investigates the differences in clothing consumption between men and women at the household level. It focuses on the impact of gender dynamics, specifically on the volume of clothing for various occasions. By promoting 'occasion' as an analytical concept, we propose a theoretical framework that considers occasion as both ordinary and special occasions, informing the expectations and norms that shape the practice of dressing. As such, this study aims to provide insight into the connections between clothing, gender and social practices by employing the concept of occasion as an analytical tool. The objective is to identify the implications of gender on clothing volumes, with a particular emphasis on how this affects women's clothing consumption. In line with Wallaschkowski (2023), we argue that it is important to acknowledge the performance of gender in clothing consumption and how prevailing stereotypes may act as barriers to achieving more sustainable clothing consumption.

This chapter begins with an overview of previous research on clothing and gender. This is followed by a theoretical section that conceptualise occasions in the practice of dressing combined with gender theory. We then explain the research design, participant characteristics and limitations. In section 'Differences Between Male and Female Wardrobes', we explore and analyse the differences in clothing volume for occasions, specialisation of clothing and expectations of variety. In section 'Discussion: Gender Dynamics and the Impact on Clothing Volumes', we discuss these differences and argue that the female wardrobes show evidence of uneven norms and expectations for women to dress according to the female sex category (West & Zimmerman, 1987). Finally, we discuss the implications of gender dynamics on clothing consumption and how this is shaped by collectively shared social practices that actively affect the volume of clothing in female wardrobes.

PREVIOUS RESEARCH ON CLOTHING AND GENDER

Most studies on clothing and fashion focus on women and their wardrobes, and there are few studies that have investigated men's clothing consumption (Maldini et al., 2023). Studies on men and fashion note how some men see clothing as a negative act and use clothing to avoid attention, thereby aiming to dress inconspicuously (van der Laan & Velthuis, 2016), while men also dress in connection with their feeling of self and may take pleasure in shopping clothes (Skjold, 2014). Barry's study on men and masculinities find that men engage in hybrid masculinities through the selection, styling and wearing of clothing in their everyday life. The varied expressions of masculinities were found to be influenced by the degree to which men identified with dominant masculine ideals in their personal and professional lives, as well as how these ideals influenced their respective environments. The participants were cautious about compromising their gender dominance and strategically used clothing choices to establish social power and reinforce an unequal gender hierarchy, irrespective of their particular identities and circumstances (Barry, 2018).

There are even fewer studies that include a comparison between men and women's clothing consumption (Maldini et al., 2023). However, there are historical studies that look at wardrobe inventories of men and women. Ulväng's (2021) study of the wardrobes of farmers in Sweden during the 18th and 19th century find that, during the industrialisation, female wardrobes decreased in value while the number of accessories and clothing increased. Women's fashion embraced greater ornamentation and variability, in contrast to men's fashion, which evolved with a more reserved approach with fewer garments of higher value (Ulväng, 2021). This dichotomy was understood as a manifestation of a societal emphasis on men as primary providers and women as homemakers, reflecting the rise of the breadwinner-homemaker ideal (Ulväng, 2021). Employing Veblen's concept of conspicuous consumption, women's clothing could be seen as a reflection of the husband's wealth and the woman's role as a homemaker (Ulväng, 2021; Veblen, 1899).

The development in the past century is highly relevant to understand current consumption patterns and the uneven gender norms that apply to clothing. Today, women are culturally constructed to be more interested in style and appearance, while also being subject to limiting norms that demand stricter body discipline (Lövgren, 2015). Studies reporting on the number of clothing in wardrobes show that there are great individual differences, but women tend to have more clothing on average (Maldini et al., 2017, 2023). Findings from representative surveys in Norway indicate that women's overall spending on clothing has increased more than men's from 1999 to 2012 (Klepp & Laitala, 2016) and on average women acquire more clothing than men (Laitala & Klepp, 2020).

Differences in the consumption patterns of women and men are often tied to gender roles (Bloodhart & Swim, 2020). A study by Wallaschkowski (2023) shows how gender stereotypes can have a big influence on fashion consumption patterns. The stereotypical woman engages in frequent and impulse shopping, has a high demand for new garments and is trend conscious. She invests effort into selecting outfits and frequently switches between garments. In contrast, the stereotypical man prioritises comfort, values durability and views shopping as a chore. He tends to maintain a pragmatic approach to dressing, wearing the same style for an extended period and using his clothes until they wear out. Men discard clothing primarily when it becomes unusable, while women may dispose of clothes due to limited use, fashion trends and an abundance of garments that are still wearable (Wallaschkowski, 2023). While there is danger of reproducing these stereotypes in a study that compares male and female wardrobes, there is a need to better understand the gender dynamics in the practice of dressing that can shed light on why women have more clothing in their wardrobes than men.

CLOTHING CONSUMPTION, GENDER AND PRACTICE THEORY

Theories of Practice Applied to Clothing Consumption

In the past two decades, theoretical works within sociology of consumption have argued for the need to see consumption as anchored in practices and routines of everyday life (Warde, 2005). This approach emerges from the 'practice turn' in consumption research (Schatzki et al., 2001), which has served as an alternative approach to the 'cultural turn'. This approach de-emphasised lifestyle, identity, taste and the symbolic aspects of consumption, shifting the focus towards understanding consumption as a cultural phenomenon (Welch et al., 2020). Theories of practice offer an analytical approach to the study of consumption that provides perspectives on how consumption is organised (Warde, 2005). Consumption, in this view, can be seen as a process rather than a practice, it is 'a moment in almost every practice' (Warde, 2005, p. 137). Practices and not individuals are the main analytical unit, and the individual is understood as a carrier of practices (Reckwitz, 2002). By engaging in practices, individuals contribute to the ongoing reproduction and maintenance of those practices as entities (Shove et al., 2012). While theories of practice have been applied to areas such as food, energy and mobility, clothing has received little attention, despite being a part of many resource-intensive practices and permeating everyday life. Clothing consumption involve several practices in which clothing is handled, such as storing, washing and repairing, in addition to the different stages of consumption, such as planning, acquisition, use and disposal. However, an essential aspect of clothing consumption is the act of getting dressed for practices, what we suggest can be conceptualised as 'the practice of dressing'.

Of the different strands within theories of practices, Schatzki's (2001) social ontology of practice shows great potential for a theoretical framework to the practice of dressing as it provides a conceptualisation of practices as integrated, organised by nexuses of actions (Schatzki, 2002). Practices are composed of a set of actions of bodily doings and sayings, which are linked through four phenomena: rules, practical understandings, general understandings and a 'teleoaffective structure' (Schatzki, 2001). Rules are explicit formulations, principles and instructions that guide people on what to do and how to do it under the notion that other people also take account and follow the same rules (Schatzki, 2002). Practical understandings refer to the skills related to the actions as part of a practice, and general understandings are broader cultural conceptions that organise and threads through practices (Schatzki, 2002; Welch & Warde, 2016). Thus, as Fig. 1 illustrates, practical understandings are the property of a particular practice while general understandings are the property of integrative practices (Welch & Warde, 2016). Finally, a teleoaffective structure is 'a range of normativized and hierarchically ordered ends, projects, and tasks, to varying degrees allied with normativized emotions and even moods' (Schatzki, 2002, p. 80). Normativity in this case refers to acceptability, as what people do is governed either by what they ought to do or what is acceptable to do (Schatzki, 2002). Put simply, a practice encompasses a collection of doings and sayings that is linked and organised by rules, understandings and a teleoaffective

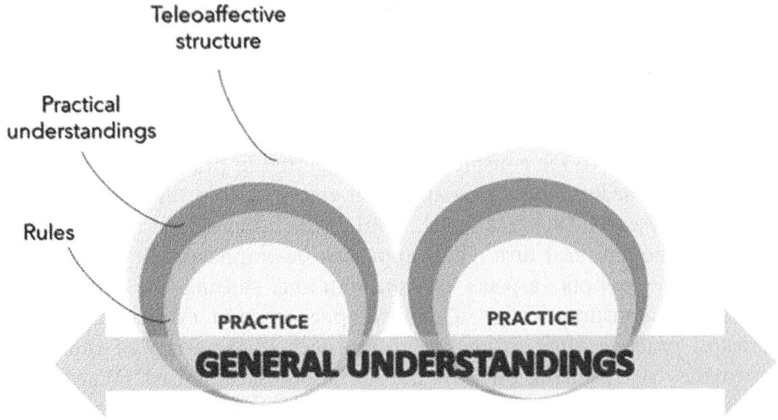

Fig. 1. The Four Phenomena of Practice.

structure. The next section will explore how these phenomena can be applied to a theoretical framework for the practice of dressing for occasions.

Conceptualising Occasion in the Practice of Dressing

The practice of dressing can be understood as an integrative practice as it interconnects with a bundle of different practices and material arrangements (Schatzki, 2005). The complexity in seeing clothing from a practice-oriented perspective is precisely this interconnectivity, as clothing inevitably threads through several practices in everyday life. Beginning with the fourth phenomenon, teleoaffectivity, the practice of dressing has an end-oriented structure as it always involves dressing for an occasion. In this sense, occasions, as a general understanding, can be understood as informing the teleoaffective structure of a practice, as practices are consciously and unconsciously guided by the occasion taking place. Employing 'occasion' as an analytical concept is not common in research on clothing or the sociology of consumption. Warde (2016) remarks how 'sociology lacks a language of occasions' (p. 60) and it is only recently that occasion has been employed as a concept in studies on food consumption (Holmes et al., 2023; Yates & Warde, 2017). 'Occasion' may imply ordinary occasions such as going to work, eating out and sleeping, but also more special occasions such as weddings, funerals and birthdays. It is somewhat aligned with the study on drinking occasions by Holmes et al. (2023), which defines 'occasion' as a period of time rather than a noteworthy event. However, the practice of dressing does not only imply temporal aspects as being 'dressed for the occasion' happens continuously and depends on many external conditions such as place, weather, time, activity and people (Klepp & Bjerck, 2009) that inevitably impact the performance of practice.

Moving on to rules and understandings, most occasions have specific demands and expectations for clothing used in the performance of the practice based on normative conceptions of doings and sayings. Rules can be understood as more explicit principles for getting dressed for occasions, such as dress codes that may apply to occasions such as work. Practical understandings are related to the skills of how to get dressed in relation to specific practices and the skill of interpreting implicit expectations adhering to occasions. While the two latter phenomena may be understood to encompass particular practices, general understandings involve larger social and cultural conceptions that link practices together (Welch & Warde, 2016). This involves dressing for occasions in accordance with membership categories such as gender and ethnicity (Welch & Warde, 2016), in addition to shared cultural notions of clothing standards. Consequently, the practice of dressing involves both conscious and unconscious actions of doings and sayings (governed by rules and understandings), leading to the clothing chosen for an occasion (organised by a teleoaffective structure).

The importance of fitting in and not standing out is part of being dressed for the occasion and relates to the need to anticipate and synchronise other people's practices and routines (Warde, 2016). As such, normativity referring to acceptability and what is considered proper can be seen as a fundamental part of the four phenomena structuring the practice of dressing (Schatzki, 2002). However, an additional exploration of normativity seems appropriate to further illustrate how clothing consumption as a mundane process takes hold in the practice of dressing. Halkier (2022) suggests a new framework to better understand mundane normativity in consumption patterns through two categories: expectable and acceptable consumption. Expectable consumption refers to the social expectations regarding specific practices and situations, highlighting the importance of adhering to societal norms and expectations (Halkier, 2022). Acceptable consumption refers to the legitimacy and social acceptance of specific patterns and ways of performing a practice (Halkier, 2022). The categories are not separate but overlapping, and the main difference is that acceptable consumption may involve more explicit negotiations and expectable consumption is often implicit and taken for granted. For example, studies suggest that, in households with men and women, women traditionally shoulder the responsibility for managing men's clothing and cleanliness (Klepp, 2007; Sundt, 1869). This can be understood as expectable consumption. Furthermore, this responsibility has implications, as the man appearing with dirty clothing may reflect badly on the woman (Klepp, 2007). Negotiating the man's cleanliness in terms of clothing that is too dirty to be worn may therefore be a case of acceptable consumption.

Combining these categories with rules, understandings and teleoaffectivity, it provides a framework for analysing different ways of consuming clothing from a practice theorical view, rooted in normative notions of what it means to be well-dressed for occasions. Expectable and acceptable consumption of clothing entail different apprehensions and performances, yet both are influenced by the occasion for which one is dressing. These occasions, informed by a teleoaffective structure, are intertwined with rules and practical and general understandings that are relevant for each specific occasion. Especially gender, as a general understanding, has a significant relevance on expectable and acceptable consumption of clothing.

Gender as a General Understanding

The practice theoretical perspective aligns well with gender scholars who see gender as something people do through their actions rather than something they are (Butler, 1990). Gender is repeated and situated action that adheres to normative conceptions of attitudes and activities appropriate for one's gender category (West & Zimmerman, 1987). Judith Butler (1990) argues for viewing gender as performative, as a repeated set of actions rather than a fixed identity. Dressing in a certain way can be seen as a performance, as well as conforming to societal norms in order to create an appearance of a stable gender identity. Butler also emphasises how gender is intertwined with other aspects of identity, such as race, class and sexuality and how these intersecting identities influence how people perform their gender and how they are perceived by society (Butler, 1990).

Combining the notion of gender as performance with gender as a general understanding have potential to advance gender as an analytical concept in theories of practice (Mechlenborg & Gram-Hanssen, 2020). Gender as a general understanding implies that gender as a larger phenomenon is present in multiple practices, organising and shaping the way they are performed (Mechlenborg & Gram-Hanssen, 2020; Welch & Warde, 2016). Consequently, gender is performed in both doings and sayings, not as an overarching structure, but by 'threading through multiple practices' (Mechlenborg & Gram-Hanssen, 2020, p. 6). This does not mean that gender explains how practices are performed, but rather that gender plays a role in shaping the performance of practices (Mechlenborg & Gram-Hanssen, 2020), intertwined with rules, practical understandings and teleoaffective structures.

Fig. 2 illustrates how the practice of dressing for occasions involves an interplay between gender and occasion as general understandings. There are different ways of doing gender that are not generic but dynamic, and what is being practiced or performed are femininities and masculinities (Gherardi, 2019). Being dressed for occasions will therefore involve a performance and negotiation

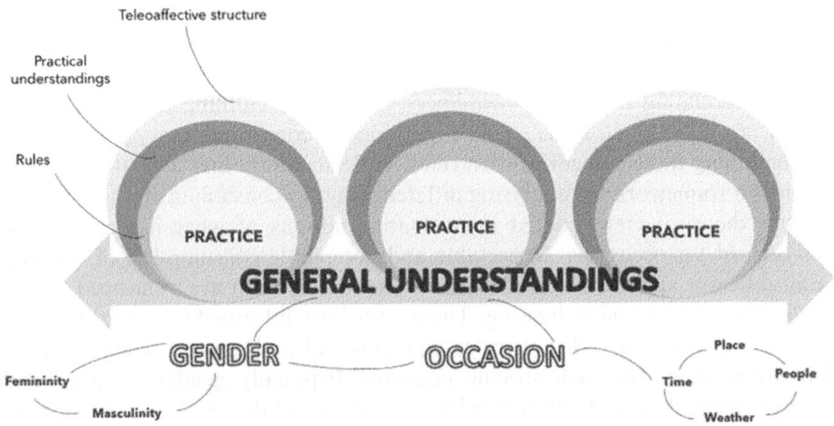

Fig. 2. The Practice of Dressing for Occasions.

of gender where the materiality of clothing has a significant impact on adhering to gender identities. In line with studies that argue for exploring social norms and conventions that have a significant influence on consumption patterns (Ellsworth-Krebs et al., 2021; Krog Juvik & Halkier, 2024), exploring gender as a general understanding in the practice of dressing can give insight to how gender dynamics perpetuate the broader social and cultural conventions of clothing consumption and the implications for the volume of clothing in wardrobes.

METHODOLOGY

Wardrobe Studies

The method employed in this research is a qualitative and quantitative wardrobe study of men and women with focus on the volume of clothing for occasions that feature different practices. Thus, the analytical unit are the social practices that clothing, as a material, is an integrated part of. The wardrobe refers to all the clothing a person owns or has access to (Klepp & Bjerck, 2014) and the methodological approach is to analyse the relationship between clothing, practices and volume. While interviews are still used in wardrobe studies, they are combined with other methods that focus on the material and individual garments. In this way, the aim is to avoid general and normative answers and instead unpack specific practices and occasions related to each garment (Fletcher & Klepp, 2017). The physical presence of the garments serves as a reminder and can evoke tacit knowledge.

Recruitment and Participants

The field research for the study was conducted between November 2022 and January 2023. Participants were recruited through purposeful sampling via participant calls on social media platforms such as Facebook and Instagram. The sampling aimed to include households with a man and a woman, as this would enable a gendered comparison between couples that take part in many of the same practices and share the everyday life. An additional aim of this recruitment strategy was to more easily reach men who may not typically volunteer for studies about clothing. Therefore, the main criteria for participation were that the household included a man and a woman. Potential participants were asked to fill out a brief online survey that gathered information about self-identified gender, age, household, housing, location, occupation, hobbies and interest in clothing. Based on these answers, a varied sample was selected.

Table 1 shows an overview of the participants. Most participants were white Norwegians and owned the house or apartment they lived in. Four of the participants had moved to Norway as adults, three from Europe and one from Asia. All households except one were signed up for participation by the woman. Some of the female participants reported an interest in clothing, but most of the participants did not express a particular interest. Several of the men also confirmed during the interview that they would not have signed up for this without their female partner.

Table 1. Overview of Participants.

Household	Gender	Age	Occupation	Location	
H1	W	30–39	Teacher	Big city	Oslo
	M	30–39	IT		
H2	W	40–49	Teacher	Town	Viken
	M	40–49	IT		
H3	W	30–39	Public sector	Big city	Oslo
	M	30–39	Advisor		
H4	W	60–69	Retired (teacher)	Small city	Vestfold
	M	70–79	Retired (Private sector)		
H5	W	30–39	Nurse	Town	Viken
	M	30–39	Electrician		
H6	W	30–39	IT	Town	Viken
	M	30–39	IT		
H7	W	70–79	Retired (Consultant)	Small city	Vestfold
	M	70–79	Retired (Chef/smith)		
H8	W	20–29	Public sector	Big city	Oslo
	M	20–29	IT		
H9	W	40–49	Public sector	Big city	Oslo
	M	40–49	Finance sector		
H10	W	50–59	Nurse	Small city	Viken
	M	50–59	Teacher		
H11	W	40–49	Doctor	Big city	Viken
	M	50–59	Freelancer/Physio therapist		
H12	W	30–39	Private sector	Small city	Nordland
	M	30–39	Group managing director		
H13	W	60–69	Retired (social worker)	Small city	Nordland
	M	70–79	Retired (Engineer)		
H14	W	60–69	Retired/Disability benefit (nurse)	Small city	Nordland
	M	60–69	Public sector		
H15	W	60–69	Teacher	Small city	Nordland
	M	60–69	Retired (graphic designer)		

Limitations

This study focuses on cisgender heterosexual couples, excluding other gender identities and sexual orientations. These limitations are a result of the recruitment criteria, which aimed at better understanding the performance of femininity and masculinity through clothing. Participants' narratives might not fully represent the diversity of perspectives and experiences that exist within this group, and they might feel compelled to provide socially desirable responses or conform to gender norms, potentially leading to the underreporting of certain experiences or to biases in the data. We as researchers, identifying as cisgender females, may unknowingly bring our own biases or assumptions about gender roles, stereotypes or relationship dynamics, which could inadvertently influence data collection, analysis and interpretation. Additionally, focusing solely on couples may introduce bias, as societal expectations around clothing and household management differ for single individuals and could influence their consumption patterns.

Wardrobe Study: Counting Exercise

This study involved home visits to each of the households, where a wardrobe study was conducted. Both authors of this chapter were present during the visits. The wardrobe study involved a short introduction, followed by a wardrobe counting exercise. The participants were asked to count all the garments in their wardrobe while one researcher asked about the occasion for each garment and the other researcher used a template form to fill out the numbers per garment category (e.g. pants, shorts, etc.). The participants were also asked to mention clothing they had not used during the past year and clothing they had knitted/sewn and bought second hand.

The wardrobe in this case refers to all the clothing the participants had access to, including underwear, socks and accessories and clothing stored in other places such as cabins and summer houses. Shoes were excluded to limit the time of the home visit. During the counting exercise, the participants would often move around the house to places clothing were stored and, in most cases, this involved several rooms and floors in the house. Each visit lasted between 2 and 4 hours and the counting of each wardrobe would take between 30 minutes to 3 hours, depending on its size. Some informants had already counted smaller garments such as underwear and socks prior to the visit. In one of the households, only the woman was present for the counting, and she also counted her partner's wardrobe and named the occasions that he would wear the clothing to. All the other participants counted their own wardrobe and sometimes the partners would observe each other's counting and make some comments.

Analytical Procedure

The quantitative data gathered from the counting exercise was analysed by organising the wardrobe forms into separate Excel sheets. Each sheet included the individual occasions reported by the participants and the corresponding count of items for each occasion. Each individual occasion is based on the occasion first associated with a garment by the participants. This means that several of the garments in each wardrobe could also be used for other occasions, but it was the main occasion that was noted. To provide an overview of the occasions for all participants, the decision was made to group similar individual occasions together. For instance, occasions such as 'rain', 'summer' and 'winter' were categorised as everyday occasions. Additionally, occasions labelled as 'everyday plus' and 'party' were categorised as dressed up/special occasions. Clothing that was not currently in use were categorised as passive. This classification process resulted in the identification of six overarching occasion types: everyday, work, sports/outdoors, dressed up/special, home, and passive. The next phase of the analysis involved deductive coding of the transcriptions in NVivo software. This coding aimed first to identify the main differences between the male and female wardrobes, and the section 'Differences Between Male and Female Wardrobes' of this chapter will explore these differences in terms of volume of clothing for occasions, the specialisation of clothing and expectations of variety. The next stage of the analysis aimed to understand these differences in relation to gender as performance and gender as a general understanding. This will be explored in the final section leading up to the conclusion.

DIFFERENCES BETWEEN MALE AND FEMALE WARDROBES

This section explores the main differences between the male and female wardrobes based on quantitative and qualitative data. The first part compares the differences in terms of the volume of clothing for occasions. The following section will explore the specialisation of clothing and expectations of variety as two aspects that significantly differentiated the male and female participants. These aspects will be further explored as potential influences, alongside other relevant factors, on the observed volume of clothing in female wardrobes.

Volume of Clothing for Occasions

Table 2 shows the total number of items in the wardrobes of all participants and the difference between partners. The biggest female wardrobe contained 1,547 items (*H6*, 30–39) and the smallest 248 items (*H1*, 30–39). The men's wardrobes varied from 375 items (*H14*, 70–79) to 195 items (*H7*, 70–79).

The women had on average 497 items and the men had 258. When comparing the volume of items between the couples, the women had on average 241 more items than their partner. The couple (*H14*) that were closest in number of items were in their 70s and the woman had 13 more items than the man. This was also the biggest male wardrobe.

Based on the counting exercise and the participant's individual reported occasions, we found six overarching occasion that emerged from the data. Fig. 3 shows the average number of garments based on occasions. Everyday is the biggest occasion type and involves various ordinary practices. The work occasion type is clothing that was mainly used for work and not for other occasions. The dressed up/special occasion includes many different types of occasions that calls for clothing that is more dressed up than everyday, but also special occasions that have specific expectations of formality, such as weddings and funerals. The grouped occasions in the sports/outdoors occasion include items for practices such as hiking, swimming, dancing, cycling, sailing, kayaking, fishing, skiing, snowboarding, climbing, running, football and exercise at the gym. The items grouped in the home occasion have in common that they are mainly worn around the house and include practices such as sleeping, gardening, painting, refurbishing and generally being at home. The passive occasion includes garments that have not been used during the past year and no longer have an occasion. Some of these are 'at mercy' (Klepp, 2001), meaning that the owner is considering disposing of the garment, for example due to size, but it is kept, sometimes because there is hope that the garment will fit in the future. Passive is therefore a different type of

Table 2. Overview of Wardrobes Based on Occasions and Total Number of Garments.

Household	Location	Housing	Gender	Age	Total Number of Occasions	Total Number of Garments	Difference Between Partners
H1	Oslo	Terrace house	Woman	30–39	15	248	37
			Man	30–39	14	211	
H2	Viken	House	Woman	40–49	14	255	53
			Man	40–49	19	202	
H3	Oslo	Apartment	Woman	30–39	25	452	255
			Man	30–39	19	197	
H4	Vestfold	House	Woman	60–69	18	382	79
			Man	70–79	19	303	
H5	Viken	House	Woman	30–39	22	409	207
			Man	30–39	13	202	
H6	Viken	House	Woman	30–39	26	1,547	1,335
			Man	30–39	11	239	
H7	Vestfold	Apartment	Woman	70–79	16	388	191
			Man	79–79	13	195	
H8	Oslo	Apartment	Woman	20–29	19	799	563
			Man	20–29	17	236	
H9	Oslo	Terrace house	Woman	40–49	25	393	117
			Man	40–49	17	276	
H10	Viken	House	Woman	50–59	22	412	124
			Man	50–59	18	288	
H11	Viken	House	Woman	40–49	23	573	305
			Man	50–59	18	268	
H12	Nordland	House	Woman	30–39	18	456	84
			Man	30–39	15	372	
H13	Nordland	House	Woman	60–69	19	468	183
			Man	70–79	19	285	
H14	Nordland	House	Woman	60–69	17	388	13
			Man	60–69	29	375	
H15	Nordland	House	Woman	60–69	17	285	68
			Man	60–69	11	217	
Total average			**Women**		**19**	**497**	**241**
			Men		**16**	**258**	

occasion as it refers to garments that are no longer in use and not involved in any practices at the moment.

The occasion with the highest clothing volume is everyday, for both women and men, followed by sports/outdoors. Female participants have more clothing for everyday and dressed up/special occasions and male participants have more clothing for work occasions. From a volume perspective, the female participants have more clothing for all occasions except work. The everyday occasion stands

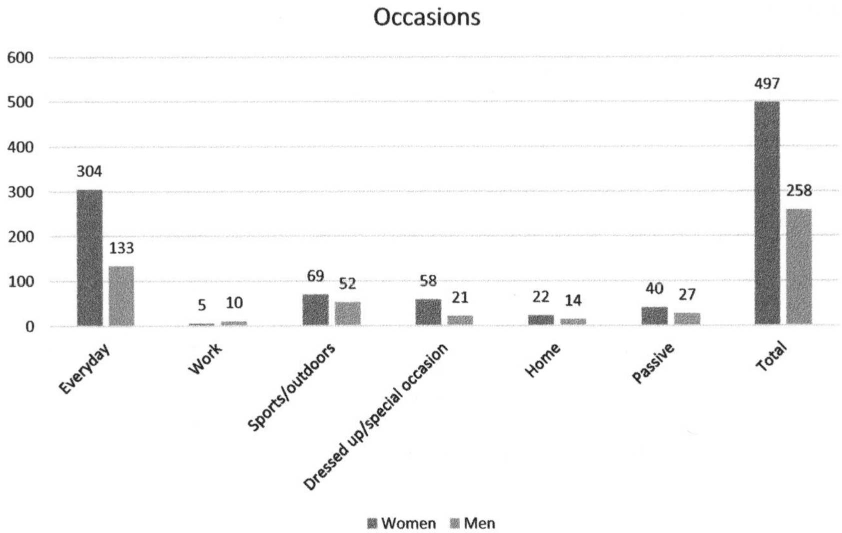

Fig. 3. Average Garments Based on Occasion Types.

out as the occasion where the female participants have a much higher volume of items than the male participants.

When analysing the percentage of the wardrobe allocated to each occasion, we find that 61% of the items in the female wardrobes are intended for everyday, while for men, this number is 52%. A larger part of the men's wardrobe consists of sports and outdoor clothing, accounting for 20% of their items, while for women this is 14%. The male wardrobes also have a larger number of passive items, with 11% being categorised as passive. For the female participants, passive items make up 8% of the wardrobe.

Figs. 4 and 5 indicate that the male and female participants have several similarities in their wardrobe contents. The distribution of clothing is similar, and all participants had garments in each of the six occasion types. In addition, over half of the items in the male and female wardrobes are characterised as everyday occasions. Comparing Fig. 3 with Figs. 4 and 5 highlights that the main difference between male and female wardrobes is due to the number of items per occasion. While the wardrobe counting data show the occasions in which female participants have more items than men, it does not show why they have more clothing. To explore this further, the following sections will present the main distinctions found in the qualitative data that impact the female participants having more clothing.

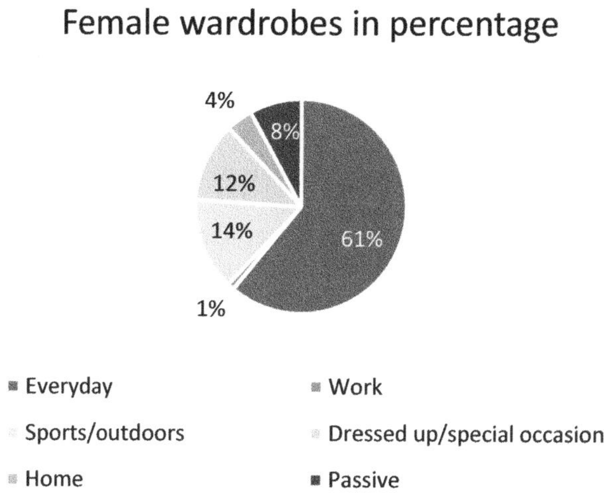

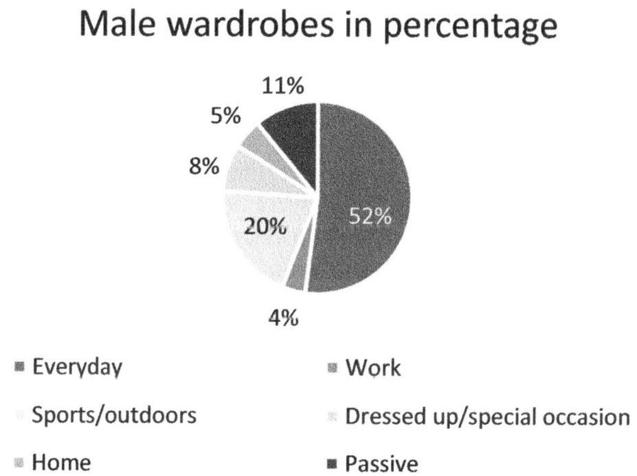

Figs. 4 and 5. Wardrobe Content in Sections.

Specialisation of Clothing

Shove (2003) links an increased range of specific occasions in contemporary society to more differences in clothing, resulting in more frequent changes of dress. Gear and equipment, including garments, have in the past decade become more specialised for practices (Shove, 2003). Since the Norwegian culture can be seen a physically active society, characterised by several distinctive occasions in the form of seasonal changes and clothing for leisure and outdoor activities (Klepp & Skuland, 2013), the specialisation of clothing is highly relevant for the number of clothing for occasions in Norwegian wardrobes.

The female participants mentioned more occasions than the male participants on average, and to some extent there was a connection between more occasions and higher volume of clothing. The man in *H14* (50–59), who owned the most clothing of all the men, also had the most occasions. He had a greater variety of different practices and occasions, both in terms of leisure activities and doing chores around the house, in addition to being in a choir that performed at various special occasions. However, another reason for the volume of clothing in his wardrobe was his age, as many of his garments were old and he rarely did a clean out of the wardrobe.

The tendency that clothing has become specialised for practices comes to show in both male and female wardrobes, which applies especially to the sports/outdoors occasion. In some cases, the male participants would have more sports clothing than their female partner for practices such as football and climbing. In terms of wardrobe content, 20% of the male wardrobes were for sports/outdoors while this was 14% for the female participants. However, the female participants still had more clothing for sports/outdoor occasions that was linked to specialised practices for similar occasions. For example, most of the female participants had different types of bathing suits and bikinis for going to the beach, going swimming in a public pool or being in a sauna during winter. The male participants would rarely differentiate between clothing for these occasions, which also relates to bodily conditions and the female body being more on display in occasions that calls for less clothing.

The beach is an example of an occasion that was mentioned by several of the female participants but none of the male. The female participants mentioned occasions such as being pregnant, which were not relevant for the men, but they also mentioned more specific occasions in relation to specific types of clothing. For example, two of the female participants had 'job interview' as a specific occasion, referring to a garment they had acquired for that occasion. Several of the women also referred to an occasion named 'everyday plus' or 'everyday dressed up', in which the garments were characterised by appearing more dressed up than ordinary everyday garments. The categories most referred to in relation to this occasion was dresses and tops such as blouses and shirts.

> Woman (H13, 60–69): yes, everything is like tops. There's a top that's kind of casual, the same with a jacket that's worn with pants and a slightly dressy pair of pants, and one lace top that I would characterise as dressy, and then there's one top here that's kind of casual and one dressy, and there's one dressy blouse.

The everyday dressed up occasion would appear in different ways in the female wardrobes, but the garments referred to in this occasion had in common that they could be worn to dress up but not to the extent that the women would seem *too* dressed up for everyday occasions. It is then a matter of what is appropriate for the occasion in terms of acceptable consumption – when is it not proper to be too dressed up. The handling of this balance between dressed up and everyday was also mentioned by some of the male informants, and they could be conscious of not wearing some garments that could make them look like they had dressed up. This shows gendered negotiations and tensions in dressing for occasions that is felt by both the male and female participants, but in different ways as practical understandings and rules adhering to specific practices are shaped by feminine and masculine ideals.

Expectations of Variety

Varying clothing is a key feature of the practice of dressing that can be performed in various ways and for different purposes. The importance of variety in dress may depend on the occasion, and having enough garments to rotate is crucial for enabling variety. In the analysis, variety does not refer to changing clothing between different occasions, but to changing clothing for the same occasions. Variety is also about novelty and appearing new, which is another expectation that applies more to the women than men (Klepp, 2005). Novelty in this case does not necessarily imply brand new clothing as novelty may be the result of varying between different garments.

Based on the wardrobe study, two different forms of variety appeared: aesthetic variety and practical variety. Aesthetic variety refers to a noticeable change in dress for the same occasion, for example varying between garments for the same everyday occasion or for special occasions, such as not wearing the same dress to a wedding twice (Lövgren, 2015). Practical variety refers to varying between dress for the same occasions due to perceived cleanliness, and this was a feature more common in the men's wardrobes. Even though some of the male informants expressed that they rotate between certain garments for everyday occasions, they had a lot less garments to choose from and many of them would have a similar appearance. This means that their dress would not change much even though they put on a different t-shirt. An example of practical variety is from the male participant in *H10* (50–59) who worked as a teacher and would be conscious about how often he varied his clothes when standing in front of his students:

> Man: I don't think it's okay to wear the same shirt for 3 days in a row, it doesn't look good, it looks sloppy, but I can't wear one shirt for a day and then throw it in the laundry, that's too much work, that's why things hang out to be rotated a bit and then I use it for a couple of days a week and maybe two weeks pass until next time, you know, but I don't spend a lot of time getting dressed, seriously, I don't.

This participant was aware of how he was on display every day for his students, but the variety is practical in the sense that his collection of shirts for work and everyday all had similar square patterns to the extent that the appearance would not change much even though he varied between different shirts. The women had a lot more aesthetic variety in terms of how their everyday garments looked, with different colours, garment types, style and fashion. A female participant who also worked as a teacher expressed the need to vary in order to not look the same:

> Researcher: ... but do you vary clothing from day to day?
>
> Woman: Yes, I do. For example, I won't come to work in this t-shirt tomorrow, and I don't wear the same sweater every day. I try to vary my outfits so that I don't look the same every day (*H15*, 60–69).

The female participants rarely spoke explicitly about variety as it can be seen as embodied knowledge that is highly routinised and internalised in the practice of dressing. This also demonstrates how variety in this case is an example of expectable consumption, as it is taken for granted that clothing should be varied for everyday occasions. However, for the men, variety was more often a case of acceptable consumption, as they consider how acceptable it is to wear the same clothing before they need to vary. When variety was referred to, it could be in relation to some specific occasions that the couple had in common, but where there was a noticeable difference between them. The couple in *H8* (20–29) discussed differences in the number of garments they bring on holiday:

> Man: But you also bring more on holiday than me, for example.
>
> Woman: Yes, I want freedom of choice.
>
> Man: Yes, you would rather pack 4–5 extra items or not just items but outfits.
>
> Woman: Yes, when I go on holiday, I try not to pack too much, so I try to plan outfits in advance and think, "I can wear this on that day." But it always ends up like this, maybe I add one more item because I know it can go with this and that, and then it always happens, I have the heavier suitcase between the two of us.
>
> Man: Yes, because I notice it more the longer the holiday is, I start thinking, "I can wear this for 5 days."
>
> Woman: Yes, but I change outfits every day.

The high number of garments for everyday and dressed up occasions in the female wardrobes show that it is less accepted for women to wear the same similar looking clothing every day. This relates to how women's physical appearance act as an important indicator of their worth, while for men this is primarily based on performance and actions (Lövgren, 2015). Thus, women vary more between their everyday dress and for special occasions as their performance of practices involve practical understandings with more expectations to vary. Aesthetic variety can therefore be understood as a feminine practice, and as a clothing norm, it affects the dynamic of the wardrobe in several ways. For example, the woman in *H11* (40–49) mentioned the need to look presentable and professional at the same time at various work occasions:

> Woman: . . . and then it's like when I have to present my research and then I feel like I have to look very proper, and I am a representative and substitute for some board of directors, so I have to travel a bit for those things, but I have plenty, more than enough to vary many times.

The female participants have several dresses for birthdays and Christmas parties, and for other social and casual occasions. In terms of volume, the expectation of variety has a big impact on the number of garments in the everyday occasion type. The female participants had twice as much clothing for everyday, which may imply that the ordinary and recurrent occasions are also the ones that require the most volume of clothing in order to achieve variety.

There was less of a gender discrepancy in the variety and volume of clothing for special occasions such as weddings. Some special occasions such as funerals can involve the same clothing, but other special occasions can require new garments. If the same people attend an event, it could be seen as important to have a different outfit than at the last event (Lövgren, 2015). However, the ritual and celebratory occasions, such as weddings, funerals, Christmas, Constitution Day, Confirmation and Baptism may have more defined clothing codes for the type of clothing that is considered suitable.

If the dressed up occasions and the special occasions are analysed separately, the male participants have more clothing for special occasions. One reason for this is that the suit items were often worn only to special occasions, and some of these occasions called for different types of suits. For example, a suit usually worn to funerals could be seen as not appropriate to use in other special occasions. For most of the female participants, only three to five of the dresses were considered as special occasion dresses. The women had 18 dresses in average for dressed up/special occasions and the majority of these were for occasions such as birthday parties and dining out. This also aligns with how occasions that occur more often have more pressing expectations of variety and may lead to higher clothing volumes.

DISCUSSION: GENDER DYNAMICS AND THE IMPACT ON CLOTHING VOLUMES

The expectations of variety and specialisation of clothing are aspects of the practice of dressing that is manifested in the performance of gender. The following sections discuss the differences identified above in relation to gender dynamics. The first section delves into how performing gender, as a general understanding, informs the practice of dressing and contributes to the observed higher volume in women's wardrobes. The second part discusses the implications of gender dynamics on clothing consumption in terms of broader social and cultural meanings and conventions.

Performing Gender in the Practice of Dressing

The display of gender is highly interconnected with occasions in everyday life as most occasions imply an implicit or explicit distinction between gender. Dressing for occasions are gendered in the sense that the outcome of clothing and adornment work will be interpreted as gender-appropriate or gender-inappropriate as a way of doing gender (West & Zimmerman, 1987). It is often more accepted that women wear garments associated with men's wear, than men wearing clothing that appear feminine (Lövgren, 2015). Literature on men's dressing norms is often more explicit and clearer than women's, which could imply that men would face more sincere consequences should they deviate from masculine clothing standards (Døving & Klepp, 2009).

Performing gender for the male participants would in many cases appear in how they emphasised their low interest in clothing and that they would not bother that much with how they dressed in the everyday life. Several of the men explained that sometimes they just grab what is on the top of a pile in their wardrobe to illustrate their low effort. This indicates that while the men expressed a low interest to get dressed for both ordinary and special occasions, dressing appropriately masculine is very much a case of expectable consumption for the male participants. Therefore, their disinterest in clothing and the resulting outfit can be understood as the appropriate masculine way of doing gender through the practice of dressing (Wallaschkowski, 2023). The male participants would often mention that they did not like to wear a suit unless it was necessary. 'I realized that I could get away with not wearing a suit if I bought some nice blazers instead, I hate wearing a suit' (Man *H11*, 50–59). The full suit would for most of the men only be worn to weddings, funerals and baptisms, but it also happened that they could 'get away' with something less formal for these occasions. This ability to dress less formally can be viewed as a negotiation of acceptable consumption, as they considered the level of formality that was deemed appropriate for special occasions.

Gender was also important for the only occasion type where the men in average had more clothing, which was work. Some of the men expressed expectations of dressing more formally at their workplace to occasions such as important meetings, which led to that some of their shirts were only worn to those work occasions. These shirts would often be too dressed up for how they preferred to dress in everyday life, which is what made the garments specific for work. For example, one man (*H3*, 30–39) had recently started a new job and at his new workplace they had a less strict dress code than the previous one. This meant that he now had several shirts in his wardrobe which he did not use as he preferred more casual clothing in everyday occasions.

These examples illustrate that several of the male participants preferred to dress casually. This was also expressed by the women, but in a different way, as women may feel more expectations to dress according to feminine dress codes, which are not as casual as the masculine dress codes in everyday occasions. For example, some of the women talked about how they are not 'good' at dressing up and refer to expectations of how women should pay attention to their appearance. 'I use the coat if I'm forced to wear a skirt in the winter or if I'm going to a funeral, mostly not otherwise. I use skirts and dresses very rarely, I'm typically a jeans girl' (Woman *H9*, 60–69). The female participants expressed expectations to appear feminine by wearing dresses more often, but that this was not something they necessarily preferred. However, the fact that they had passive dresses could also be spoken about negatively: 'Yeah, when I want to dress up in something other than the old t-shirts, I'm terribly bad at dressing up. 12, gosh, I have 14 dresses, I almost never use them, it's too bad' (Woman *H14*, 60–69). The female participants would often talk about something they found difficult or that was negative about their wardrobe, and it could be cases where they said they were not good at disposing of passive garments or that they had too many dresses. This was also surrounded by an overarching narrative of their wardrobes being overflowing with too much clothing. The ideal often referred to by the public media regarding clothing consumption is to have fewer clothes and only keep those that are actively used. However, most of the female participants did not feel that they could incorporate this ideal in their practices.

The counting exercise was more difficult and stressful for the women due to the volume of clothing they had to count but also because they tied their personal selves to how they maintained their wardrobes. The men were more likely to blame external factors such as fast fashion and poor quality, or that the garment was gifted, rather than themselves if they had too many passive garments. Some of the women could also say that they were embarrassed to show how many garments they had and felt responsible for the volume. 'Again, I feel that it's very embarrassing how many clothes I have, I'm too fond of clothes' (Woman *H11*, 40–49). Some of the women were also honest about that they liked clothing, and the three biggest wardrobes were owned by women who expressed an interest in clothing.

During the wardrobe counting, many of the women would refer to wardrobe ideals about keeping an organised wardrobe, such as Marie Kondo with having a tidy wardrobe and garments that spark joy (Kondo, 2014), and a capsule wardrobe with garments that go well together (Wolfe, 2018). The way the women referred to these ideals show that there was an expectation for the women to have a plan around their wardrobe. Having a capsule wardrobe is something they could do to achieve a more organised wardrobe. Another way this came to show is when the women talked about the 'one garment in, one garment out' ideal, referring to when they acquired something new, they should also dispose of something to not end up with too many clothes. Even though few followed this ideal strictly, it could explain why the women more often than the men would go through their wardrobe and do a wardrobe clean up to compensate for their higher frequency of acquiring garments. Consequently, the practice of cleaning up and going through garments is part of expectable consumption for the women and becomes a way of maintaining and being in control of their wardrobe.

The different gendered expectations and levels of acceptability in appearance were evident in the fact that the men had a significantly higher amount of clothing showing physical signs of wear and tear. Several of the men explained how they did not want to waste clothing and it was important that clothes were completely 'used up' before they were discarded. However, the worn-out clothing was typically considered inappropriate and not acceptable for most public occasions. As a result, many of these clothes were moved from being worn in everyday situations to becoming designated for home occasions after being used for a while. This was also the case for most of the female participants, but the men had a lot more of these types of clothing, also because the men did not engage in wardrobe clean ups as frequently. Sometimes the men could be told not to wear the worn-out garments outside the house and one man (*H10*, 50–59) had been told not to wear one of his shirts in public:

> Man: … so it's typical that when you first have home trousers, you need to have a home shirt too, I've been told, you don't wear this one outside.
>
> Researcher: oh, because it is..?
>
> Man: no, because I've repaired holes and I'm not as good as my mother-in-law, you see.

Similar situations were also described by several of the men. This could imply that the women had a bigger say in what was acceptable for the men to wear than the other way around. In all households, the women were to a bigger or lesser extent in charge of the clothing-related practices and in the households with children this was more explicit. It would often happen during the wardrobe counting that the man asked the woman if he had forgotten something and the location of certain items, or the women corrected the men if they reported fewer garments than they had. This suggest that, within the households studied, the women had more influence in determining what was deemed acceptable for the men to wear, highlighting the gender dynamics in clothing-related practices.

Implications of Gender Dynamics on Clothing Volumes

The section above demonstrates uneven expressions of expectable and acceptable consumption that lead to gendered varieties in dressing for occasions. The practice of dressing is shaped by rules, practical and general understandings and a teleoaffective structure, which contribute to the reproduction of gendered doings and sayings in dressing for various occasions. There are other factors besides gender that also have an impact on clothing consumption, such as age, income, bodily conditions and life changes, in addition to previous experience with certain types of styles, shapes and colours of clothing (Skjold, 2014). However, we argue that gender is highly relevant to gain insight on the volume in wardrobes. The identified dynamics above contributing to higher volume in female wardrobes can be understood as part of embodied habits, temporal routines and established norms in social networks that 'push' the practice of dressing beyond individual control (Warde, 2016).

An implication of the volume of clothing are feelings of shame and guilt (McIntyre, 2019). Wardrobes are seen as overflowing with clothing and there is a lot of organisational work and concern for what to keep and what to dispose of. The female participants would talk about their clothing as if it was something they could have been better at. This is related to how women may feel a greater responsibility to have sustainable consumption patterns (Bloodhart & Swim, 2020). They feel the pressure to take part in ideals within wardrobe planning that may lead to a more organised and sustainable wardrobe and show more willingness than men to reduce their clothing consumption (Sigaard & Laitala, 2023). For example, the female participants expressed how they should be better at wearing some clothes more often or that they should be better at not having too much. Being better is not just about having less clothing, and it can also be about not having enough of some specific garment types, such as dresses, or feeling self-conscious or making excuses for not frequently wearing dresses or skirts.

The female participants talked about challenges they face in finding a balance in their dressing for various occasions, avoiding extremes such as being overly dressy or too feminine. This highlights the multifaceted risks and associated sanctions women face when dressing: the risk of being overdressed (and therefore perceived as foolish and superficial), the risk of being dressed too provocatively (and becoming a legitimate target), the risk of not dressing according to age (too young or too old) and the risk of being underdressed (and appearing sloppy). These are all risks that apply more to women than men and the responsibility for not falling into any of these lies solely on the woman herself (Klepp, 2004). The numerous risks and associated sanctions for women's dressing practices may influence the volume of clothing in wardrobes, due to the complexity of navigating the appropriate way of dressing. Men would also encounter risks to some extent, but the greater risk for men would be to not dress in accordance with expectations of masculinity and appear too feminine. The boundaries of acceptable consumption in terms of dressing for occasions are more clearly defined for men and more nuanced for women, which is likely to have an impact on the volume of clothing required to navigate being appropriately dressed.

In order to conform to the various gender expectations, women can be seen to be more engaged in the practice of dressing. This engagement came to show in how the women talked about what type of garments they like, the style, shape and colours they prefer, and in general had a much richer language for talking about their wardrobe compared to their male partner. This is also found in Skjold's (2014) wardrobe study of men that found it difficult to verbally describe their clothing preferences. The level of engagement in practices has implications for how routinised the practice becomes for individuals. People are less reflective in ordinary practices and more in special ones (Warde, 2016). Occasions may differ in the level of engagement and is likely to be higher in occasions that occur less often, which also have formal clothing standards and norms. People who are less engaged in the practice of dressing may therefore have a more routinised way of dressing with less deliberation of what to wear in everyday occasions.

The women expressed more need to devote time to appearance work, which can be spending time on finding the right garments for occasions. The literature from fashion studies focuses on how this is part of showing sides of the self, of communicating identity, as a way to take control (Lövgren, 2015). However, this focus may also reinforce the idea that women need to communicate a part of their selves through dress. For the men, appearance work was less articulated even though it may be just as important as they have more restrictive possibilities in terms of materials and gender expressions. The fact that women feel the need to be expressive through clothing as a way to show they are taking care of their self, and being an individual, may be interpreted as part of broader societal understandings of gender in the practice of dressing that initially affects women's sense of feeling the need to look their best.

Furthermore, this dimension of being expressive through clothing also impacts the women's male partners. The female participants could be conscious of how their partner appeared in public, for example the shirt in *H10* that had been badly repaired. The women were often responsible for organising and keeping track of not only her own clothing consumption but also her male partner's and their children as a way of practicing partnering. Consequently, when a partner is dressing in worn out or shabby looking clothes in public, it may be seen to reflect badly on the woman as keeper of the household. This essentially stand in opposition to what Veblen (1899) observed about conspicuous consumption. Now, it is the man's clothing that may reflect on the woman's role as homemaker. Even though the breadwinner-homemaker ideal has developed since the 1900s, this ideal is still at play in Norway with women taking the role as caretaker of the home (Godin & Langlois, 2021; Magnussen, 2020). Women keep track of what their partners wear and may take a very active role in keeping their partners clean (Klepp, 2005). However, this role may lead to tensions for women as it does not support gender equality in housework. This may result in what Kaufmann refers to as the 'trap': the dilemma where a woman appears to support a system she would typically oppose, causing inner conflict (Kaufmann, 1998). Therefore, it poses a double burden for women as they are not only expected to navigate the complexities and bundles of clothing-related practices for their own clothing consumption but also for their household, while also striving for gender equality and rejecting such expectations. This highlights how gender dynamics in clothing consumption upholds traditional ideals in contemporary society.

CONCLUSION

This study has provided new insights into the influence of gender and occasions in the practice of dressing and the impact on the differences in clothing volume between men and women. The connectivity between rules, practical and general understandings and teleoaffective structures in practices, involving gendered societal expectations and norms, play a significant role in shaping individuals' clothing consumption and the content of wardrobes. The female wardrobes show evidence of higher expectations to have a variety of clothing for the same occasions and more specialised clothing for practices, in order to adhere to feminine dress codes, leading to a higher volume of clothing. These expectation stems from societal notions of femininity and the need for women to appear well-dressed and put-together. In turn, the male participants tended to emphasise a low interest in clothing and prefer casual dressing. The men focused more on perceived cleanliness and functionality when dressing rather than aesthetic variations, aligning with societal expectations of masculinity.

The findings illustrate how the current environmental discourse, with its focus on the quantity and size of wardrobes, impacts women more than men. Women take on a greater responsibility for being environmentally conscious while also trying to fulfil expectations and unclear norms to dress for occasions, creating a paradox. This paradox also applies to the risks and associated sanctions of being appropriately feminine. Women are expected to excel in both appropriately embracing femininity and maintaining a lower clothing acquisition rate. However, finding this balance is challenging due to the ambiguous and diverse clothing standards that apply to women.

It is crucial to recognise the dynamics of gender in clothing consumption and its different impacts on individuals. Efforts towards reducing clothing consumption should find ways to prompt how understandings in practices can be altered, for example by lowering clothing standards and challenge feminine conceptions in the practice of dressing. However, changing perceptions of gender as a general understanding can be challenging, as it is deeply ingrained in established practices and routines, particularly in relation to women's care work and responsibilities.

Moreover, this study acknowledges that its focus on binary heterosexual perspectives limits conclusions regarding the differences in clothing consumption for various gender identities. Future research should explore the nuances of clothing consumption among diverse gender identities to gain a comprehensive understanding.

Overall, by examining the practice of dressing as an integrative practice shaped by rules, understandings and a teleoaffective structure, and by considering the interplay between gender and occasions, we can gain a better understanding of the factors influencing clothing volumes and the complexity attached to the practice of dressing. Applying practice theory in clothing consumption research allows for a more nuanced and deeper understanding of what contributes to variations in clothing volumes and the significance of gender dynamics. This approach opens up new avenues for exploring the organisation and impact of clothing consumption, providing valuable insights into the interconnectedness of actions that comprise the practice of dressing for occasions.

REFERENCES

Barry, B. (2018). (Re)Fashioning masculinity: Social identity and context in men's hybrid masculinities through dress. *Gender & Society*, *32*(5), 638–662. https://doi.org/10.1177/0891243218774495

Banim, M., & Guy, A. (2001). Dis/continued selves: Why do women keep clothes they no longer wear? In A. Guy, E. Green, & M. Banim (Eds.), *Through the wardrobe: Women's relationships with their clothes* (pp. 203–219). Berg.

Bloodhart, B., & Swim, J. K. (2020). Sustainability and consumption: What's gender got to do with it? *Journal of Social Issues*, *76*(1), 101–113. https://doi.org/10.1111/josi.12370

Breward, C. (1999). *The hidden consumer: Masculinities, fashion and city life 1860–1914*. Manchester University Press.

Butler, J. (1990). *Gender trouble: Feminism and the subversion of identity*. Routledge.

Døving, R., & Klepp, I. G. (2009). Avlæring av ansvar. Normer og kunnskap om klæri skikk og brukbøker. In K. Asdal & E. Jacobsen (Eds.), *Forbrukernes ansvar* (pp. 113–144). Cappelen akademisk forlag.

Ellsworth-Krebs, K., Reid, L., & Hunter, C. J. (2021). Home comfort and "Peak household": Implications for energy demand. *Housing, Theory and Society*, *38*(1), 1–20. https://doi.org/10.1080/14036096.2019.1694579

Fletcher, K., & Klepp, I. G. (Eds.). (2017). *Opening up the wardrobe: A methods book*. Novus.

Gherardi, S. (2019). *How to conduct a practice-based study: Problems and methods*. Edward Elgar Publishing.

Godin, L., & Langlois, J. (2021). Care, gender, and change in the study of sustainable consumption: A critical review of the literature. *Frontiers in Sustainability*, *2*. https://doi.org/10.3389/frsus.2021.725753

Halkier, B. (2022). Mundane normativity and the everyday handling of contested food consumption. *Consumption and Society*, *1*(1), 51–66.

Holmes, J., Sasso, A., Hernández Alava, M., Stevely, A. K., Warde, A., Angus, C., & Meier, P. S. (2023). Change and stability in British drinking practices and culture between 2009 and 2019: A longitudinal latent class analysis of drinking occasions. *SSM – Population Health*, *24*, 101548. https://doi.org/10.1016/j.ssmph.2023.101548

Kaufmann, J.-C. (1998). *Dirty linen: Couples and their laundry*. Middlesex University Press.

Klepp, I. G. (2001). Hvorfor går klær ut av bruk? Avhending sett i forhold til kvinners klesvaner. https://hdl.handle.net/20.500.12199/5390

Klepp, I. G. (2004). Farlige farger [Dangerous colours]. *Norsk antropologisk tidsskrift*, *15*(4), 227–240.

Klepp, I. G. (2005). Demonstrations of feminine purity: The meaning of cleanliness and the growth of laundry. In G. Hagemann & H. Roll-Hansen (Eds.), *Twentieth-century houseqives. Meanings and implications of unpaid work*. Unipub.

Klepp, I. G. (2007). Patched, louse-ridden, tattered: Clean and dirty clothes. *Textile: The Journal of Cloth and Culture*, *5*(3), 254–275. https://doi.org/10.2752/175183507X249459

Klepp, I. G., & Bjerck, M. (2009). *Klær og utstyr for en hver anledning – Friluftslivets spesialisering*. Forskning i Friluft 2009. FRIFO-rapport.

Klepp, I. G., & Bjerck, M. (2014). A methodological approach to the materiality of clothing: Wardrobe Studies. *International Journal of Social Research Methodology*, *17*(4), 373–386. https://doi.org/10.1080/13645579.2012.737148

Klepp, I. G., & Laitala, K. (2016). Klesforbruk i Norge. https://hdl.handle.net/20.500.12199/5331

Klepp, I. G., & Skuland, S. (2013). The rationalisation of consumption reasons for purchasing outdoor recreational outfits. In M. Vaccarella & J. L. Foltyn (Eds.), *Fashion wise* (pp. 43–52). Inter-Disciplinary Press.

Kondo, M. (2014). *The life-changing magic of tidying: A simple, effective way to banish clutter forever*. Random House.

Krog Juvik, A., & Halkier, B. (2024). Pathways to more resource-intensive consumption through convenient bundles and complexes of food, mobility and housing practices. *Consumption and Society*, *3*(1), 2–20. https://doi.org/10.1332/27528499y2023d000000002

Laitala, K., & Klepp, I. G. (2020). Klær og miljø: Innkjøp, gjenbruk og vask. https://hdl.handle.net/20.500.12199/3065

Lövgren, K. (2015). *Squirrels and nostalgia: About wardrobe collections of older women*. In L. Karlsson, M. Liliequist, A. S. Lundgren, K. Lövgren, & A. Sjöstedt Landén (Eds.), *Ageing, culture and identity* (pp. 95–120). Umeå University.

Magnussen, M.-L. (2020). Men's family breadwinning in today's Norway: A blind spot in the strive for gender equality. *NORA – Nordic Journal of Feminist and Gender Research*, *28*(4), 302–313. https://doi.org/10.1080/08038740.2020.1790658

Maguire, H., & Fahy, F. (2022). Practising fashion and wardrobe studies: A geographical reframing? *Area*, *54*(1), 69–77. https://doi.org/10.1111/area.12761

Maldini, I., Duncker, L., Bregman, L., Piltz, G., Duscha, L., Cunningham, G., Vooges, M., Grevinga, T., Tap, R., & Balgooi, F. v. (2017). *Measuring the Dutch Clothing mountain data for sustainability-oriented studies and actions in the apparel sector*. https://research.hva.nl/files/3144178/Measuring_the_Dutch_Clothing_Mountain_final_report_002_.pdf

Maldini, I., Haugrønning, V., & de León, L. (2023). Studying clothing consumption volumes through wardrobe studies a methodological reflection. In *Paper presented at the PLATE - Product Lifetimes and the Environment*, Helsinki.

McIntyre, M. P. (2019). Shame, blame, and passion: Affects of (Un)sustainable Wardrobes. *Fashion Theory*, *25*(6), 735–755. https://doi.org/10.1080/1362704X.2019.1676506

Mechlenborg, M., & Gram-Hanssen, K. (2020). Gendered homes in theories of practice: A framework for research in residential energy consumption. *Energy Research & Social Science*, *67*, 101538. https://doi.org/10.1016/j.erss.2020.101538

Mittner, L. (2018). "Students can have a really powerful role…": Understanding curriculum transformation within the framework of Canon critique and critical pedagogy. *Journal for Research in Arts and Sports Education*, *2*(2).

Pilcher, J. (2011). No logo? Children's consumption of fashion. *Childhood*, *18*(1), 128–141. https://doi.org/10.1177/0907568210373668

Reckwitz, A. (2002). Toward a theory of social practices a development in culturalist theorizing. *European Journal of Social Theory*, *5*(2), 243–263. https://doi.org/10.1177/13684310222225432

Schatzki, T. R. (1996). *Social practices: A Wittgensteinian approach to human activity and the social*. Cambridge University Press.

Schatzki, T. R. (2001). Practice mind-ed orders. In T. R. Schatzki, K. K. Cetina, & E. v. Savigny (Eds.), *The practice turn in contemporary theory* (pp. 42–55). Routledge.

Schatzki, T. R. (2002). *The site of the social. A philosophical account of the constitution of social life and change*. Pennsylvania State University Press.

Schatzki, T. R. (2005). Peripheral vision: The sites of organizations. *Organization Studies*, *26*(3), 465–484. https://doi.org/10.1177/0170840605050876

Schatzki, T. R., Cetina, K. K., & Savigny, E. V. (Eds.). (2001). *The practice turn in contemporary theory*. Routledge.

Schuster, M. R., & Van Dyne, S. R. (1985). *Women's place in the academy: Transforming the liberal arts curriculum*. ERIC.

Shove, E. (2003). *Comfort, cleanliness and convenience: The social organization of normality*. Berg.

Shove, E., Pantzar, M., & Watson, M. (2012). *The dynamics of social practice: Everyday life and how it changes*. SAGE Publications Ltd.

Sigaard, A. S., & Laitala, K. (2023). Natural and sustainable? Consumers' textile fiber preferences. *Fibers*, *11*(2). https://doi.org/10.3390/fib11020012

Skjold, E. (2014). *The daily selection. (Ph.D.). Design School Kolding*. Unpublished.

Sundt, E. (1869). *Om renligheds-stellet i Norge: Til oplysning om flid og fremskridt i landet*. JC Abelsted.

Tseëlon, E. (2001). Fashion research and its discontents. *Fashion Theory: The Journal of Dress, Body & Culture*, *5*(4), 435–451. https://doi.org/10.2752/136270401778998864

Ulväng, M. (2021). Clothing economy and clothing culture: The farm Wardrobe from a gendered perspective in nineteenth-century Sweden. *Gender & History*, *33*(2), 365–389. https://doi.org/10.1111/1468-0424.12543

van der Laan, E., & Velthuis, O. (2016). Inconspicuous dressing: A critique of the construction-through-consumption paradigm in the sociology of clothing. *Journal of Consumer Culture*, *16*(1), 22–42.

Veblen, T. (1899). *Theory of the leisure class: An economic study in the evolution of institutions*. Macmillan.

Wallaschkowski, S. (2023, 31 May–2 June). Gender roles as barriers to sustainable fashion lifetimes: How a deconstruction of norms can extend the use phase of garments. In *Paper presented at the PLATE - Product Lifetimes and the Environment*, Helsinki. https://kth.diva-portal.org/smash/get/diva2:1795825/FULLTEXT01.pdf

Warde, A. (2005). Consumption and theories of practice. *Journal of Consumer Culture*, *5*(2), 131–153. https://doi.org/10.1177/1469540505053090

Warde, A. (2016). *The practice of eating*. John Wiley & Sons.

Welch, D., Halkier, B., & Keller, M. (2020). Introduction to the special issue: Renewing theories of practice and reappraising the cultural. *Cultural Sociology*, *14*(4), 325–339. https://doi.org/10.1177/1749975520954146

Welch, D., & Warde, A. (2016). How should we understand 'general understandings'?. In *The nexus of practices* (pp. 195–208). Routledge.

West, C., & Zimmerman, D. H. (1987). Doing gender. *Gender & Society*, *1*(2), 125–151. http://www.jstor.org/stable/189945

Wolfe, I. (2018). Capsule Wardrobes: How to build a sustainable closet for life. https://goodonyou.eco/capsule-wardrobes-create-your-own/

Woodward, S. (2014). Accidently sustainable? Ethnographic approaches to clothing practices. In K. Fletcher & M. Tham (Eds.), *Routledge handbook of sustainability and fashion* (p. 131). Routledge.

Yates, L., & Warde, A. (2017). Eating together and eating alone: Meal arrangements in British households. *British Journal of Sociology*, *68*(1), 97–118. https://doi.org/10.1111/1468-4446.12231

'GAMERS' CRAFTED BY CONSUMPTION: THE INFLUENCE OF CONSUMPTION ON GENDER IDENTITIES IN VIDEO GAMES

Kamilla Knutsen Steinnes

Oslo Metropolitan University, Norway

ABSTRACT

Playing online games is a highly gendered consumption activity. While female players are objectified and harassed within the gaming community, male players tend to be stigmatized through unfavorable stereotypes. More than a label of players, 'gamer' forms an identity that can grant membership in gaming communities. The gamer identity is defined through consumption, yet material elements have been granted a minor role within studies of gender identity in video games. Through 41 play-along *interviews with children and youth aged 10–24 years, this article seeks to understand how consumption patterns shape and reinforce gender identities in games, and by which market mechanisms gendered consumption patterns are maintained. By drawing on Social Identity Theory, the findings suggest 'legitimate' gaming is associated with gendered expectations for the choice of gaming consoles, types of games, and in-game products. These expectations are organized within a hierarchy among players, where certain consumption patterns are assigned greater value. When female players adhere to these consumption patterns, they may face harassment and strategic disadvantages. Additionally, transactional interactions between genders and household dynamics imply female dependence. These gendered consumption patterns are encouraged and enabled through market mechanisms such as game design and marketing ideas. The findings are discussed in terms of how gendered consumption influences membership in the gaming culture and encourages the promotion of inclusion in game design and gaming platforms.*

Consumers and Consumption in Comparison
Comparative Social Research, Volume 37, 167–187

ISSN: 0195-6310/doi:10.1108/S0195-631020240000037008

Keywords: Video games; gender; consumption; identity; commercial markets

INTRODUCTION

Mainstream video games translate into a highly commercialized multi-billion-dollar industry. Globally, the video game market is estimated to surpass $500 billion in revenue by 2025 (Statista, 2024). Hence, when players participate in commercial video games, they are operating as consumers in a market. This market is highly gendered, where significant disparities persist in the gaming experiences of boys and girls. Girls are often initiated into the gaming community through their male relationships and may be assigned the role of spectators while boys play (Bryce & Rutter, 2003; Cote, 2020b; Jenson & de Castell, 2011). Moreover, girls spend less time (Smahel et al., 2020) and money on video games (Rodriguez-Barcenilla & Ortega-Mohedano, 2022) and are often discredited as 'casual' gamers who are less skilled and less competent than male players (Kelly et al., 2023; Paaßen et al., 2017). This negative perception of women in gaming is observed among both female and male players (Beavis & Charles, 2007), and considerable research demonstrates general harassment of female players in video games (e.g., Fox & Tang, 2017; Kuss et al., 2022; Lopez-Fernandez et al., 2019).

The term 'gamer' is more than a description of the players of games. It is also a social identity that can grant community into the gaming culture (Vermeulen et al., 2016). Substantial research builds an understanding of gamers as a male-dominated group. Despite being repeatedly disproven by multiple studies, a common misconception of the 'typical' gamer is that of a white, young, and antisocial male (e.g., Nielsen, 2015; Paaßen et al., 2017; Vanderhoef, 2013). This stereotype not only fails to accurately represent male players but also alienates non-male players from identifying as gamers. Indeed, women are less likely than men to identify as gamers (e.g., Fox & Tang, 2017; Shaw, 2012) despite making up almost half of the global player population (Entertainment Software Association, 2019). Cote (2020c) refers to this as a contemporary paradox in gaming. She highlights how games are both becoming more inclusive as more women become players, but at the same time becoming more exclusionary as evidenced by a reinforcement of female player harassment.

While existing studies provide valuable insight into the interplay between gaming, gendered experiences, and identity, they often overlook the influence of material elements (George et al., 2023; Jenson & de Castell, 2010). Historically, game developers have primarily targeted male consumers (Cote, 2020c), resulting in gaming consoles that were too big for women's hands as they were initially designed for men (Fron et al., 2007). Shaw (2013) argues that such gendered game design solidifies the association between masculinity and gaming, thereby defining the gamer identity through consumption. De Grove et al. (2015) similarly suggest that consumption behaviors determine gamer identity. Recognizing this central role of consumption in gendered gamer identities, this paper asks: How do consumption patterns shape and reinforce gender identities in games, and by which market mechanisms are gendered consumption patterns maintained? Through a theoretical lens of Social Identity Theory (Tajfel & Turner, 1979), the aim is to highlight the specific ways in which gendered consumption contributes to the construction and consolidation of gender identities. This extends to discussions on how gendered consumption is encouraged through commercial elements such as marketing assumptions, game design, and domestic constraints. The results are debated in terms of how inherent gendered assumptions within the gaming industry contribute to perpetuating games as exclusionary environments.

Gendered Market Dynamics

Digital games are conveniently designed for consumption. With the rise of increasingly accessible, mobile, and flexible games, they have become highly practical to consume (Skelly et al., 2023; Thorhauge & Gregersen, 2019). Following Evans' (2022) idea about 'embeddedness' and the evolving nature of modern consumption, video game consumption is not limited to the physical hardware required to play. It also extends to the purchase of (im)material virtual items and time spent playing the game, which translates into revenue for game companies. Chess' (2017) groups gaming consumption into materials (e.g., consoles), contents (e.g., time spent playing), mechanics (e.g., fictional in-game usage of virtual items), and in-game purchases through spending either actual or fictional currency. Reich and Steinnes (2023) further group in-game purchases into six main categories that illustrate a vast product selection: cosmetic items, progression-based items, digital currencies, donations to content creators, social events, and game passes. Such in-game consumption is effectively encouraged and facilitated through design elements (Steinnes, 2024).

As the video game industry has traditionally been determined and organized by masculinity, female and male gamers have been separated into inequitable commercial categories. Cote (2020b) asserts that such gendered power imbalances persist in contemporary gaming. This includes the way modern games are designed and marketed to target a male audience (Condis & Morrissette, 2023), the underrepresentation and sexualization of female game characters (Lynch et al., 2016), and the barriers that female game developers face when trying to enter the industry (Jenson & de Castell, 2010). Fron et al. (2007) describe such masculinization of gaming as 'the hegemony of play', where the majority retain status quo over the minority by gatekeeping gaming as a male activity.

Cote (2020a) points out how the hegemony, or masculine 'core', is juxtaposed with the feminine 'casual'. Core and casual refer to specific genres, players, gendered experiences, and gaming cultures and are largely explored as mutually exclusive concepts despite their overlapping flexibility (Cote, 2020a). Core games are typically associated with masculinity and are highly regarded in terms of economic and cultural capital. Casual games, however, are marketed toward and predominantly consumed by a female audience, are characterized by their ease and accessibility, and are often perceived as illegitimate and inferior (Chess, 2017; Cote, 2020c; Shaw, 2013; Vanderhoef, 2013; Vermeulen et al., 2016). Chess (2017) points out how casual games are developed and promoted with a feminine 'designed identity' in mind. Such a feminization of casual culture poses a threat to the core culture, leading to a redefinition of casual gaming as illegitimate and to the harassment and exclusion of women from gaming (Cote, 2020a). The core and casual binary thus becomes a tool to perpetuate a gender hierarchy. However, despite being devalued among core players, the casual players are highly valued as a consumer segment by the industry. This is evident in the flourishing mobile game market which generated a profit of over 100 billion USD in 2022, surpassing the combined revenue of both consoles and computers (Statista, 2022).

Gender Identity Construction in Games

Previous literature has established that video games are arenas for identity construction, where players can identify with avatars (i.e., virtual characters representing the player) or entire social groups (e.g., Beavis & Charles, 2007; Nielsen, 2015). Jansz (2015), for example, describes games as 'identity laboratories', where players can explore and experiment with their (gender) identities. Games facilitate such exploration by allowing players to customize their avatar to virtually represent them, for instance, through cosmetic changes to the avatar's appearance (also called 'skins'). Through the avatar, players can take on multiple identities and act them out within a simulated reality (Nielsen, 2015), as the avatar invites social engagement (Lee et al., 2023). Moreover, players tend to design avatars to reflect their physical appearance, such as having the same hair color, gender identity, and height, as well as an idealized (improved) personality representation (Zimmermann et al., 2022). This positions the avatar as a symbol of identity and an important tool for categorizing players into social groups.

However, avatar customization is restricted to the specific game design of the avatar interface. Video games have traditionally been designed by men and for men (Allen, 2023; Cote, 2020c; Grimes, 2021; Lopez-Fernandez et al., 2019), lacking female character representation that girls can relate to and identify with. Female characters that are portrayed in video games tend to be hypersexualized, objectified, or subdued (Lynch et al., 2016), with some exceptions (Allen, 2023). Due to this masculine structure of video games, girls struggle to align their identities as gamers (e.g., Fox & Tang, 2017; Shaw, 2012). This may be explained by the tendency to view girls as casual players. Casual play is perceived as easier, less immersive, and less dedicated than core play, which might cause girls to internalize stereotypical views of female players as less serious and competent (Cote, 2020b). Casual players may consequently struggle to find their place, straddling the line between being partially immersed and partially detached. While previous research outlines a complex interplay between gaming, gender, and identity, it remains unclear how consumption factors into these dynamics.

THEORETICAL FRAMEWORK

This paper is informed by a theoretical framework that incorporates consumption within Social Identity Theory (Tajfel & Turner, 1979). It argues that gendered consumption patterns not only reflect but also shape and consolidate gender identity. Moreover, gendered consumption behavior, in turn, is enabled by the market logic and design of games, as well as domestic norms of consumption.

Social Identity Theory is widely applied as a theoretical lens to studies of gender identity in games. It posits that people form identities by interacting with others, both on an interpersonal and intergroup level (Tajfel & Turner, 1979). This means categorizing themselves and other people into social groups, such as 'male', 'female', or 'gamer'. By identifying with an in-group (e.g., 'gamers'), people automatically compare and distance themselves from an out-group (e.g., 'non-gamers'). That is, people are automatically categorized as either 'similar' or 'different'. This membership in given groups has important effects on a person's self-concept, where the group's social status is a partial source of the individual's self-esteem. Conversely, nonmembership can result in stereotypes and discrimination against members from out-groups. This categorization process is central within gaming spaces, as the gamer identity forms a social category imbued by gender.

Consumption plays a significant role in the expression and formation of identity (Warde, 2017a). Consumption is an inherently social activity that takes different shapes, ranging from ordinary and routinized to conspicuous and symbolic (Warde, 2017b). While recognizing that much consumption in and of games is likely to be ordinary and without symbolism, this paper focuses on consumption as a means to communicate identity. Consumption choices, such as the selection of game genres or consoles, thus enable individuals to align with specific gamer cultures – core or casual – each associated with different gender connotations. Emulating the ideas of Tajfel and Turner (1979), consumption choices in gaming become social symbols that assert an individual's group identity.

Building on Fuentes and Sörum's (2019) understanding of smartphone applications, games are acknowledged as *consumption devices* in which consumers operate. Consumption devices are intended to encourage consumption through market elements, which entails being adept at shaping consumption preferences that steer consumers toward making specific choices (Fuentes & Sörum, 2019). The video game industry, through its marketing techniques, creates distinct consumer preferences that facilitate gendered consumption. Through such marketing techniques, games have the potential to both fulfill and invent consumption needs (Hamari & Lehdonvirta, 2010). For example, Dubuisson-Quellier (2022) outlines how variety preferences are created through product diversity resulting in consumers buying different versions of the same products (e.g., a blue versus a pink game console). Creating gendered versions of games and consoles, a market logic termed 'pink games', targets a female audience based on feminine aesthetics and presumed preferences of girls in gaming (Grimes, 2021). Indeed, the binary categories of casual and (hard)core were introduced by the video game industry itself, to create two distinct consumer segments for women and men, respectively (Vanderhoef, 2013).

Game design is instrumental in facilitating gendered consumption patterns. Games are designed with specific target demographics in mind, where design choices often cater to gender stereotypes, thereby influencing consumption behavior. Shaw (2012) suggests that the masculinized gamer identity follows a market logic, as males have traditionally been viewed as the archetypal consumer target for video game marketing and development. Chess (2017) further argues that the idea of women as shoppers, rather than players, is reflected in the design and features of casual games. The 'fashion game' genre serves to illustrate this point, where the consumption practice of shopping becomes female entertainment. Casual games whose storylines are primarily focused on shopping and consumerism (e.g., *The Sims*) tend to be written off as feminine and frivolous (Chess, 2017; Cote, 2020a). These design choices not only affect who plays what games but also how players perceive themselves and others within the broader gaming culture. In other words, this market logic informs players on who fits into the gamer identity and importantly; who does not.

The material context of gaming consumption, including domestic factors, further shapes gender identities as gamers. The physical placement of gaming consoles in 'male spaces' within households provides girls with restricted access to gaming equipment (Bryce et al., 2006; Bryce & Rutter, 2003). Male members of the household are typically first in line to access gaming (Jenson & de Castell, 2010), reinforcing the association between males and games. Girls are less likely than boys to be encouraged to play, as parents are more willing to buy gaming consoles for boys than girls (Cote, 2020a; Jenson & de Castell, 2010). This differentiation is not only spatial but also symbolic, as women tend to assume passive roles rather than active participants. This is exemplified by women's tendency to purchase gaming equipment for male relatives, indicating that men are primarily *players* while positioning women primarily as *shoppers* (Chess, 2017).

Through this theoretical framework, this article explores how gendered consumption not only reflects but actively shapes gender identities in video games. Understanding the role of consumption within the dynamic interplay between gaming, gender, and identity provides a better position to address the stereotypes and gender issues that persist in contemporary gaming culture.

METHOD

The empirical foundation of this paper is semi-structured interviews with Norwegian children and youth. The interviews were supplied with an ethnographic-inspired *play-along* where researchers observed the participants' gaming sessions.

Participants

A total of 41 Norwegian children and youth participated in the study. All participants filled out a short questionnaire about their socioeconomic background and their gaming habits. The sample had a mean age of 17, ranging from 10 to 24 years.[1] Out of the 41 participants, 20 self-identified as female, 20 as male, and 1 as nonbinary. The sample was spread across 10 of the 11 counties of Norway (*Møre og Romsdal* being the only exception). The participants were recruited to include a broad understanding of 'gamers', ranging across consoles, genres, and time investment. The sample included four active streamers, four hobby game designers, and two former e-sport athletes. Table 1 gives an overview of the key demographics of the sample. The participants were partly recruited through a recruitment agency and partly through convenience sampling.

Table 1. Overview of the Key Demographics of the Sample by Frequency, $N = 41$.

		Frequency
Gender identity	Boys	20
	Girls	20
	Nonbinary	1
Age range	10–13 years	12
	14–17 years	8
	18–21 years	10
	22–24 years	11
Nationality	Norwegian	38
	Non-Norwegian	3
Economic situation (self-reported)	Average	25
	Below average	10
	Above average	5
	Not sure	1
County of residence	Vestland	7
	Viken	7
	Oslo	5
	Nordland	5
	Trøndelag	4
	Rogaland	4
	Innlandet	3
	Agder	3
	Troms og Finnmark	2
	Vestfold og Telemark	1

Procedure

The interviews were piloted in four interviews, and the interview guide was age-adapted to address the 10- to 15-year-olds compared to the 16- to 24-years-olds. Including such diverse age groups allows for exploring how gendered gaming experiences and perceptions vary across ages, offering potential insights into when certain consumption patterns become gendered.

Given the domestic constraints of girls to access games and gaming equipment within male spaces of the household, studies of gameplay consumption have mostly taken place outside the household (Jenson & de Castell, 2010). Hence, the interviews were supplied with an ethnographic-inspired *play-along* where researchers observed the participant's gaming session. This ensured ecologic validity by meeting the participants directly within their online gaming environment, reproducing how players interact through on-screen digital communication. Supplying interviews with ethnography provides a more comprehensive picture of the contextual and relational elements of social behavior (Jerolmack & Khan, 2014). Specifically, the play-along was included to provide direct insights into the game design (e.g., gendered avatar design), in-game inventory (e.g., cosmetic items owned), and mechanical use of hardware equipment (e.g., microphone communication) of the participants' game sessions.

The interviews were conducted online, both to ensure a familiar gaming setting for the participants and to ensure geographic spread across all of Norway, including children and youth from both rural and urban neighborhoods. Each interview lasted for an average of 90 minutes (ranging from 50 to 130 minutes). The data collection was conducted from December 2022 to March 2023 and received ethical approval from the Norwegian Agency for Shared Services in Education and Research. All participants (and in some cases their guardians) provided their consent before participation.[2]

Data Analysis

All interviews were recorded and transcribed verbatim and coded through the qualitative data analysis software Nvivo.[3] The data were subjected to a template (or codebook) analysis (Brooks et al., 2015). To ensure the reliability of coding, as recommended by Turner and Turner (2009), two researchers took part in both the interview process and the data analysis. The analysis of the transcripts followed the iterative six-phase approach outlined by Brooks et al. (2015). The interviews were broadly focused on topics related to gaming and consumption, including gender. For the purpose of this article, only themes and codes from the material that related to gender were selected for further analysis, totaling 22 subcodes. The following 12 codes were placed under the main theme 'gender': gender exploration, gendered preferences, gendered game design, gender norms and stereotypes, boys in games, girls in games, nonbinary in games, gender norm-breaking and social sanctions, gender identity, gender conflicts, negotiating gender, hiding gender cues. An addition of 10 codes was included from other main themes in the interview material as they revealed gendered patterns: exclusion, hate speech, sexism, romantic interactions, gamer label, gifting, type of games played, favorite game(s), gaming equipment, and game console hierarchy. The analysis of the codes was guided by 12 questions, partly derived from the theoretical framework and partly from previous literature.[4] These questions included both comparisons and interactions between genders, as well as any potential intersecting variables such as age.

The outlined methodological approach aims to answer how gaming consumption patterns influence gender identities and how market mechanisms encourage such gendered consumption patterns. Combining interviews with ethnographic insights captures the natural gaming behavior of participants and provides a direct observation of how gender is communicated through consumption.

RESULTS

The results reveal how 'gamer' as a social category is perceived as highly gendered where gender identities influence membership. Group membership is associated with gendered consumption expectations for the choice of gaming consoles, types of games, and in-game products. These are placed within a hierarchy among players, where certain (male) consumption patterns are assigned a higher value. When females conform to such higher valued consumption patterns, they tend to face harassment, which leads to strategic disadvantages and underperformance. Moreover, female dependence is implied from the transactional nature of in-game gifting and household dynamics that favor boys with gaming access. Market dynamics encourage and facilitate such gendered forms of consumption. It is important to note that the analysis largely highlights a binary understanding of gender where female players often are at a disadvantage, as this is what emerged from the material. However, the results do not undermine the increasing inclusive developments within gaming, invalidate favorable female gaming experiences, or discredit male gamer culture. The purpose of the provided insights is to explore the influence of consumption in gendered gaming and to foster discussions on how to further improve gaming. Throughout, the results highlight how gender intersects with age in various instances.

Playing the Part: Consumption Standards of the Gamer Identity

The gamer identity is highly gendered and traditionally associated with males and masculinity (e.g., Ask et al., 2016; Paaßen et al., 2017). The following sections will argue that this perception is communicated through consumption.

Identifying as a gamer is associated with specific norms for consumption, such as engaging in competitive team play, winning, wearing specific skins, adopting specific communication styles, and playing 'high-end games' on computers:

> I definitely need a keyboard and mouse, but if it's going to be a more high-end game like Fortnite, you need a better PC than usual. (Georg, 11)

> There is a certain expectation that you should be skilled. Especially if you play team-based games like shooters. For example, if you play Fortnite or Call of Duty or Overwatch. I mean, then you basically have to be quite good. (Bella, 18)

This expectation forms a performance standard that influences consumption levels and reinforces the idea that legitimate gaming requires serious investment, both in terms of time and equipment. Girls in the sample who distanced themselves from the gamer identity reported feeling like they did not play the 'correct games' or not feeling 'good enough' to identify as gamers:

> It's a very ride-or-die thing, like you have to be really into playing, and only certain games make you a gamer. And you have to really prove yourself if you're a girl. (Sofia, 23)

To illustrate, Kevin, a former e-sports athlete in a popular first-person shooter game, identified as a gamer and the associated gamer culture. He had built his own stationary computer, spoke the language, knew all the terms for strategic communication, wanted to win, and 'dislikes bad team members'. He found basic skins in games to be 'incredibly ugly' and valued the status and prestige associated with wearing exclusive skins. Identifying himself with the in-group of gamers, he considered people who play mobile games as an out-group: 'If they call themselves gamers, something feels off for many of us'. By contrast, Ulrikke did not identify as a gamer because she worried about playing the wrong games: 'Do I really fit in here? Because I haven't played too many of those [massively multiplayer online games]'. By many accounts, she might be considered the quintessential gamer, as she played daily, preferred fighting games, participated in local gaming tournaments, and designed and programed her own games.

While most boys in the sample displayed inclusive and highly positive attitudes toward female players, three boys described them as a 'red flag', 'weird', and 'not typical gamers'. Stereotypical perceptions of female players were typically based on the type of games and consoles they were associated with:

> There are few girls who play. Or, many play mobile games and Sims. I know that many girls like that; creating families and stuff. But very few play shooter games and such. And those who do, I think the majority may not necessarily be the strongest, most resourceful. (Herman, 19)

Hence, the participants were aware of the gendered expectations of a gamer, both in terms of performance and consumption. Such perceptions may reflect the gendered marketing assumptions of the industry, indicating that some players have internalized such views of girls being illegitimate players due to the games they play.

When 'Correct' Consumption Isn't Enough

The previous section has illustrated that being a gamer is associated with certain consumption patterns, such as playing the correct games on the correct consoles. However, the following text will argue that 'correct' consumption may not always or necessarily compensate for being female. Moreover, being a girl in a hostile environment can lead to silencing or cause a lack of utilization of available equipment, which consequently makes them underperform as players.

Several of the girls in the sample used strategies to conceal their gender identity from other players. These strategies included the use of gender-neutral and male nicknames, staying silent in voice-chats, and avoiding certain games altogether. Amina for example, who engaged in competitive shooter games, avoided using a microphone despite acknowledging that this gave her a strategic disadvantage in the game. She reflected on the fact that the flow of information is a key part of competitive games and that her not talking resulted in poor communication with her team members which could potentially make her a burden more than a resource to her team. These occurrences were in contrast to many of the boys' experiences, who demonstrated through the play-along to automatically resort to their microphones in voice-chats with their team.

Reflections like these led some participants to discuss the possibility of designing games without the voice-chat function to provide a better experience for girls in gaming.

Harassment in hostile environments typically worsened if girls disproved the perceptions by excelling in competitive core games, thereby defying the normative consumption patterns described earlier. Some girls in the sample had experienced disbelieving comments such as 'you are hacking', 'you are just faking', and 'that is just luck'. Sidra reported an instance from the first time she tried to play *Call of Duty*. When she started talking through her microphone, and consequently revealing herself as a girl, her team members screamed at her to 'shut up', and 'die'. Girls like Sidra and Bella therefore avoided certain games due to past negative experiences and generally stayed clear of games that had a voice-chat function:

> Most [girls] now choose to chat and not use a microphone. At least, that's what I do if I'm going to play those kinds of games because I've had bad experiences, and it's usually better when you just write in the chat (...) often, I think most people have a very neutral and non-gender-based profile. (Bella, 18)

Although Bella had the appropriate equipment to participate in effective team communication, she chose not to, as a coping mechanism to escape harassment. Upon revealing their gender through consumption, female players are denoted as illegitimate players, regardless of their skill. That is, some girls refrain from utilizing available consumption tools that can enhance their performance as gamers. Sometimes, such underutilization was imposed on girls by other players, for instance, by muting them like Danielle describes:

> If you play well as a woman, it's always like, 'Oh, you're probably just a fat pig sitting in your room every day and not going outside,' (...) 'go play something else', 'why don't you play Hello Kitty' or something (...) I feel like maybe if I were a boy, it would be easier to join most conversations. But I feel many boys don't think that girls have anything in common with them in a way, in a lobby. So there are times when I notice that I have been muted by the entire lobby. Then I'm basically just talking to myself. (Danielle, 20)

The girls' gaming descriptions can be understood as a form of 'masculinized female play' (Jenson & de Castell, 2010, p. 63), where girls engage in genres and playstyles that are typically associated with boys. Cote (2020b) finds that women who adopt such play can still be excluded from a gamer community due to their gender identity. These gendered experiences indicate that it is insufficient for girls to own and use the appropriate consumer products aligned with the gamer identity. That is, engaging in the 'right' consumption does not provide full membership in the gaming community for girls. In addition, by concealing their identities through underutilizing gaming equipment, girls inadvertently perpetuate the invisibility of female core gamers. Thus, 'correct' consumption that aligns with notions of legitimate gaming does not ensure acceptance into the gamer identity.

Boys Provide What Girls Need: Transactional Relationships and Domestic Consumption Norms

The gaming experiences of the participants revealed subtle power imbalances that positioned males as *providing* help or equipment, and females as *needing* help or equipment. The subsequent sections will demonstrate how this is achieved through transactional relationships and household dynamics.

Some players used in-game consumption to engage in transactional communication between genders. Specifically, 11 participants discussed the prevalence of gifting of in-game items between players, primarily *between* girls and *from* boys *to* girls. They stated that they engaged in gifting in games either as givers or receivers of gifts. Out of these were seven girls, three boys, and one nonbinary participant. Gifting appears to be a built-in social design element, particularly in casual games, that strengthens social ties and a sense of belonging. For instance, Bea regularly got in-game tasks in *Adopt Me!* that encouraged her to buy gifts for other players. Other examples included Ellie receiving money from male friends to buy loot boxes in *Counter-Strike: Global Offensive*, Jennie getting in-game bundles from her boyfriend and friends in *Royale High*, and Danielle borrowing skins from male players in *Valorant*. Danielle reflected on gifting in games as a transactional relationship where girls receive in-game items, and boys receive interaction with girls. In her opinion, this was one of the few benefits of games that girls could exploit to their advantage.

Although gifting can foster a sense of community between players, it can also indicate a dependency dynamic. In other words, receiving gifts can be viewed as a form of help given from boys to girls. Cote (2020b) points out that male players often offer to help female players solely based on their gender identity and argues that this forms a power imbalance that positions girls as incapable damsels in distress. Offering female players gifts in the form of consumable items also presumes women as consumers or shoppers first, and players second. This serves as another instance to demonstrate how consumption reinforces the dominant perception of male players in gaming, both through their ability and willingness to gift (implying considerable resources) and through the assumption that female players are in need or want of gifts. The underlying implication of such transactional relationships is that males are inherently superior players, which can contribute to the low self-esteem of female players.

The gamer identity as male is further perpetuated by associating gaming equipment with male spaces and male members in the household. For example, both Markus and Fadi started playing because their fathers bought them a PlayStation when they were respectively 4 and 8 years old. Iver 'simply learned to play from Dad' where his father 'taught me all the buttons and how I should play'. Moreover, Andreas built his gaming computer with his father, and Oliver's dad 'had this [gaming] equipment for a *very* long time, and then he gave it to me'. Yvon, who identifies as nonbinary, was gifted an Xbox from their older brother, who also covered half of their expenses for a new gaming computer. Several of the girls explained how they would borrow gaming equipment from their male siblings or boyfriends. For instance, Amalie borrowed a gaming computer and console from her younger brother, and Nora started to play when she could borrow her brothers' gaming equipment. Ellie explained how her parents more easily facilitated her brother's gaming than hers:

> It's mainly because of my brother that I started playing because he's also very interested in gaming. And my parents were more inclined to give him games than me. If he had games first, then I could play those games too. (Ellie, 21)

This finding connects to Bryce et al.'s (2006) idea about domestic constraints within the household, where male members of the household reproduce the idea of gaming as a predominantly male activity. Within households where there is a gender bias in gaming encouragement, there might be differences in both the willingness to identify as gamers and in the economic investment in gaming equipment. This is evident in how parents might be more inclined to facilitate boys' gaming by purchasing equipment for them, while girls may have to borrow or share equipment. Such household dynamics provide easier access to gaming equipment for male members, which then consolidates gaming within male spaces.

More boys than girls in the sample had built their own gaming computer. Girls who had built their computers had asked for assistance from a male friend or sibling as they did not feel competent enough to do it alone. This low confidence in their technical abilities might point to the low social status that girls traditionally have in technology and gaming, as pointed out by Kivijärvi and Katila (2022). According to Social Identity Theory (Tajfel & Turner, 1979), girls may compare themselves to male peers who are stereotypically viewed as more competent. This comparison can exacerbate feelings of inferiority or lower competence, reinforcing the belief that they do not belong or are not as skilled. This belief is highlighted by their perceived need to seek help from male friends or siblings when building their computers. Such internalization is central to how social identity influences individual self-esteem. It also reflects domestic norms of game consumption, reinforcing games as male spaces.

The normative consumption patterns within households described above perpetuate the idea that gaming is primarily a male activity and position girls and women as secondary users. This gendered distribution of gaming equipment shapes initial interest in gaming and affects who identifies as gamers. As many boys are encouraged to engage with video games from an early age, they may enhance their self-concept as gamers. Boys are provided with economic investment in their gaming experiences (e.g., buying them consoles), which reinforces the male gamer identity through consumer products from a young age. Girls may find it harder to claim this identity due to less facilitation and access to equipment, as they often find themselves borrowing or sharing equipment. By owning and managing equipment, and thus gaming access, boys find their consumption patterns validate their identities as gamers. Even when girls decide to engage in gaming by building their own computers, they often seek help due to a lack of confidence in their technical abilities – a sentiment not commonly reported among boys. The next section will argue that broader game marketing messages likely contribute to this difference by framing core gaming as male-dominated.

Gendered Market Dynamics Shape Preferences for Gaming Hardware and Software

The following sections argue that market mechanisms contribute to encouraging gendered consumption patterns in games, as reflected in the observed and reported motivations and preferences of different genders.

The participants played a range of different games across genres and game consoles. Together, they mentioned over 80 different games they actively played or used to play. This reflects the wide variety of games offered in the market. However, gendered patterns emerged in the types of games they played on which game consoles. For instance, many of the girls in the sample typically played on mobiles and tablets, whereas many of the boys mostly played on computers and PlayStation:

> I mostly play on the phone if I'm at someone else's house. Otherwise, it's normally iPad, because it's a bigger screen and stuff, and it's more practical to play with. (Sidra, 14)

> You need a PC that can handle a bit, to play games that are actually fun. (Aron, 14)

Crawford and Gosling (2005) also find gendered preferences for game consoles, where girls tend to play more on mobile platforms than boys, which aligns with the casual and core segmentation of the game industry. These gendered patterns might impact girls' identity work as gamers, as the stereotypical gamer label is usually associated with playing on computers or consoles such as a PlayStation or Xbox (Kelly et al., 2023). Indeed, many of the participants shared an idea of a hierarchy of gaming consoles, where computers are at the top, consoles like PlayStation and Xbox are in the middle, and mobiles and tablets are at the bottom:

> If you're a true gamer, you play on PC. And then you think everyone else is stupid. If you're kind of a gamer, you play on a console and think PC people are a bit stupid and a bit nerdy. And mobile gamers are really stupid no matter what, among gamers. Because they know nothing, they sit and play Hay Day and are stupid. (Herman, 19)

This hierarchy yields a strategy of *social creativity* (Tajfel & Turner, 1979), where core gamers claim renewed dominance by introducing new forms of comparisons to the out-group (Cote, 2020c). This is achieved by elevating the status of certain consoles associated with males (i.e., computers), and devaluing the status of other consoles associated with female players (i.e., mobiles). To illustrate, the gendered preferences for game consoles require different consumption levels. Computers typically require the most skill, the most expensive hardware (e.g., keyboard, headset, microphone, RAM, processor), and the most challenging games. PlayStation and similar consoles are attractive to players due to console-exclusive games. Mobile games require the least skill and hardware, as mobiles and tablets are often not considered as proper gaming consoles. Hence, it is perceived as the least exclusive to play mobile games because 'everyone has a phone' as Erlend pointed out. Andreas further stated that 'if you say you're a gamer and play Candy Crush: it's a bit wrong'. Cote (2020a) also points out how core games on computers and consoles are associated with higher costs compared to casual mobile games. The consoles and associated games that girls prefer are consequently devalued, as they are placed at the bottom of the hierarchy, which in turn may cause girls to internalize that playing games on tablets and mobiles does not qualify as legitimate gaming:

> If you say you're a 'gamer' and play on mobile, I think you get very looked down upon very quickly. It's not quite the, I mean, it's maybe not quite considered a, what should I say, gaming console. (Bella, 18)

Beyond game consoles, ethnographic insights from the play-along revealed that boys and girls also displayed different choices of games. A majority of the girls chose to play role-playing games like *Adopt Me!* on Roblox, social simulation games like *Heyday, Animal Crossing, Stardew Valley,* and *Sims*, and sandbox games like *Minecraft.* Most of the boys in the sample chose battle-royale games like *Fortnite*, multiplayer-online-battle-arena (MOBA) games like *League of Legends*, first-person-shooter games like *Counter-Strike: Global Offensive* and *Call of Duty*, and sports games like *FIFA* and *Rocket League*. Although these gendered preferences of gaming genres are supported by previous studies (Crawford & Gosling, 2005; Nielsen, 2015), there were many nuances and exceptions to these gendered patterns, as the participants played a substantial range of diverse games across consoles and genres.

Moreover, the play-along uncovered that many of the boys in the sample had bought cosmetics that cosmetically altered the appearance of avatars (i.e., 'skins') or weapons (i.e., 'wraps'). Some games were labeled 'childish', 'cringe', and 'for little kids', and most of these games were either tied to the consoles or the specific games girls preferred. This labeling was most prevalent among the younger boys in the sample who tended to categorize games into 'boy games' and 'girl games':

> Girl games and boy games. That's not what they are, but some people call it that. For example, if a boy plays Candy Crush, I mean, it's… and there are many boys who call it a girls' game. You can, for example, get bullied for it at school if they talk about it. Or if a girl plays Fortnite, and she writes in the chat that she's a girl (...) they get talked to very rudely; they don't belong here, they're sluts. (Erlend, 12)

Many of the girls in the sample tended toward purchasing decorative items for their in-game homes, as well as animals, clothes, and accessories for their avatar to make it look 'cuter' and 'prettier'. For example, Lilly was excited about the opportunity to buy clothes and a 'prettier body' for her avatar in Royale High so that she could 'look like a princess':

> When it's that kind of game where you can spend money on weapons and stuff, I don't find it that interesting. It doesn't interest me at all, weapons and such. But I think it's much more fun to spend money on cute clothes. (Jennie, 23)

These patterns of gendered in-game consumption are encouraged by game design. Danielle, for instance, talked about the option to purchase a 'pink gun' in *Valorant*, Ariel reported having more options to dress up her avatar if she chose a female avatar instead of a male one, and Noah reflected on the gendered 'preppy' avatar styles in Roblox that he associated with specific groups of girls:

> You get a few choices. I think it's four or five hairstyles you can choose from if you're a girl, and two or three if you're a boy. That's what you start with. (Ariel, 11)

> There's a style called preppy, and it is girls who always go, "Wow, wow, wow! Oh my god, you're so cute, yaas", those kinds of girls. Hate them. I don't hate girls; I hate those types of girls. (Noah, 10)

This indicates that some games include design elements that communicate ideas about girls' appearance being more important than boys'. The marketing and targeting of gendered gaming experiences to girls – 'pink games' – are argued to be the result of the longstanding male domination of the gaming industry, creating a clear differentiation of games for boys and girls (Grimes, 2021). This core-casual binary is not merely a matter of preferences but is actively shaped by the industry's market mechanisms that design and encourage specific games to specific genders. This points to market-driven designs that steer boys toward competitive, strategy, and action games, while girls are targeted with casual and family-oriented games. By forming two distinct consumer segments, the industry communicates gendered gaming assumptions that also affect the perceived legitimacy of different genres, consoles, and consumption patterns. The observed gendered patterns within the sample align with the industry's marketing assumption of casual and core play. The outcome is a gendered game design that reproduces a binary gender understanding.

DISCUSSION AND CONCLUSION

While substantial research has addressed gender issues in video games, this article proposes that the mechanisms through which games are marketed, designed, and consumed contribute to a highly gendered landscape. The gamer identity is associated with gendered consumption patterns which shape and consolidate gender identity and can grant membership in the gaming culture. However, displaying the 'correct' consumption patterns does not necessarily compensate for being a female player within hostile environments. Specific consumption behaviors can also situate girls as dependent on boys, both in terms of in-game transactions and access to equipment. Market dynamics, such as game design and marketing assumptions, play an important part in facilitating and encouraging such gendered consumption patterns. The following sections will elaborate on this argumentation.

Taking on a gendered social identity means attaching meaning to it based on the social context in which it is enacted, which often can lead to reinforcing gender norms and stereotypes (Carter, 2014). The gamer identity is thus defined by what is perceived as expected and widespread behavior in gaming environments. Dominant discourses surrounding what it means to be a 'true gamer' result in in-groups and out-groups, where players of other gender identities than males may struggle to fit in. The term 'gamer' primarily refers to a social identity rather than a description of the activity of 'playing'. As this article has shown, the gamer identity comes with specific expectations, such as being a skilled player in the 'right' games on the 'right' consoles. Identifying as a 'gamer' thus serves as an identity marker, which is made salient through consumption, and can grant membership in the gaming culture (Tajfel & Turner, 1979). Girls, more so than boys, have to prove themselves as gamers and tend to distance themselves from the label. Cote (2017) postulates that girls may be seen as intruders to the male space of gaming, disrupting what is otherwise perceived as a well-functioning and homogenous social group. Vermeulen et al. (2016) refer to this as a male 'gamer status threat'. The presence of female players might 'soften' the gaming environment (Cote, 2017), which can lead to some male players feeling pressure to moderate their behavior and language.

Shaw (2013) and De Grove et al. (2015) state that consumption is what defines the gamer identity. As shown in this article, boys and girls demonstrate different consumer choices which are partly influenced by the gendered patterns in the games they prefer. Specifically, gendered consumption patterns are evident in gaming hardware and software choices, as well as game activities and social interactions. Boys generally chose to play sports and shooter games, while girls tended to play role-playing games and simulations of everyday life where consumption is an essential part. Their choice of games allows for different ways to enact gender. For instance, in *Adopt Me!* players parent and care for animals, while players of *Fortnite* compete to win over other players. Consumption preferences for game consoles, game genres, and in-game items, consequently become visible symbols of gender identity and thus (non)membership to the gamer community (Tajfel & Turner, 1979).

Certain forms of gaming consumption, such as having access to consoles and playing 'legitimate' core games, can give women *partial* authorization to enter male-dominated gaming spaces (Chess, 2017). The article posits that certain consumption patterns contribute to upholding subtle power imbalances, inhibiting casual gamers a *full* authorization. For instance, adopting the expected consumption associated with the gamer identity may not be sufficient for female players, who may underutilize available tools to avoid harassment. The current results further support the notion of domestic constraints (Bryce et al., 2006), where games are associated with male members of the household. This might perpetuate gender stereotypes and limit girls' access to gaming equipment, thereby influencing their consumption choices (e.g., choosing more accessible game consoles like mobiles and tablets). Such household norms, as well as transactional relationships, form a dependency dynamic that perpetuates ideas of females as less competent players. These interplays might lead to girls being socialized to internalize and confirm the negative stereotypes of women in gaming.

Through group interactions, gender identities become more salient and developed as they can be played out in a social setting (Carter, 2014). That is, the more players interact with other players in video games, the more they reinforce their gender identity. Because boys tend to play more competitive team-based games, they might consolidate their identities as legitimate core gamers, while girls in turn reinforce their identities as casual mobile gamers. Moreover, girls tend to cope with harassment by making themselves invisible in games by using gender-neutral nicknames and muting their microphones. Such strategies effectively harm their performance in team communications, and contribute to the invisibility of female gamers in core cultures. As more girls and players with diverse gender identities become visible in gaming environments, virtual worlds may become more inclusive and less gendered. However, exposure to female players alone may not be sufficient to tackle gender stereotypes and issues in video games (Kelly et al., 2023). The dominant gendered understanding around the gamer identity – emphasized through consumption and market logic – can contribute to obscuring the great diversity among players and create a barrier to inclusion. By challenging this understanding, gaming communities and game developers are encouraged to move away from rigid, binary, and narrow understandings of gamers and gaming culture.

Recognizing the potential of game design to reproduce gendered behavior (Jensen et al., 2023), this article argues that gendered design elements and underlying market assumptions are contributing factors to the consumption patterns outlined above. This involves offering more clothing options for female avatars and creating separate markets for 'boy' and 'girl' games – or core and casual. Girl games include nurturing and feminine activities like tending to animals, dressing up, interior decorating, and playing family. Hence, gendered market elements shape different consumption preferences (Dubuisson-Quellier, 2022), position female players as shoppers (Chess, 2017), and contribute to the visibility of gender differences. According to Grimes (2021), designing games on the assumption that boys and girls have fundamentally different game preferences only reproduces gender stereotypes in gaming. Findings from Fox and Tang (2017) suggest that the way game companies respond to misogyny and implement measures to protect female players from harassment has a significant impact on their continued participation. Hence, game companies have an important position in designing gender-inclusive games. Rather than designing games specifically directed at girls, the focus ought to shift to designing games to be more inclusive for all players.

In conclusion, consumption plays a significant role in shaping the gamer identity as a socialized gendered category. As perceived legitimate gaming is predominantly associated with male players, it creates in-groups and out-groups of core and casual gamers. Gendered consumption patterns, influenced by market mechanisms, shape and consolidate gender identity. To foster inclusivity, future endeavors are encouraged to shift from narrow perceptions, urging players and game developers to embrace diversity and challenge prevailing stereotypes in gaming culture.

NOTES

1. Following the United Nations (1981) definition of youth up to 24 years.
2. All participants are given pseudonyms throughout the manuscript to protect their anonymity.
3. Throughout the manuscript, statements from the participants have been translated from Norwegian to English by the author.
4. The following analytical questions guided the coding of the material: What is expected by the gamer identity? How are gender identities negotiated? How is consumption enacted?

How do players identify as gamers? Which gender stereotypes emerge, if any? Does gender influence membership in gaming environments? What type of gender conflicts emerge? What games are boys and girls playing? Do gender identities manifest themselves differently across ages? Are some consumption patterns understood as gender-specific? Are there any consumption norms associated with being a gamer? Are there any social sanctions in response to not adhering to gender or consumption norms?

REFERENCES

Allen, M. L. (2023). "How is it that someone like you: Paragon, Damn near Saint; could love this world so Damn much but no one in it?": Horizon Zero Dawn's Aloy and the disruption of hetero-amatonormative benevolent sexism in female-led games. *Games and Culture*. https://doi.org/10.1177/15554120231179511

Ask, K., Svendsen, S. H. B., & Karlstrøm, H. (2016). Når jentene må inn i skapet: Seksuell trakassering og kjønnsfrihet i online dataspill. *Norsk medietidsskrift*, *23*(1), 1–21. https://doi.org/10.18261/issn.0805-9535-2016-01-03

Beavis, C., & Charles, C. (2007). Would the 'real' girl gamer please stand up? Gender, LAN cafés and the reformulation of the 'girl' gamer. *Gender and Education*, *19*(6), 691–705. https://doi.org/10.1080/09540250701650615

Brooks, J., McCluskey, S., Turley, E., & King, N. (2015). The utility of template analysis in qualitative psychology research. *Qualitative Research in Psychology*, *12*(2), 202–222. https://doi.org/10.1080/14780887.2014.955224

Bryce, J. O., & Rutter, J. (2003). Gender dynamics and the social and spatial organization of computer gaming. *Leisure Studies*, *22*(1), 1–15. https://doi.org/10.1080/02614360306571

Bryce, J., Rutter, J., & Sullivan, C. (2006). Digital games and gender. In J. Bryce & J. Rutter (Eds.), *Understanding digital games* (Vol. 1, pp. 185–204). Sage.

Carter, M. J. (2014). Gender socialization and identity theory. *Social Sciences*, *3*(2), 242–263. https://www.mdpi.com/2076-0760/3/2/242

Chess, S. (2017). Playing with consumption. In *Ready player two* (pp. 121–148). University of Minnesota Press. https://doi.org/10.5749/j.ctt1pwt7z7.8

Condis, M., & Morrissette, J. (2023). Dudes, boobs, and GameCubes: Video game advertising enters adolescence. *Media, Culture & Society*, *45*(6). https://doi.org/10.1177/01634437231159533

Cote, A. C. (2017). "I can defend myself": Women's strategies for coping with harassment while gaming online. *Games and Culture: A Journal of Interactive Media*, *12*(2), 136–155. https://doi.org/10.1177/1555412015587603

Cote, A. C. (2020a). Core and the video game industry: Changing perceptions of power. In *Gaming sexism: Gender and identity in the era of casual video games*. New York University Press.

Cote, A. C. (2020b). Girly games and girl gamers: Inferential sexism and its impacts. In *Gaming sexism: Gender and identity in the era of casual video games*. New York University Press.

Cote, A. C. (2020c). Introduction: Diversification and resistance in gaming's casualized era. In *Gaming sexism: Gender and identity in the era of casual video games*. New York University Press. https://doi.org/10.18574/nyu/9781479838523.001.0001

Crawford, G., & Gosling, V. (2005). Toys for boys? Women's marginalization and participation as digital gamers. *Sociological Research Online*, *10*(1), 46–56. https://doi.org/10.5153/sro.1024

De Grove, F., Courtois, C., & Van Looy, J. (2015). How to be a gamer! Exploring personal and social indicators of gamer identity. *Journal of Computer-Mediated Communication*, *20*(3), 346–361. https://doi.org/10.1111/jcc4.12114

Dubuisson-Quellier, S. (2022). How does affluent consumption come to consumers? A research agenda for exploring the foundations and lock-ins of affluent consumption. *Consumption and Society*, *1*(1), 31–50. https://doi.org/10.1332/uhiw3894

Entertainment Software Association. (2019). Essential facts about the computer and video game industry. https://www.theesa.com/wp-content/uploads/2019/2005/2019-Essential-Facts-About-the-Computer-and-Video-Game-Industry.pdf

Evans, D. M. (2022). Why consumption, why society, why now? Consumption studies and societal challenges. *Consumption and Society*, *1*(1), 231–241. https://doi.org/10.1332/lajc5187

Fox, J., & Tang, W. Y. (2017). Women's experiences with general and sexual harassment in online video games: Rumination, organizational responsiveness, withdrawal, and coping strategies. *New Media & Society*, *19*(8), 1290–1307. https://doi.org/10.1177/1461444816635778

Fron, J., Fullerton, T., Morie, J. F., & Pearce, C. (2007). The hegemony of play. In *Situated Play: Proceedings of DiGRA 2007 Conference*. Tokyo, Japan. https://ict.usc.edu/pubs/The%20Hegemony%20of%20Play.pdf

Fuentes, C., & Sörum, N. (2019). Agencing ethical consumers: Smartphone apps and the socio-material reconfiguration of everyday life. *Consumption Markets & Culture*, *22*(2), 131–156. https://doi.org/10.1080/10253866.2018.1456428

George, L., Singh, A., Bianchi-Berthouze, N., Hobbs, L., & Gibbs, J. (2023). Jamming-as-exploration: Creating and playing games to explore gender identity. In *Conference Proceedings for the 2023 CHI Conference on Human Factors in Computing Systems* (p. 22). ACM. https://doi.org/10.1145/3544548.3580646

Grimes, S. M. (2021). *Digital playgrounds: The hidden politics of children's online play spaces, virtual worlds, and connected games*. University of Toronto Press.

Hamari, J., & Lehdonvirta, V. (2010). Game design as marketing: How game mechanics create demand for virtual goods. *International Journal of Business Science and Applied Management*, *5*(1), 14–29.

Jansz, J. (2015). 14. Playing out identities and emotions. In F. Valerie (Ed.), *Playful identities* (pp. 267–280). Amsterdam University Press. https://doi.org/10.1515/9789048523030-017

Jensen, K. H., Fynbo, L., & Hansen, N. N. (2023). The interplay between game design and social practice. *New Media & Society*. https://doi.org/10.1177/14614448231187820

Jenson, J., & de Castell, S. (2010). Gender, simulation, and gaming: Research review and redirections. *Simulation & Gaming*, *41*(1), 51–71. https://doi.org/10.1177/1046878109353473

Jenson, J., & de Castell, S. (2011). Girls@Play. *Feminist Media Studies*, *11*(2), 167–179. https://doi.org/10.1080/14680777.2010.521625

Jerolmack, C., & Khan, S. (2014). Talk is cheap: Ethnography and the attitudinal fallacy. *Sociological Methods & Research*, *43*(2), 178–209. https://doi.org/10.1177/0049124114523396

Kelly, D., Nic Giolla Easpaig, B., & Castillo, P. (2023). 'You game like a girl': Perceptions of gender and competence in gaming. *Games and Culture*, *18*(1), 62–78. https://doi.org/10.1177/15554120221077730

Kivijärvi, M., & Katila, S. (2022). Becoming a gamer: Performative construction of gendered gamer identities. *Games and Culture*, *17*(3), 461–481. https://doi.org/10.1177/15554120211042260

Kuss, D. J., Kristensen, A. M., Williams, A. J., & Lopez-Fernandez, O. (2022). To be or not to be a female gamer: A qualitative exploration of female gamer identity. *International Journal of Environmental Research and Public Health*, *19*(3). https://doi.org/10.3390/ijerph19031169

Lee, H. W., Chang, K., Uhm, J. P., & Owiro, E. (2023). How avatar identification affects enjoyment in the metaverse: The roles of avatar customization and social engagement. *Cyberpsychology, Behavior, and Social Networking*. https://doi.org/10.1089/cyber.2022.0257

Lopez-Fernandez, O., Williams, A. J., & Kuss, D. J. (2019). Measuring female gaming: Gamer profile, predictors, prevalence, and characteristics from psychological and gender perspectives [Original Research]. *Frontiers in Psychology*, *10*. https://doi.org/10.3389/fpsyg.2019.00898

Lynch, T., Tompkins, J. E., van Driel, I. I., & Fritz, N. (2016). Sexy, strong, and secondary: A content analysis of female characters in video games across 31 years. *Journal of Communication*, *66*(4), 564–584. https://doi.org/10.1111/jcom.12237

Nielsen, D. (2015). Identity performance in roleplaying games. *Computers and Composition*, *38*, 45–56. https://doi.org/10.1016/j.compcom.2015.09.003

Paaßen, B., Morgenroth, T., & Stratemeyer, M. (2017). What is a true gamer? The male gamer stereotype and the marginalization of women in video game culture. *Sex Roles*, *76*(7), 421–435. https://doi.org/10.1007/s11199-016-0678-y

Reich, C. J., & Steinnes, K. K. (2023). *Children's consumption in video games and how it affects social relations – Interim report 2 from the project "Pay to play"* (Consumption Research Norway, report 13–23). https://hdl.handle.net/11250/3101053

Rodriguez-Barcenilla, E., & Ortega-Mohedano, F. (2022). Moving towards the end of gender differences in the habits of use and consumption of mobile video games. *Information*, *13*(8), 380. https://www.mdpi.com/2078-2489/13/8/380

Shaw, A. (2012). Do you identify as a gamer? Gender, race, sexuality, and gamer identity. *New Media & Society*, *14*(1), 28–44. https://doi.org/10.1177/1461444811410394

Shaw, A. (2013). On not becoming gamers: Moving beyond the constructed audience. *Ada: A Journal of Gender, New Media & Technology*, (2). https://doi.org/10.7264/N33N21B3

Skelly, T. A. M., Haulund Jensen, K., & Halkier, B. (2023). The convenience of gaming. *Consumption and Society*, *2*(1), 102–121. https://doi.org/10.1332/plws2488

Smahel, D., Machackova, H., Mascheroni, G., Dedkova, L., Staksrud, E., Olafsson, K., Livingstone, S., & Hasebrink, U. (2020). EU kids online 2020: Survey results from 19 countries. *EU Kids Online*. https://doi.org/10.21953/lse.47fdeqj01ofo

Statista. (2022). Games market revenue worldwide in 2021. *Video Gaming & eSports*. https://www.statista.com/statistics/278181/global-gaming-market-revenue-device/

Statista. (2024). Video game market revenue worldwide from 2019 to 2029. https://www.statista.com/statistics/1344668/revenue-video-game-worldwide/

Steinnes, K. K. (2024). Architecting virtual storefronts: How in-game shops are designed to encourage consumption. *Consumption Markets & Culture*, 1–18. https://doi.org/10.1080/10253866.2024.2385562

Tajfel, H., & Turner, J. (1979). An integrative theory of intergroup conflict. In M. J. Hatch & M. Schultz (Eds.), *Organizational identity*. Oxford University Press.

Thorhauge, A. M., & Gregersen, A. (2019). Individual pastime or focused social interaction: Gendered gaming practices among Danish youth. *New Media & Society*, *21*(7), 1444–1464. https://doi.org/10.1177/1461444818823546

Turner, P., & Turner, S. (2009). Triangulation in practice. *Virtual Reality*, *13*(3), 171–181. https://doi.org/10.1007/s10055-009-0117-2

Vanderhoef, J. (2013). Casual threats: The feminization of casual video games. *Ada: A Journal of Gender, New Media, and Technology*, (2), 1–28.

Vermeulen, L., Vanden Abeele, M., & Van Bauwel, S. (2016). A gendered identity debate in digital game culture. *Press Start*, *3*(1), 1–16.

Warde, A. (2017a). The development of the sociology of consumption. In A. Warde (Ed.), *Consumption: A sociological analysis* (pp. 33–55). Palgrave Macmillan. https://doi.org/10.1057/978-1-137-55682-0_3

Warde, A. (2017b). Introduction. In A. Warde (Ed.), *Consumption: A sociological analysis* (pp. 1–12). Palgrave Macmillan. https://doi.org/10.1057/978-1-137-55682-0_1

Zimmermann, D., Wehler, A., & Kaspar, K. (2022). Self-representation through avatars in digital environments. *Current Psychology*. https://doi.org/10.1007/s12144-022-03232-6

BETWEEN DISTRIBUTED AGENCY AND CHOICE ARCHITECTURE: COMPARING NUDGE AND PRACTICE THEORETICAL APPROACHES TO CHANGING CONSUMPTION

Johanna Sofia Adolfsson, Arve Hansen and Ulrikke Wethal

University of Oslo, Norway

ABSTRACT

How to change consumption patterns remains one of the most wicked global sustainability challenges, and it is increasingly acknowledged that such wicked problems require interdisciplinary solutions. In this chapter, we ask what can be learnt from contrasting two approaches to sustainable consumption that only to a very limited extent interact. First, psychological approaches to consumption have been immensely influential concerning individual behavioural change, particularly through their theorisations of 'nudge' and 'choice architecture'. Second, social practice theories (SPTs) have obtained a dominant position in sociocultural approaches to consumption, focusing on how bodily, social and material elements combine into taken for granted daily routines that make up shared patterns of (unsustainable) social life. Interestingly, despite the theoretical approaches' different ontologies and analytical loci, nudge theory and practice theories seem to end up in surprisingly similar recommendations for facilitating sustainable change. In this chapter, we explore the differences and similarities of two theoretical bodies that rarely interact, with the aim to explore the room for breaking out of disciplinary silos and investigate potentials for cross-field pollination. We

Consumers and Consumption in Comparison
Comparative Social Research, Volume 37, 189–213

ISSN: 0195-6310/doi:10.1108/S0195-631020240000037009

use the empirical case of continuity and change in meat consumption, but the dynamics discussed are arguably relevant for all fields of consumption. We demonstrate that while cross-pollination between nudge and practice theories could potentially increase political attention as well as be used to deliver more precise and tailored interventions, the diverging ontological underpinnings of these directions of thought significantly reduce the potential for further co-development.

Keywords: Consumption patterns; behavioural change; social practice theories; nudge theory; environmental consciousness

INTRODUCTION

Household consumption patterns are increasingly placed at the core of contemporary climate and environmental challenges, estimated to contribute to over 70% of global greenhouse gas (GHG) emissions (Dubois et al., 2019) and between 50 and 80% of total resource use in affluent societies (Ivanova et al., 2016). Recent years have seen renewed attention to 'demand-side mitigation' (IPCC et al., 2022) and lifestyle changes (Wiedmann et al., 2021), and widespread acknowledgement that solutions to global environmental challenges ultimately requires understanding and changing human behaviour (Kurz et al., 2015). Policy makers also tend to lean towards the belief that, confronted with an individualised citizenry and social complexity, the most effective – if not the only – way to tackle wicked problems like the climate crisis is by encouraging citizens themselves to act, such as choosing to live more sustainably (Chatterton, 2016; Leggett, 2014; Reid and Ellsworth-Krebs, 2019). Yet tackling unsustainable consumption has proved challenging and there is no consensus on how to best do so. The mainstream sustainability agenda has tended to bifurcate into either focusing on how to make the production of household goods more energy efficient or increasing the knowledge and information available for consumers to make 'greener' choices (Klitkou et al., 2022). Despite a growing recognition that solving wicked problems demands interdisciplinary approaches, research on consumption and sustainability tends to stay firmly within disciplinary boundaries.

A wide range of fields have sought to explain how specific consumption patterns take hold and evolve, as well as why many environmentally unsustainable consumption patterns are often highly stubborn to change (see, for example Hansen & Nielsen, 2023; Quoquab and Mohammad, 2020; Sandberg, 2021 for overviews). While it is increasingly acknowledged that consumption patterns are not mere products of individual choices, a dividing line across many of these fields is still the understanding of consumption as either determined mainly by cognitive processes *or* sociocultural and material contexts. In this chapter, we ask what can be learnt from contrasting two approaches to sustainable consumption that only to a very limited extent interact. First, behavioural and psychological approaches to consumption have been immensely influential concerning individual behavioural change, including through their influence on behavioural economics, but also in consumer research within fields such as marketing and environmental sciences. Theorisations around 'planned behaviour', 'agency', 'cognitive dissonance' and 'nudging' define much of mainstream thinking on sustainable change at the level of the individual. Second, although quite far from the impact of behavioural approaches, social practice theories (SPT) have obtained a dominant position in social-scientific research on sustainable consumption beyond psychology and economics. For the sake of the discussion in this chapter, we group this diverse research field together as 'sociocultural approaches' due to their shared focus on understanding consumption as a fundamentally collective phenomenon, examined through 'lenses of culture, materials and practices, thereby emphasising its social embeddedness' (Warde, 2022, p. 12). There have recently been theoretical developments that we understand as an opening for closer conversation across disciplinary divides. For example, some psychological approaches have sought to expand behavioural models to increasingly consider broader aspects of 'context' in determining choices (Graça et al., 2019; Mitchie et al., 2011). Within practice approaches, often accused of neglecting the consumer all together (see Evans et al., 2017; Welch et al., 2020), there have been recent attempts to open more analytical space for reflexive consumers, or at least the bounded agency of individual 'practitioners' (see Christensen et al., 2024; Wethal et al., 2024). This slight 'convergence' has however mostly taken place without much direct interaction (for notable exceptions see Kutz et al., 2015; Blue et al., 2016; Reid and Ellsworth-Krebs, 2019), and many studies continue to lean on stubborn caricatures of 'the other' (Kutz et al., 2015).

The overarching goal of this chapter is to see what can be gained from bringing different conceptualisations of consumption and change into closer conversation. Specifically, we bring SPT into conversation with one of the most influential behavioural approaches over the recent decades, emerging through a combination of behavioural economics and psychology; nudge theory. While these entry points are somewhat different in scope, size and influence, and represent 'fundamentally different perspectives on the nature of human action' (Reid & Ellsworth-Krebs, 2019, p. 297; see also Welch, 2016), we find it particularly intriguing that nudge theory and SPT often seem to end up in relatively similar recommendations for how to facilitate change. In particular, both approaches seem to agree that changes to the material environment in which consumption takes place can play a crucial role in shaping consumption patterns (Cass et al., 2018; Thaler et al., 2012; Wilhite, 2008). Also, both approaches place strong focus on habits and agency. That said, the theory of change behind these suggestions differs considerably, as we discuss further below. We will also draw on examples from broader behavioural approaches within psychology to situate nudge theory within wider psychological discussions and make it more contrastable with the plurality and heterogeneity underneath the umbrella term 'theories of practice' (Welch, 2016).

We use meat consumption (and reduction) as the empirical case for exploration. As a contested consumption domain that attracts much popular attention among consumers and in the media and which has considerable environmental impact (Parlasca & Qaim, 2022), meat eating and attempts to change or reduce meat consumption has attracted considerable academic attention over the recent decade (see Dagevos, 2021; Hansen et al., 2023 for recent overviews). As is characteristic for the field in general, this research has largely taken place within academic 'silos' with little cross-disciplinary integration (see Graça et al., 2019). After a theoretical introduction where we focus on behavioural and practice approaches to change and zoom in on and compare central conceptualisations within nudge and SPT, we examine how both fields engage with meat consumption and change. We end with a discussion on policy implications, limitations and future avenues for interdisciplinary research.

BEHAVOURIAL AND SOCIOCULTURAL APPROACHES TO CHANGE

In recent decades, cognitive psychology has established itself as one of the most influential disciplines concerning how mental processes influence behaviour, and how to promote individual behavioural change (Faux, 2014; Lembcke et al., 2019). Psychology has had a large influence on behavioural economics, creating a hybrid of economic and psychological theories to better understand individual decision-making processes. After the publication of the first edition of Richard Thaler and Cass Sunstein's book *Nudge: Improving Decisions About Health, Wealth and Happiness* in 2008, the concept almost immediately gained significant attention, and has since been applied in various climate and environmental policies across the world, particularly regarding how to alter individuals' consumption patterns. Nudge theory is a conceptual framework that promotes an implementation of subtle and indirect interventions, termed *nudges*, to influence human behaviour and choice-making in a positive and predictable way. Nudge theory is generally said to have its ontological origins in behavioural sciences, among other psychology and behavioural economics (Marchiori et al., 2017; Pedwell, 2017; Reid & Ellsworth-Krebs, 2019). In line with these roots, nudge theory views human behaviour as influenced and shaped both by individual psychology and the material environment (see more below). The central idea behind nudge is inspired by decades of psychological research on cognitive biases and logical fallacies (Gigerenzer & Todd, 1999; Kahneman & Tversky, 1979; Tversky & Kahneman, 1974) and rests on the principle that people, due to cognitive limitations, often make irrational decisions that hamper their health, wealth and happiness. Therefore, by understanding human psychology and by using strategical changes in the way choices are framed, the use of nudges 'gently pushes' individuals into making 'better' decisions (Thaler & Sunstein, 2008), which improves their well-being. Several techniques can be employed to nudge individuals in the 'right' direction, and the most central include; Providing clear and easily accessible information, for example displaying information about nutrition, environmental impact, etc.; Using social norms, for instance providing information about the positive behaviour of others to encourage individuals to adopt the same manners; Employing default options, e.g. setting a desired choice as standard; Using non-monetary or monetary rewards and incentives to affect a desired outcome; Employing visual elements and situational cues to draw attention to a particular behaviour or choice, such as displaying images that encourage environmental-friendly options (Ledderer et al., 2020). Overall, nudge theory emphasises transparency; individuals should always be able to understand the interventions they are targeted by, and always be able to opt out of nudges if they wish. Therefore, the inventors of nudge argue that such incentives can be ethically sound and cost-effective approach for policymakers and organisations to improve outcomes (Thaler & Sunstein, 2008). The most applied nudge-policies in this field regard issues related to recycling, waste reduction, reduced energy usage and healthier and more sustainable food consumption (see Crago et al., 2020; Hansen et al., 2021; John et al., 2009; Kurz, 2018).

Studies on individuals' climate actions typically centre on their effect – specifically targeting the most impactful actions to countering climate change. As put by Cameron et al. (2023, p. 1), conventional Western psychology remains centred on 'the science of behaviour prediction and control', and regarding the environmental crisis, its primary focus lies in addressing 'short-term behavioural and/or emotional dimensions.' These approaches have been repeatedly and heavily criticised by consumption researchers from other fields. For example, according to Welch (2016) 'the holy grail (of behaviour change) is as allusive as ever and behaviour change initiatives have delivered only marginal gains in tackling the unfolding crises of environmentally damaging consumption and non-communicable diseases.'

Within what can be labelled as sociocultural approaches to consumption, and particularly within the sociology of sustainable consumption (see Sahakian et al., 2022), theories of practice have taken hold as the leading ontological entry point. These exist in a wide variety of forms, most of which are united through focusing on social practices, rather than individuals or 'structures' as the main unity of analysis. This includes more than just adding social context to understand individual behaviour. While arguably less coherent than nudge theory, SPT operate with a social ontology in which social life is constituted by practices and the relations between them (see Schatzki, 2016). For the field of consumption, this means that focusing on individual consumers as the main agents of change from this perspective is unproductive, as human action only becomes meaningful as part of practice (e.g. Shove, 2010). Instead, SPT analyses focus on how broader social and material (hereafter socio-material) configurations complicate efforts to make consumption patterns more sustainable (Sahakian & Wilhite, 2014), even among highly motivated consumers (see Volden & Hansen, 2022; Wethal et al., 2024).

The resurgence of practice theories within consumption studies during the early 2000s largely emerged as a critique of existing approaches dominated either by rational choice and utilitarian models of sovereign consumers or by an emphasis on conspicuous consumption and cultural expressivism through style, taste and identity (Warde, 2014). Theories of practice build on long traditions of social theory, with Pierre Bourdieu and Anthony Giddens as central scholars. Practice theories have been influential in turning the gaze towards the sustainability implications of ordinary, mundane and taken-for-granted forms of consumption (see Shove, 2003; Sahakian & Wilhite, 2014). One strength of practice theories further lies in explaining how bodily, social and material elements combine into taken-for granted daily routines that make up shared patterns of (unsustainable) social life. As such, practices are often studied together as sequences of events rather than as isolated entities (Castelo et al., 2021), for instance how commute and shopping tend to be intertwined (Greene et al., 2022). Consumption, then, occurs as 'moments' in broader sets of interrelated practices (Warde, 2005), meaning that changing consumption patterns demands a transformation of the practices in which individuals participate, not informing or persuading individuals to make better choices (Hargreaves, 2011). White et al. (2022, p. 2) thus argue that practice theory 'is particularly useful in the exploration of pro-environmental behaviours as it allows for the decentralisation of individuals from analysis and for attention to instead be drawn towards the social and collective organisation of practices.'

We argue that behavioural theorists tend to misunderstand practice theories as merely involving adding social context to individual behaviour. On the other hand, social practice theorists tend to demonstrate considerable scepticism towards behavioural and psychological approaches to consumption, including nudge theory. Elizabeth Shove (2010), one of the most influential scholars of contemporary practice-oriented consumption research, has indeed argued that there is a 'yawning gulf' between the potential contribution of social sciences and the conceptualisations of social change that tend to dominate environmental policy, focusing on 'the ABC' of attitudes, behaviour and choice (see also the discussion between Whitmarsh et al. (2011) and Shove (2012) in response to Shove's original text). As Shove argues, this gulf comes from the fact that these are inherently different ways of understanding society. They represent different ontological entry points, or different understandings of 'the fundamental nature, structure, dimension or elements' of social phenomena (Schatzki, 2016, p. 28). In the following section, we approach some of the central conceptualisations within each of the approaches.

Contrasting conceptualisations

Habits

Both nudge and practice approaches have given ample attention to the role of habits in structuring behaviour and in turn consumption, although from different starting points. The nudge framework incorporates the renowned psychologist Daniel Kahneman's (2011) theory on two cognitive systems of thinking, commonly known as *System 1* and *2*. These two systems make up different modes of thinking that affect our decision-making. In short, System 1 thinking operates rapidly, automatic, instinctive, intuitive, habitual and unconscious. System 2 thinking – in contrast – involves a process that requires concentration; it is slow, deliberate, effortful, logical and conscious. While System 1 thinking is understood to be influenced by cognitive biases, which are based on quick assessments, habits, emotions, associations and experiences, System 2 on the other hand, operates with complexity: requiring concentration, analyses, evaluation and critical thinking. The System 2 thinking's effortfulness, analytical and rational feature may help us overcome cognitive biases and 'short cuts' characterised by System 1 thinking. Thus, by recognising the interplay between the two systems, we may make more informed choices (Kahneman, 2011). The policy challenge, then, becomes how to 'unlock or break habits: freeing (people) to choose more sustainable ways of life and drawing their behaviour back into the zone of (anticipated) policy influence' (Shove, 2012, p. 101; see also Lehner et al., 2016).

From a social practice approach, a habit is similarly considered an automated form of regular and contextualised behaviour, but practice theorists are more concerned with how different shared patterns of behaviour interrelate, and 'seek to map the sociohistorical trajectories of sets of practices and the ways in which their co-ordinated habitual performance can become established (or derailed) as a normalised aspect of the everyday social world' (Kutz et al., 2015, p. 115). A habit is considered a particular form of social practice, and (somewhat resembling System 1 thinking) one that does not employ cognition and reflexivity (Wilhite, 2012) but is 'recurrently and relatively consistently reproduced' (Shove, 2012, p. 101). Habits are deeply shaped by practitioners' habitus and practical knowledge (Bourdieu, 1977), meaning that they build on experience with and fields of dispositions for action within a certain social and cultural space. Habits are shaped and strengthened by embodied knowledge. Processes of enculturation and training can embed practical knowledge within the body, in turn creating 'embodied agency' in which bodies 'intend certain situations' (Wilhite, 2012, p. 89). In other words, in certain contexts people act without necessary reflection upon why and how they act, and these unreflective forms of acting are strengthened by repetition (see also Jacobsen & Hansen, 2021). Habits are further shaped and strengthened by materially embedded knowledge, meaning that 'things take on different uses and meanings in different sociocultural settings', in turn influencing how to behave in different social settings (Wilhite, 2012, p. 90). The strength of habits, then, is shaped by their bodily embeddedness, social significance and the material context in question (Wilhite, 2012). Habits are from this perspective not considered actions inferior to those based on more active choice, but are considered 'effective, often rewarded and socially honourable' mechanisms of the social world in themselves (Warde, 2016, p. 198). More importantly in this context, habits are not individual achievements, but collective processes steered by shared conventions, infrastructures and goals (Wilhite, 2012).

Material Surroundings

As indicated above, both SPT and nudge theory agree that material surroundings can play an important role in shaping human behaviour (se also Warde, 2016). Indeed, this is one of the fundamental ideas of nudge – changing the 'hard' context in which action takes place can change how people act (McNeill, 2023). This is captured by the concept of *choice architecture*, in turn stressing the importance of carefully designing environments for optimal decision-making (Thaler & Sunstein, 2008). That is, the choice architecture emphasises that the ways in which decisions are presented and promoted will have fundamental impact on *how* and *what* individuals choose, and these are in turn and in different ways designed by 'choice architects'; institutions and individuals that construct the choice-context. Nudges are thus the tools with which the choice architecture may be altered to steer people's decision-making (Thaler & Sunstein, 2008). Changing the material environment where choices take place has been a popular implementation of nudge, with common examples including the placement of healthy food in stores or the use of smaller plates to get people to eat less. But also speed bumps, traffic signs or any kind of alteration to the material world surrounding us that does not force but encourage certain behaviour can be considered a nudge. Moreover, 'the choice architecture is also inevitable' (Legget, 2014, p. 5), that is, it is not possible to avoid introducing options and choices to people in one way or the another. Therefore, supporters of nudging can dismiss ethical concerns regarding what might be argued to be manipulation: 'to put any information, policy or product into the world necessarily involves framing the choices of – or nudging – the end user in some way' (Legget, 2014, p. 5; Qizilbash, 2009). This framework justifies choice architects' attempt to influence or shape the way people make decisions. To further elucidate nudge as an approach, it is useful to briefly address the ideology of *libertarian paternalism* (Brachem et al., 2019), coined by Thaler and Sunstein (2003, p. 179) as a framework 'that preserves freedom of choice but authorised both private and public institutions to steer people in directions that will promote their welfare.' That is, the concept of libertarian paternalism relies on the assumption that it is possible to promote favourable choices while simultaneously respecting and caring for individual autonomy. In essence, nudge is often seen as a method or tool used within the libertarian paternalism approach (Thaler & Sunstein, 2008).

Within practice theories, social life is considered to transpire through 'a mesh' of practices and material arrangements, making it both depend on and be co-shaped by material infrastructures, devices, technologies and artefacts (Schatzki, 2010, p. 130). Indeed, all social practices depend on a range of material structures and objects being existent and available (Shove & Walker, 2014), in turn prefiguring practices by making some actions more accessible, attractive, or convenient than others (Schatzki, 2002). However, material arrangements are not considered external to the social practices themselves, as they are only given meaning through the performance of certain practices (Shove & Walker, 2014). As put by Cass et al. (2018, p. 164), inspired by Star and Ruhleder (1996), 'material arrangements, technologies and systems can stand in infrastructural relation to practices.' Hence, materials can take different shapes depending on whether they are in the 'background' of practices (such as power grids) or used actively by participants (e.g. the mobile phone) (see Shove, 2017). Material arrangements then fundamentally shape (and are shaped by) practices. Some strands of practice-theoretical consumption research have found inspiration in conceptualisations of 'material scripts' (Akrich, 1992; Latour, 1992) to analyse such relationships. Scripts are considered 'pathways' built into infrastructures and technologies in order to encourage and enable particular forms of actions (see Fuentes & Fuentes, 2022) that, together with social expectations, frame certain performances as convenient, acceptable and desirable (Hansen & Wethal, 2023). As such, while SPT scholars would expect changes to occur incrementally and slowly, they would agree with cognitive sciences and nudge that altering the material environments in which consumption occurs might be a fruitful place to trigger change in behaviour (Warde, 2016).

Agency

Conventional behaviour and psychological approaches are epistemologically and ontologically centred on cognition, and typically do not attribute agency to surroundings, e.g. the cultural and contextual stuff surrounding the individual (Toomela, 2014). Hence, although nudge theory recognises that the environment influences how decisions are made, it does not attribute agency to the environment itself (Thaler & Sunstein, 2008). Put simply, psychological and behavioural approaches treat social settings as the context in which individuals make choices. This context may shape behaviour by altering the availability or likelihood of choices, but it do not take on agency. However, as noted above, the importance of social influence through established social norms is considered, given how nudge can use knowledge on prevalent norms to encourage individuals to change behaviours. Agency, then, sits firmly with the individual making choices. Thaler and Sunstein have placed much importance on nudges as non-coercive instruments. They are *not* explicitly commanding or prohibiting 'bad' choices, they are *not* compromising or restricting our individual autonomy and freedom to make fewer good decisions; if we wish to drop the seatbelt, eat candy for lunch and stick with un-eco-friendly behaviour, nudges are not designed to stop us. Rather, in a non-intrusive manner, nudges are understood to improve people's decision-making towards more beneficial and desired cognition and behaviour (Thaler & Sunstein, 2008, 2009).

In contrast, within practice theories, human behaviour is inherently collective and socially embedded in the contexts in which they operate. By focusing on practices and the connections between them, SPT seeks to overcome traditional agent-structure dilemmas within social theories (Giddens, 1984). As noted above, practice ontology understands social practices, not individuals, to represent the basic units of society. In other words, everything is social, and it makes little sense to separate individuals from the contexts that define them and their acts. This approach redirects the focus towards how consumption as part of practice occurs as result of normative expectations for proper performance. In sum, consumption is considered deeply 'embedded in wider socioeconomic, political and cultural configurations' (Welch et al., 2020, p. 3; see also Warde, 2022). Moreover, from a practice theoretical approach, the fact that actions are mediated by the material world is understood as more than the context for choices – it involves the material world itself taking on agency. Agency, then, is considered to be distributed between bodily, social and material processes (Sahakian & Wilhite, 2014; Shove & Watson, 2012). To explicate, Wilhite (2012, p. 90) proposes that agency is distributed between the body and the material world, but that both 'result from exposure to the social world'. SPT here takes inspiration from Science and Technology Studies and Bruno Latour's (2005) theorisations around material agency where agency is not an inherent quality of humans, but the result of actor networks consisting of both humans and non-humans (Fuentes & Fuentes, 2022; see also Verbeek, 2006).

In this section, we have explored some of the ontological and theoretical starting points that define nudge theory and social practice theory. While both SPT and nudge theory emphasise the importance of understanding the social and material context in which consumption takes place, this insight emerges from very different ontological entry points. As we return to in the section below, this has implications for approaches to how to change consumption, particularly in the long run. In the following, we explore how these theorisations are employed, and how they overlap and divert, within the empirical context of meat reduction.

APPROACHING MEAT CONSUMPTION

Globally, we eat twice as much meat per person compared to 60 years ago. Significant parts of this increase have taken place in developing and emerging economies, but overconsumption of meat in affluent societies stands out as a core sustainability challenge (Parlasca & Qaim, 2022; Poore & Nemecek, 2018). Indeed, estimations show that Western citizens must decrease their consumption of red meet by 90% to meet global climate targets (Froggatt & Wellesley, 2019). Due to the ways in which meat eating is societally embedded and simultaneously highly habitual and normatively contested, meat is an illustrative case of the complexity of consumption (see Hansen et al., 2023). While research shows that consumers increasingly identify as meat reducers – reportedly as much as 30% of the population in Belgium and 40% in the Netherlands, for example (see Dagevos, 2021; Dagevos & Verbeke, 2022) – 'meaty routines' (Sundet et al., 2023) have proven highly resilient to change. For example, recent studies in Denmark, Norway, the Netherlands and the United Kingdom have shown how high levels of meat consumption persist alongside rapidly growing interest among consumers to eat less meat, and how even devoted meat reducers (who are not vegetarians or vegans) struggle to eat less meat in everyday life (see Dagevos & Verbeke, 2022; Mylan, 2018; Sundet et al., 2023; Wendler, 2023). Perhaps due to a combination of its obvious importance for the environment and for people's everyday life as well as how difficult many find it to break out of meat-intensive habits and lifestyles, the literature on meat eating, meat reduction and meat avoidance have blossomed over the past decade (see, for example Bjørkdahl & Syse, 2023; Dagevos, 2021; Kanerva, 2021; Hansen & Syse, 2021). Outside behavioural sciences, and beyond a large literature on meat production (see, e.g. Winders & Ransom, 2019), approaches to study meat consumption are dispersed across many different disciplines and, again, often with little direct interaction (see Hansen et al., 2023; Morris et al., 2021 for recent overviews). In the following, we approach meat consumption and reduction both through theories of social practice *and* from the perspective of behaviour and psychology with a focus on nudge.

Psychologists have regarded meat consumption as an interesting case for exploring how individuals rationalise behaviour, navigate moral decisions and 'negotiate intrapersonal conflicts' (Rothgerber, 2020, p. 1). Understanding how meat-eating individuals justify their consumption behaviour – particularly when facing external challenges – is seen as imperative for better understanding why meat consumption, albeit the massive focus on its detrimental impact on the climate, proves so difficult to change. As cultural psychologist Rozin asserts, 'meat should be of special interest to psychologists, because it is a quintessential example of the interesting and important state of ambivalence' (2007, p. 404). This ambivalence is considered to stem from the discrepancies between people's attitudes and ideals and their behaviour, creating a value-action gap (Kollmuss & Agyeman, 2002; Meistrup & Klitmøller, 2023). That is, although individuals are concerned about the negative impact of meat eating on animal welfare and the environment, they simultaneously continue to consume meat. To explain this 'meat paradox' (Loughnan et al., 2010; Loughnan et al., 2014) psychologists have focused on Cognitive Dissonance Theory (CDT) (Collier et al., 2021), concerned with the mental strategies individuals apply to deal with and reduce the negative arousals from cognitive dissonance (e.g. the discomfort that individuals experience when they hold two or more conflicting values, attitudes and beliefs simultaneously). To resolve the meat paradox individuals either 'bring their behaviour in line with their beliefs, e.g. by not eating meat, or they bring their beliefs in line with their behaviour, e.g. by engaging in moral disengagement or avoidant strategies' (Bastian & Loughnan, 2017; Collier et al., 2021, p. 2; Loughnan et al., 2014). For example, perceiving animals as distinctively differently living beings than humans is frequently employed as a method, emerging when individuals who cherish their pets, advocate for animal rights and stand up for animal welfare, simultaneously consume animal products (Çoker & van der Linden, 2022; Loughnan et al., 2010; Loughnan et al., 2014). The meat paradox has been a significant framework in the psychological examination of meat consumption (Rothgerber & Rosenfeld, 2021). Thus, by rationalising and justifying a questioned behaviour, for instance on the basis of meat consumption being necessary, natural, normal and nice (see Joy, 2020; Piazza et al., 2015), individuals may uphold a positive self-image, and keep on with beliefs, attitudes and behaviours that might otherwise evoke feelings of guilt (Collier et al., 2021; Piazza et al., 2015).

SPT scholars also acknowledge *value-action gaps* as occurring when people cannot fully bring their behaviour in line with their attitudes and ideals, but this is neither considered an individual matter nor an object of study in itself. Rather, such gaps are given, occurring as conflicts between social, material and bodily elements of practice, or through the interlinkage of and negotiations between the different practices that make up everyday life. Meat reduced eating can, for example come at odds with what is considered appropriate when hosting guests, or meat consumption may align with the social expectations of a neighbourhood barbeque or the practices of proper parenting in certain contexts (Hansen &

Wethal, 2023). For instance, in what Sundet et al. (2023) conceptualise as scripted social sites, self-declared meat reducers encounter meaty social norms, expectations and cultures that together complicate the actual implementation of their meat reduction projects. Along similar lines, through a qualitative study of Danish meat reducers, Wendler (2023) explores how arrangements of social encounters can create very different terms for the construction of mainly plant-based diets as normal. Focusing more on material surroundings, scholars have for instance, analysed how immediate food environments, such as supermarkets and restaurants, take on agentive capacities and deeply contribute to shaping the performance and meat-intensity of food practices (Biermann & Rau, 2020; Hansen & Jakobsen, 2020; Hansen & Wethal, 2023). In this vein, Fuentes and Fuentes (2022) employ the concept of 'scripted materialities' to explore how landscapes are 'programmed' by way of encouraging and enabling (but not determining) certain actions as more acceptable and desirable than others, for instance how much convenience food comes with meat consumption as an embedded expectation, or how food outlets in many contexts are highly meat intensive (Hansen & Wethal, 2023).[1] Such insights are in many ways shared by behavioural approaches, based on evidence from intervention studies where changing the context in which people make choices has contributed to changing their meat consumption (Byerly et al., 2018), although, as discussed below, the conceptualisation of agency within these situations remain different.

Practice theoretical approaches further challenge the basic assumption that people are intentionally choosing what they eat, instead seeing food consumption as often 'mindless', outside of rational and deliberate thought (Warde, 2016). While similar findings are common in much behavioural work (Graves & Roelich, 2021; Mazar et al., 2021), explanations there remain with people making decisions (Torma et al., 2018; Warde, 2016). With SPT as point of departure, instances of 'thoughtless' eating, for example situations where flexitarians eat or serve meat without giving it much thought because the situation expects it of them (see Sundet et al., 2023) are explained by distributed agency and embodied knowledge, where food environments and social settings give certain cues for what behaviour is appropriate in each situation. Bodies act as 'repositories of experiences' (Wallenborn & Wilhite, 2014, p. 63), storing knowledge about what kinds of behaviours different material and social cues hint at, in turn shaping what and how we eat. Taken together, from a practice perspective, consumption patterns taking place through 'meat-accustomed bodies' operating in meat-inducive environments can be very difficult to change (Sundet et al., 2023). Again, behavioural, psychological and sociocultural approaches would largely agree on this, but they would have very different explanations of why this is the case. While SPT scholars would refer to the social and material structures of food environments as socio-material arrangements, for nudge theorists, these would be examples of choice architectures, i.e. contexts in which choices are made, with reference to the mental infrastructures outlined by Kahneman's system 1 and system 2 thinking. This brings us back to the ontological differences discussed above, with the former understanding agency as distributed between social, material and bodily 'pillars' (Sahakian & Wilhite, 2014), and the latter understanding anything beyond the individual as external influences and agency always grounded in human cognition. Moreover, SPT has been more concerned with understanding the various factors that have led to the development of meaty consumption patterns, whereas behavioural and psychological approaches appear to be more focused on how individuals operate within status quo, as well as how to change this behaviour.

Changing Meat Consumption

SPT is often criticised for being stronger in explaining patterns of behaviour (or criticising other approaches' recommendations) than to suggest *how* to bring about change. Still, there is general agreement among practice theorists that attempts to change consumption patterns need to move beyond 'the ABC' of attitudes, behaviour and change (Shove, 2010) and instead focus on changing the broader patterns of practices within which consumption takes place. What exactly this means, however, and what the role of individual consumers is, is not always clear. When it comes to meat consumption, Wendler (2023, p. 38) calls for policies in favour of plant-friendly social interaction, focusing on 'diffusing and making available not just knowledge and information, but also social interactions that support and normalise plant-based eating.' Halkier and Lund (2023) call for a combination of information campaigns, social marketing and developing learning tools that promote plant-based eating, while Sundet et al. (2023) have suggested focusing on changing meat-intensive conventions beyond individual consumers in order to enable reinterpretations of practice. However, as conventions in turn are co-shaped by interactions between the bodily, social and material, this is not necessarily a straightforward action. Given how meat consumption is understood to be deeply embedded in infrastructures and 'foodscapes' (Hansen & Wethal, 2023; Hansen & Jakobsen, 2020), policies aiming to change the places where people buy and eat food are also obvious policy recommendations, particularly to reduce the amount of social and practical work involved in creating a meat reduced diet (Wendler & Halkier, 2023). Fuentes and Fuentes (2022) have also shown how material reconfigurations can create space for more plant-based food practices, for instance through the expanding availability of plant-based foods, social media platforms communicating plant-based cooking and the multiple scripts of material entities.

Although not labelled as such, the recommendations above are somewhat in line with nudge thinking. Indeed, nudge approaches have in general been much more efficient in proposing and influencing policy, further strengthened by the fact that much research on nudge has focused on experimenting with actual nudges, in other words focusing on causing or trying to cause change. This gives a very different empirical material (and impact) than most practice-based research, which mainly relies on observations and qualitative interview data focusing on the performance of current practices. Typical interventions used to influence people to reduce or avoid meat consumption often employ nudges that mobilise and capitalise on the 'herd mentality.' People are generally reluctant to deviate from what they consider to be normal. Thus, these nudges leverage social norms and the tendency to conform or comply with accepted behaviour, guiding individuals toward decisions that align with the perceived norm in a specific context (see Brachem et al., 2019; Çoker et al., 2022; Griesoph et al., 2021). Other examples include making vegetarian meals more visible, increasing vegetable servings and decreasing meat portion sizes, and making vegetarian options default (Kwasny et al., 2022; Torma et al., 2018). Many studies find that such 'green defaults' are effective in nudging people towards eating less meat (see Kurz, 2018; Meier et al., 2022; Randers & Thøgersen, 2023), Venema and Jensen (2023) find that nudges towards vegetarian options can be particularly effective for customers with 'weak location-bound preferences', i.e. individuals who have little experience with making choices in the specific context or environment. Other nudge-informed policy interventions would typically include 'meat-free alternatives' in institutions like workplaces and schools (Park & Barker, 2020), price increase on meat products (Rose, 2018), health information campaigns (McBey et al., 2019) and engaging influencers and celebrities to promote plant-based diets (Osman & Nelson, 2019).

While there are some obvious overlaps in terms of recommendations for facilitating change in meat consumption, there are also some clear differences. Firstly, while nudge seeks to change behaviour in one particular setting by manipulating the choice architecture surrounding it, there is little focus on long-term change. As an example, an intervention study by Coucke et al. (2022, p. 1) showed a 67% increase in sales of meat substitutes after adding them to the butchery section and next to equivalent meat products. However, when removing the nudges, sales numbers reverted to the baseline level, and the authors call for more research on the long-term effects of nudging (see also Lin et al., 2017; Mols et al., 2015 for similar critique). SPT can demonstrate less direct effects on meat consumption habits, due to different methods and fewer intervention studies, but has stronger focus on embodiment and learning and thus also on building longer term competences (Wilhite, 2014). As indicated above, past learning and experiences shape the competences for performance of practice, and new competences might need to be developed to change meat consumption. Hence, SPT scholars would find strong weaknesses in recommendations for information campaigns without also equipping consumers with the opportunity for building experiences with new ways of performing practices. Through a practice theoretical lens, changing unsustainable consumption patterns requires a transformation of the practices themselves (Hargreaves, 2011), which need to occur both through social learning of alternative ways of performing and a profound re-shaping of the socio-material environments in which consumption takes place (Wilhite, 2012). Moreover, focusing on one separate practice will be inadequate to effectuate change, as it ignores the connections, alliances and conflicts between the different practices that make up everyday life (Hargreaves, 2011, p. 95).

DISCUSSION: SOCIO-MATERIAL AND MENTAL INFRASTRUCTURES; PRACTICES VERSUS BEHAVIOUR?

In the above, we have sought to outline main similarities and differences in how the two approaches understand and conceptualise meat consumption and how to change it. We consider these findings to be relevant also for other fields of contested consumption, beyond meat. Partly, the similarities between the two theoretical approaches are masked by the way academic disciplines work and the lack of cross-fertilisation across fields of study, partly also by publishing processes incentivising scholars to make their points sound more unique than they are. For instance, Kurz et al. (2015, p. 123) argue that SPT scholars tend to create a caricature of behavioural and psychological approaches and that 'the precise mechanisms of change involved in interventions concordant with the social practice approach largely concur with the social psychological perspective.' Psychological and behavioural approaches on their hand, rarely take other approaches into account at all.

Considering that SPT and nudge theory are among the dominant approaches in their respective fields dealing with consumption-related behaviour, there is potential for a gainful exchange of ideas between them. However, albeit overlaps between the theories, some fundamental ontological differences remain, in turn hindering fruitful combination. While both approaches would agree on the limitations of targeting cognitive reason alone in order to affect change, SPT has a robust emphasis on socio-material infrastructures and nudge theory has an equally robust focus on mental infrastructures; understanding premises for change as either practice-driven or behaviour-driven. These different perspectives of human habits, agency and the role of material surroundings have – as explored above – developed from different historical trajectories, which set premises for how individual and collective change is to be understood.

SPT places little emphasis on individuals' cognitive system; instead concentrating on social relations, norms and material arrangements. From this perspective, to analyze isolated individuals does not consort with SPT's ontological stance. Individuals are understood as socially constructed and always embedded in webs of historical, cultural and structural processes (Reid & Ellsworth-Krebs, 2019). Consequently, SPT has encountered criticism for 'losing the individual' by ignoring the explicit role of individuals in constructing their behaviour (Warde, 2005; Welch et al., 2020). Likewise, nudge theory has faced criticism for neglecting external environmental influences; for placing too strong emphasis on the immediate cognitive processes and behavioural tendencies of individuals (see Brown, 2012; Legget, 2014). While the long-term efficacy of nudges is debated, the SPT framework is also criticised for its perceived lack of performative ambition and its inclination towards understanding and explaining underlying social structures over designing and prescribing guidance and interventions. Thus, because of SPTs vague and often complicated conceptualisation of how change is to be achieved, it has received limited policy interest (Hampton & Adams, 2018).

Behavioural and psychological approaches like nudge theory offer support strategies for strengthening and encouraging individuals to continue taking steps to a changed behaviour. However, nudges cannot provide individuals with guidance on how to break with the structures and institutions that dictate the sociocultural context. The social facts and social realities that societies together establish to be efficient, valid and true – be it religious traditions, food taboos or norms regarding child-upbringing – are embodied by us and make up our social worlds (Shweder, 2003). To use the above meat example, the meaty norms, practices and behaviours that both create and are created by processes of 'meatification' (Weis, 2013) have increasingly become part of both our mental and socio-material infrastructures. This is further complicated by the fact that 'eating' is not like other habits, unwired to our survival instincts, like drinking coffee at a certain hour from a specific mug or doing yoga on Mondays. Beings need nutrition to survive, and throughout human history, meat has been among the most valued sources of protein. This is again complicated by the fact that historically and presently, throughout most parts of the world, meat symbolise economic and physical well-being. Even if the levels of meat consumption seen in many affluent societies today are a quite recent phenomenon that have been made possible by global trade networks and industrialised meat production (Weis, 2013), the normalisation of these consumption patterns through bringing meat from the margins to the centre of diets is related to meat's historical role and position in many societies. Consequently, even though humans have historically eaten very little meat compared to today, changing meaty consumption patterns often meets opposition due to meat's position in longstanding historical and cultural food norms, traditions and knowledges (e.g. Hansen & Syse, 2021).

SPT's strong focus on socio-material and cultural aspects could be a valuable contribution to the nudge framework as it could potentially help explain how nudges interconnect with broader shared patterns of behaviour and their interlinkages, which render them more – or less – efficient. For instance, from SPTs perspective, meat consumption is understood as deeply connected to cultural practices and social norms (e.g. Hansen, 2021). This would then help explain why the efficacy of nudges that promotes meat reduction might vary both within and between societies depending on the populations' cultural background (Sunstein et al., 2019). That is, meaty behaviours might be the effect of religious and cultural influences, but there might also be other socio-material explanations, like the exposure of meat products in food stores, restaurant menus, commercials and expectations in social gatherings. Additionally, to efficiently nudge people in a certain population, choice architects would need to consider the social norms that are embedded in that specific cultural context. Accordingly, paying attention to how patterns of social practices influence behaviour, choice architectures can be tailored to better fit cultural contexts, in turn potentially contributing to more long-term impacts of nudge interventions. Consequently, the holistic and theoretical perspective that SPT offers, may provide nudge theory the opportunity to broaden its understanding of the individual, adding context and culture to the microlevel approach.

Similarly, nudge theory's insights into how individual decision-making is based on cognitive processes may also contribute to SPT's understanding of change. As noted, nudge interventions have proved efficient for influencing decision-making in various settings and, although SPT often shy away from prescribing specific interventions (although see, e.g. Daly, 2020; Hoolohan & Browne, 2020; Jack, 2013), applying nudge strategies could complement its more holistic and theoretical focus. That is, SPTs empirical evidence may arguably be strengthened by acknowledging how both individual cognition and immediate contexts, although embedded and co-shaped, may influence dynamics and outcomes of social practices. For example, SPT's conception of meat consumption as ingrained in socio-material and cultural practices, might, when applying nudge theory's understanding of cognitive biases, like the 'default effect' (people's tendency to stick with default options) add a valuable nuance. Accordingly, the microlevel framework that nudge theory provides may offer SPT the possibility to better place the individual within social practices. Potentially opening opportunities for understanding and explaining social norms from a more sociocultural perspective, an even more holistic perspective of the 'doings of actions' may emerge.

However, for most practice theorists, nudging would represent only a very small step on the way to deeper societal transformation, potentially brushed off as symptom relief rather than addressing the underlying causes of high levels of meat consumption (see also Hampton & Adams, 2018). As noted above, nudges offer context-specific short-term changes, with evidence suggesting that behaviours often resort to 'normal' after removing the nudge. Pedwell (2017, p. 62) discusses how 'many nudge-style policies draw heavily on corporate techniques and are largely "market-corrective" in orientation', with the goal of upholding people's freedom and choice. SPT scholars, on the other hand, would support interventions that seek to change several of the elements that hold a practice together at once, substitute practices altogether or unlock the linkages between practices (Spurling et al., 2013). This in turn means more complex solutions, and sometimes governance solutions that potentially interfere with freedom of choice in order to ignite deeper transformative change. Reasons for why policy recommendations still come out fairly similar across the SPT-nudge-divide might be that SPT scholars are less trained (or interested) in formulating recommendations based on their analyses or simply an acknowledgement from SPT scholars that hard-wired recommendations of changing the institutions and legislation around production, marketing and sale will be challenging to sell within contemporary liberal, capitalist societies.

CONCLUSION

How to change consumption patterns remains one of the most wicked global sustainability challenges, and it is increasingly acknowledged that such wicked problems require interdisciplinary solutions. In this chapter, we have sought to bring nudge theory – as an influential representative of behavioural and psychological approaches – into conversation with practice theoretical approaches. We have focused on the differences and similarities of two bodies of approaches that rarely interact, with the aim to explore the room for breaking out of disciplinary silos and investigate potentials for cross-field pollination. To do so, we have used the empirical case of continuity and change in meat consumption, but the dynamics discussed are arguably relevant for other fields of consumption.

As we have argued, nudge theory and practice theories agree on the limitations of solely targeting cognitive reason to create change but differ in how they explain behaviour and change. In essence, we argue, SPT has a robust emphasis on socio-material infrastructures and nudge theory has an equally robust focus on mental infrastructures. Combining insight from both could potentially be a way of accommodating critique of SPT for neglecting the individual, as well as critique of behavioural and psychological approaches in failing to understand how broader socio-material contexts co-shape consumption behaviours. Hence, the cross-pollination of nudge and SPT may potentially contribute to a more nuanced and holistic – even interdisciplinary – understanding both of socially shaped and cognitive-b(i)ased decision-making, by recognising the intricate interplay between socio-material and mental infrastructures. The potential outcome may be increased political attention as well as more precise and tailored interventions, incorporating both the socio-embedded and practice-driven, and cognitive behaviour-driven being. Importantly, while we do see some potential in such cross-pollination, there would probably be clear limits to how far this could be taken. Nudge and SPT operate at different levels of intervention and carry with them deep-seated ontological differences. Nudge attempts to provide optimal conditions for rationally acting individuals, not merely describe how decisions are made. As such, nudge tries to tap into the System 1 thinking to 'nudge' individuals towards rational choices – characterised by System 2. Thus, in an effort to nurture and sustain a liberal society, nudging approaches provide practical and applicable strategies for influencing behaviour. SPT, on the other hand, and akin to much of sociocultural theorisation, appears to lack a similar performative ambition. Rather, the focus is on understanding and explaining underlying social structures and dynamics than directly affecting change. These differences can in many ways explain both the inability of nudge in effecting long-term behavioural change and SPTs limited impact on policy. Thus, while cross-disciplinary engagements certainly have the potential to bring vital new insights into how to transform consumption patterns in a more sustainable direction, bringing fundamentally different theoretical approaches into closer conversation is a challenging task with uncertain outcomes.

NOTE

1. From a practice perspective, price signals can be understood as part of the material environment in which practices are performed, which, together with other forms of scripting, frame-specific actions as more doable and desirable. However, price mechanisms alone are not considered main drivers of consumption behaviour (see Warde, 2022).

REFERENCES

Akrich, M. (1992). The de-scription of technical objects. In W. Bijker & J. Law (Eds.), *Shaping technology/building society: Studies in sociotechnical change* (pp. 205–224). MIT Press.

Bastian, B., & Loughnan, S. (2017). Resolving the meat-paradox: A motivational account of morally troublesome behavior and its maintenance. *Personality and Social Psychology Review*, *21*(3), 278–299.

Biermann, G., & Rau, H. (2020). The meaning of meat: (Un) sustainable eating practices at home and out of home. *Appetite*, *153*, 104730.

Bjørkdahl, K., & Lykke, K. V. (2023). *Live, die, buy, eat: A cultural history of animals and meat* (p. 321). Taylor & Francis.

Blue, S., Shove, E., Carmona, C., & Kelly, M. P. (2016). Theories of practice and public health: Understanding (un) healthy practices. *Critical Public Health*, *26*(1), 36–50.

Bordieu, P. (1977). *Outline of a theory of practice*. Cambridge University Press.

Brachem, J., Krüdewagen, H., & Hagmayer, Y. (2019). *The limits of nudging: Can descriptive social norms be used to reduce meat consumption? It's probably not that easy* Georg-August-University Göttingen Georg-Elias-Müller-Institute of Psychology. Göttingen, Germany. manuscript (4). pdf (uio.no).

Brown, P. (2012). A nudge in the right direction? Towards a sociological engagement with libertarian paternalism. *Social Policy and Society*, *11*(3), 305–317. http://doi.org/10.1017/S1474746412000061

Byerly, H., Balmford, A., Ferraro, P. J., Hammond Wagner, C., Palchak, E., Polasky, S., Ricketss, T. H., Schwartz, A. J., & Fisher, B. (2018). Nudging pro-environmental behavior: Evidence and opportunities. *Frontiers in Ecology and the Environment*, *16*(3), 159–168.

Cameron, E., Tateo, L., & Bacigalupe, G. (2023). Call for papers: "Environmental justice and psychology: Alternative ideas on environmental issues": A topical issue of International Perspectives in Psychology: Research, Practice, Consultation. *International Perspectives in Psychology*, *12*(2), 132–133. https://doi.org/10.1027/2157-3891/a000077

Cass, N., Schwanen, T., & Shove, E. (2018). Infrastructures, intersections and societal transformations. *Technological Forecasting and Social Change*, *137*, 160–167.

Castelo, A. F., Schäfer, M., & Silva, M. E. (2021). Food practices as part of daily routines: A conceptual framework for analysing networks of practices. *Appetite*, *157*, 1–10. https://doi.org/10.1016/j.appet.2020.104978

Chatterton, T. (2016). An introduction to theories of behaviour. In F. Spotswood (Ed.), *Beyond behaviour change* (pp. 27–48). Policy Press.

Christensen, T. H., Halkier, B., Gram-Hanssen, K., Freudendal-Pedersen, M., & Krog Juvik, A. (2024). Exploring routinization and reflexivity in change and reproduction of consumption towards lower climate impact. *Journal of Consumer Culture*, *24*(1), 211–229. https://doi.org/10.1177/14695405231207599

Çoker, E. N., Pechey, R., Frie, K., Jebb, S. A., Stewart, C., Higgs, S., & Cook, B. (2022). A dynamic social norm messaging intervention to reduce meat consumption: A randomized cross-over trial in retail store restaurants. *Appetite*, *169*. https://doi.org/10.1016/j.appet.2021.105824

Çoker, E. N., & van der Linden, S. (2022). Fleshing out the theory of planned of behavior: Meat consumption as an environmentally significant behavior. *Current Psychology*, *41*(2), 681–690. https://doi.org/10.1007/s12144-019-00593-3

Collier, E. S., Oberrauter, L. M., Normann, A., Norman, C., Svensson, M., Niimi, J., & Bergman, P. (2021). Identifying barriers to decreasing meat consumption and increasing acceptance of meat substitutes among Swedish consumers. *Appetite*, *167*, 105643.

Coucke, N., Vermeir, I., Slabbinck, H., Geuens, M., & Choueiki, Z. (2022). How to reduce agri-environmental impacts on ecosystem services: The role of nudging techniques to increase purchase of plant-based meat substitutes. *Ecosystem Services*, *56*. https://doi.org/10.1016/j.ecoser.2022.101444

Crago, C. L., Spraggon, J. M., & Hunter, E. (2020). Motivating non- households with feedback and social nudges: A cautionary tale. *Energy Policy*, *145*, 1–10. https://doi.org/10.1016/j.enpol.2020.111764

Dagevos, H. (2021). Finding: Current studies on meat eaters and meat reducers. *Trends in Food Science & Technology*, *114*, 530–539. https://doi.org/10.1016/j.tifs.2021.06.021

Dagevos, H., & Verbeke, W. (2022). Meat consumption and flexitarianism in the low countries. *Meat Science*, *192*, 1–8. https://doi.org/10.1016/j.meatsci.2022.108894

Daly, J. (2020). A social practice perspective on meat reduction in Australian households: Rethinking intervention strategies. *Geographical Research*, *58*, 240–251. https://doi.org/10.1111/1745-5871.12399

Dubois, G., et al (2019). It starts at home? Climate policies targeting household consumption and behavioral decisions are key to low-carbon futures. *Energy Research & Social Science*, *52*, 144–158.

Evans, D., Welch, D., & Swaffield, J. (2017). Constructing and mobilizing 'the consumer': Responsibility, consumption and the politics of sustainability. *Environment and Planning A*, *49*(6), 1396–1412.

Faux, R. (2014). Cognitive theory. In T. Teo (Ed.), *Encyclopedia of critical psychology*. Springer. https://doi.org/10.1007/978-1-4614-5583-7_451

Fuentes, M., & Fuentes, C. (2022). Reconfiguring food materialities: Plant-based food consumption practices in antagonistic landscapes. *Food, Culture & Society*, *25*(3), 520–539.

Froggatt, A., & Wellesley, L. (2019). *Meat analogues: Considerations for the EU*. Chatham House - The Royal Institute of International Affairs.

Giddens, A. (1984). *The constitution of society: Outline of the theory of structuration*. University of California Press.

Gigerenzer, G., & Todd, P. M. (1999). *Simple heuristics that make us smart*. Oxford University Press.

Graça, J., Godinho, C. A., & Truninger, M. (2019). Reducing meat consumption and following plant-based diets: Current evidence and future directions to inform integrated transitions. *Trends in Food Science & Technology*, *91*, 380–390. https://doi.org/10.1016/j.tifs.2019.07.046

Graves, C., & Roelich, K. (2021). Psychological barriers to pro-environmental behaviour change: A review of meat consumption behaviours. *Sustainability*, *13*(21), 1–18. https://doi.org/10.3390/su132111582

Greene, M., Hansen, A., Hoolohan, C., Süßbauer, E., & Domaneschi, L. (2022). Consumption and shifting temporalities of daily life in times of disruption: Undoing and reassembling household practices during the COVID-19 pandemic. *Sustainability: Science, Practice and Policy*, *18*(1), 215–230. https://doi.org/10.1080/15487733.2022.2037903

Griesoph, A., Hoffmann, S., Merk, C., Rehdanz, K., & Schmidt, U. (2021). Guess what...?—How guessed norms Nudge climate-friendly food choices in real-life settings. *Sustainability*, *13*(15), 1–18. https://doi.org/10.3390/su13158669

Halkier, B., & Lund, T. B. (2023). Exploring everyday life dynamics in meat reduction – A cluster analysis of flexitarians in Denmark. *Appetite*, *183*, 106487.

Hampton, S., & Adams, R. (2018). Behavioural economics vs social practice theory: Perspectives from inside the United Kingdom government. *Energy Research & Social Science*. https://doi.org/10.1016/j.erss.2018.07.02346214224

Hansen, A. (2021). Eating a capitalist transformation: Economic development, culinary hybridization, and changing meat cultures in Vietnam. In A. Hansen & K. Lykke Syse (Eds.), *Changing meat cultures: Food practices, global capitalism, and the consumption of animals* (pp. 99–120). Rowman Littlefield Publishers.

Hansen, A., & Jakobsen, J. (2020). Meatification and everyday geographies of consumption in Vietnam and China. *Geografiska Annaler: Series B, Human Geography*, *102*(1), 21–39. https://doi.org/10.1080/04353684.2019.1709217

Hansen, A., & Nielsen, K. B. (2023). Consumption, sustainability and everyday life. In A. Hansen & K. B. Nielsen (Eds.), *Consumption, sustainability and everyday life* (pp. 3–26). Palgrave Macmillan.

Hansen, P. G., Schilling, M., & Malthesen, M. S. (2021). Nudging healthy and sustainable food choices: Three randomized controlled field experiments using a vegetarian lunch-default as a normative signal. *Journal of Public Health*, *43*(2), 392–397. https://doi.org/10.1093/pubmed/fdz154

Hansen, A., & Syse, K. L. (Eds.). (2021). *Changing meat cultures: Food practices, global capitalism, and the consumption of animals*. Rowman & Littlefield.

Hansen, A., & Wethal, U. (2023). 'It's just pølse': Convenient meat consumption and reduction in Norway. *Appetite*. https://doi.org/10.1016/j.appet.2023.106611

Hansen, A., Wethal, U. B, Efstathiou, S., & Volden, J. R. (2023). Towards plantification: Contesting, negotiating and re-placing meaty routines. *Consumption and Society*. https://doi.org/10.1332/WPKF9257

Hargreaves, T. (2011). Practice-ing behaviour change: Applying social practice theory to pro-environmental behaviour change. *Journal of consumer culture*, *11*(1), 79–99.

Hoolohan, C., & Browne, A. L. (2020). Design thinking for practice-based intervention: Co-producing the change points toolkit to unlock (un)sustainable practices. *Design Studies*, *67*, 102–132. https://doi.org/10.1016/j.destud.2019.12.002

Ivanova, D., Stadler, K., Steen-Olsen, K., Wood, R., Vita, G., Tukker, A., & Hertwich, E. G. (2016). Environmental impact assessment of household consumption. *Journal of Industrial Ecology*, *20*(3), 526–536.

IPCC. (2022). *Climate change 2022: Impacts, adaptation, and vulnerability*. Contribution of working group II to the sixth assessment report of the intergovernmental panel on climate change. [H.-O., Pörtner, D. C., Roberts, M., Tignor, E. S., Poloczanska, K., Mintenbeck, A., Alegría, M., Craig, S., Langsdorf, S., Löschke, V., Möller, A., Okem, & B., Rama (Eds.).]. 3056 pp. Cambridge University Press. https://doi.org/10.1017/9781009325844

Jack, T. (2013). Nobody was dirty: Intervening in inconspicuous consumption of laundry routines. *Journal of Consumer Culture*, *13*(3), 406–421. https://doi.org/10.1177/1469540513485272

Jacobsen, M. H., & Hansen, A. R. (2021). (Re)introducing embodied practical understanding to the sociology of sustainable consumption. *Journal of Consumer Culture*, *21*(4), 747–763. https://doi.org/10.1177/1469540519846213

John, P., Smith, G., & Stoker, G. (2009). Nudge nudge, think think: Two strategies for changing civic behaviour. *The Political Quarterly*, *80*(3), 361–370. https://doi.org/10.1111/j.1467-923X.2009.02001.x

Joy, M. (2020). *Why we love dogs, eat pigs, and wear cows: An introduction to*. Red Wheel.

Kahneman, D (2011). *Thinking, fast and slow*. Penguin Random House.

Kahneman, D., & Tversky, A. (1979). Prospect theory: An analysis of decision under risk. *Econometrica*, *47*(2). https://doi.org/10.1142/9789814417358_0006

Kanerva, M. (2021). *The new meatways and sustainability: Discourses and social practices* (1st ed.). transcript Verlag.

Klitkou, A., Bolwig, S., Huber, A., Ingeborgrud, I., Pluciński, P., Rohracher, H., Schartinger, D., Thiene, M., & Żuk, P. (2022). The interconnected dynamics of social practices and their implications for transformative change: A review. *Sustainable Production and Consumption*, *31*, 603–614. https://doi.org/10.1016/j.spc.2022.03.027

Kollmuss, A., & Agyeman, J. (2002). Mind the gap: Why do people act environmentally and what are the barriers to pro-environmental behavior? *Environmental Education Research*, *8*(3), 239–260.

Kurz, V. (2018). Nudging to reduce meat consumption: Immediate and persistent effects of an intervention at a university restaurant. *Journal of Environmental Economics and Management*, *90*, 317–341. https://doi.org/10.1016/j.jeem.2018.06.005

Kurz, T., Gardner, B., Verplanken, B., & Abraham, C. (2015). Habitual behaviors or patterns of practice? Explaining and changing repetitive climate-relevant actions. *Wiley Interdisciplinary Reviews: Climate Change*, *6*(1), 113–128.

Kwasny, T., Dobernig, K., & Riefler, P. (2022). Towards reduced meat consumption: A systematic literature review of intervention effectiveness, 2001–2019. *Appetite*, *168*. https://doi.org/10.1016/j.appet.2021.105739

Latour, B. (1992). Where are the missing masses? The sociology of a few mundane artifacts. *Shaping Technology/Building Society: Studies in Sociotechnical Change*, *1*, 225–258.

Latour, B. (2005). *Reassembling the social – An introduction to actor-network-theory*. Oxford University Press.

Ledderer, L., Kjær, M., Madsen, E. K., Busch, J., & Fage-Butler, A. (2020). Nudging in public health lifestyle interventions: A systematic literature review and metasynthesis. *Health Education Behavior*, *47*(5), 749–764. https://doi.org/10.1177/1090198120931788

Leggett, W. (2014). The politics of behaviour change: Nudge, neoliberalism and the state. *Policy Politics*, *42*(1), 3–19. https://doi.org/10.1332/030557312X655576

Lehner, M., Mont, O., & Heiskanen, E. (2016). Nudging–A promising tool for sustainable consumption behaviour? *Journal of Cleaner Production*, *134*, 166–177. https://doi.org/10.1016/j.jclepro.2015.11.08

Lembcke, T. B., Engelbrecht, N., Brendel, A. B., & Kolbe, L. M. (2019). To nudge or not to nudge: Ethical considerations of digital nudging based on its behavioral economics roots. In *Proceedings of the European conference on information systems. Twenty-Seventh European Conference on Information Systems (ECIS2019), Stockholm-Uppsala, Sweden* (pp. 1–17).

Lin, Y., Osman, M., & Ashcroft, R. (2017). Nudge: Concept, effectiveness, and ethics. *Basic and Applied Social Psychology*, *39*(6), 293–306. https://doi.org/10.1080/01973533.2017.1356304

Loughnan, S., Bastian, B., & Haslam, N. (2014). The psychology of eating animals. *Current Directions in Psychological Science*, *23*(2), 104–108.

Loughnan, S., Haslam, N., & Bastian, B. (2010). The role of meat consumption in the denial of moral status and mind to meat animals. *Appetite*, *55*(1), 156–159.

Marchiori, D. R., Adriaanse, M. A., & De Ridder, D. T. (2017). Unresolved questions in nudging research: Putting the psychology back in nudging. *Social and Personality Psychology Compass*, *1*(1), 12–13. https://doi.org/10.1111/spc3.12297

Mazar, A., Tomaino, G., Carmon, Z., & Wood, W. (2021). Habits to save our habitat: Using the psychology of habits to promote sustainability. *Behavioral Science & Policy*, *7*(2), 75–89. https://doi.org/10.1177/237946152100700207

McBey, D., Watts, D., & Johnstone, A. M. (2019). Nudging, formulating new products, and the lifecourse: A qualitative assessment of the viability of three methods for reducing Scottish meat consumption for health, ethical, and environmental reasons. *Appetite*, *142*. https://doi.org/10.1016/j.appet.2019.104349

McNeill, D. (2023). Can economics help to understand, and change, consumption behaviour?. Consumption and public life. In A. Hansen & B. K. Nielsen (Eds.), *Consumption, Sustainability and everyday life*. Palgrave Macmillan. https://doi.org/10.1007/978-3-031-11069-6_12

Meier, R., Blaimer, B. B., Buenaventura, E., Hartop, E., von Rintelen, T., Srivathsan, A., & Yeo, D. (2022). A re-analysis of the data in Sharkey et al.'s (2021) minimalist revision reveals that BINs do not deserve names, but BOLD Systems needs a stronger commitment to open science. *Cladistics*, *38*(2), 264–275.

Meistrup, L. I., & Klitmøller, J. (2023). Stop chasing unicorns of climate inaction: Annulling the value–action gap, introducing persons. *Theory & Psychology*, *33*(5), 717–735.

Mitchie, S., Ashford, S., Sniehotta, F. F., Dombrowski, S. U., Bishop, A., & French, D. P. (2011). A refined taxonomy of behaviour change techniques to help people change their physical activity and healthy eating behaviors: The CALO-RE taxonomy. *Psychology and Health*, *26*, 1479–1498.

Mols, F., Haslam, S. A., Jetten, J., & Steffens, N. K. (2015). Why a nudge is not enough: A social identity critique of governance by stealth. *European Journal of Political Research*, *54*(1), 81–98. https://doi.org/10.1111/1475-6765.12073

Morris, C., Kaljonen, M., Aavik, K., Balázs, B., Cole, M., Coles, B., . . . White, R. (2021). Priorities for social science and humanities research on the challenges of moving beyond animal-based food systems. *Humanities and Social Sciences Communications*, *8*(1), 1–12.

Mylan, J. (2018). Sustainable consumption in everyday life: A qualitative study of UK consumer experiences of meat reduction. *Sustainability*, *10*(7), 2307.

Osman, M., & Nelson, W. (2019). How can food futures insight promote change in consumers' choices, are behavioural interventions (eg nudges) the answer? *Futures*, *111*, 116–122. https://doi.org/10.1016/j.futures.2019.04.00

Park, T., & Barker, J. (2020). Nudging diet change for health and sustainability. (Consumer-insights-sightandlife.pdf). *Sight Life*, *34*, 57–61.

Parlasca, M. C., & Qaim, M. (2022). Meat consumption and sustainability. *Annual Review of Resource Economics*, *14*(1), 17–41.

Pedwell, C. (2017). Habit and the politics of social change: A comparison of nudge theory and pragmatist philosophy. *Body & Society*, *23*(4), 59–94. https://doi.org/10.1177/1357034X17734619

Piazza, J., Ruby, M. B., Loughnan, S., Luong, M., Kulik, J., Watkins, H. M., & Seigerman, M. (2015). Rationalizing meat consumption. The 4Ns. *Appetite*, *91*(1), 114–128. https://doi.org/10.1016/j.appet.2015.04.011

Poore, J., & Nemecek, T. (2018). Reducing food's environmental impacts through producers and consumers. *Science*, *360*, 987–992. https://doi.org/10.1126/science.aaq0216

Qizilbash, M. (2009). *Well-being, preference formation and the danger of paternalism (No. 0918)*. Papers on economics and evolution. Max Planck Institute of Economics. http://hdl.handle.net/10419/32663

Quoquab, F., & Mohammad, J. (2020). A review of sustainable consumption (2000 to 2020): What we know and what we need to know. *Journal of Global Marketing*, *33*(5), 305–334.

Randers, L., & Thøgersen, J. (2023). Meat, myself, and I: The role of multiple identities in meat consumption. *Appetite*, *180*, 106319.

Reid, L., & Ellsworth-Krebs, K. (2019). Nudge (ography) and practice theories: Contemporary sites of behavioural science and post-structuralist approaches in geography? *Progress in Human Geography*, *43*(2), 295–313. https://doi.org/10.1177/0309132517750773

Rose, D. (2018). Environmental nudges to reduce meat demand. *The Lancet Planetary Health*, *2*(9), 374–375. https://doi.org/10.1016/S2542-5196(18)30185-2

Rothgerber, H. (2020). Meat-related cognitive dissonance: A conceptual framework for understanding how meat eaters reduce negative arousal from eating animals. *Appetite*, *146*, 104511.

Rothgerber, H., & Rosenfeld, D. L. (2021). Meat-related cognitive dissonance: The social psychology of eating animals. *Social and Personality Psychology Compass*, *15*(5), 1–16.

Rozin, P. (2007). Food and eating. In S. Kitayama & D. Coven (Eds.), *Handbook of cultural psychology* (Vol. 2, pp. 447–477). The Guilford Press.

Sahakian, M., & Wilhite, H. (2014). Making practice theory practicable: Towards more sustainable forms of consumption. *Journal of Consumer Culture*, *14*(1), 25–44.

Sahakian, M., Wahlen, S., & Welch, D. (2022). (Un)sustainable consumption: A contested, compelling and critical field. *Consumption and Society*, *1*(2), 244–254.

Sandberg, M. (2021). Sufficiency transitions: A review of consumption changes for environmental sustainability. *Journal of Cleaner Production*, *293*, 126097.

Schatzki, T. R. (2002). *The site of the social: A philosophical account of the constitution of social life and change*. Penn State Press.

Schatzki, T. (2010). Materiality and social life. *Nature and culture*, *5*(2), 123–149.

Schatzki, T. (2016). Practice theory as flat ontology. In G. Spaargaren, D. Weenik, & M. Lamers (Eds.), *Practice theory and research: Exploring the dynamics of social life* (pp. 44–58). Routledge.

Shove, E. (2003). *Comfort, cleanliness and convenience: The social organization of normality*. Berg.

Shove, E. (2010). Beyond the ABC: Climate change policy and theories of social change. *Environment and Planning A*, *42*(6), 1273–1285.

Shove, E. (2012). Habits and their creatures. In A. Warde & D. Southerton (Eds.), *The habits of consumption* (Vol. 12). Helsinki Collegium for Advances Studies. Collegium. Studies across disciplines in the humanities and social sciences.

Shove, E. (2017). Matters of practice. In A. Hui, T. Schatzki, & E. Shove (Eds.), *The nexus of practices: Connections, constellations, practitioners*. Routledge.

Shove, E., & Walker, G. (2014). What is energy for? Social practice and energy demand. *Theory, Culture & Society*, *31*(5), 41–58. https://doi.org/10.1177/026327641453

Shweder, R. A. (2003). *Why do men barbecue?: Recipes for cultural psychology*. Harvard University Press.

Spurling, N. J., McMeekin, A., Southerton, D., Shove, E. A., & Welch, D. (2013). Interventions in practice: Reframing policy approaches to consumer behaviour. In Y. Strengers & Y. C. Maller (Eds.), *Social practices, interventions and sustainability: Beyond behaviour change*. Routledge.

Star, S. L., & Ruhleder, K. (1996). Steps toward an ecology of infrastructure: Design and access for large information spaces. *Information Systems Research*, *7*(1), 111–134.

Sundet, Ø., Hansen, A., & Wethal, U. (2023). Performing meat reduction across scripted social sites: Exploring the experiences and challenges of meat reducers in Norway. *Consumption and Society*, *2*(2), 238–257. https://doi.org/10.1332/ZGZV3476

Sunstein, C. R., Reish, L. A., & Kaiser, M. (2019). Trusting nudges? Lessons from an international survey. *Journal of European Public Policy*, *26*(10), 1417–1443. https://doi.org/10.1080/13501763.2018.1531912

Thaler, R. H. (2012). *The winner's curse: Paradoxes and anomalies of economic life*. Simon and Schuster.

Thaler, R. H., & Sunstein, C. R. (2003). Libertarian paternalism. *The American Economic Review*, *93*(2), 175–179.

Thaler, R. H., & Sunstein, C. R. (2008). *Nudge: Improving decisions about health, wealth, and happiness*. Yale University Press.

Thaler, R. H., & Sunstein, C. R. (2009). *Nudge: Improving decisions about health, wealth, and happiness*. Penguin.

Toomela, A. (2014). Mainstream sychology. In T. Teo (Ed.), *Encyclopedia of critical psychology*. Springer. https://doi.org/10.1007/978-1-4614-5583-7_611

Torma, G., Aschemann-Witzel, J., & Thøgersen, J. (2018). I nudge myself: Exploring 'self-nudging' strategies to drive sustainable consumption behaviour. *International Journal of Consumer Studies*, *42*(1), 141–154. https://doi.org/10.1111/ijcs.12404

Tversky, A., & Kahneman, D. (1974). Judgment under uncertainty: Heuristics and biases. *Science*, *185*, 1124–1131. https://doi.org/10.1126/science.185.4157.1124

Venema, T. A., & Jensen, N. H. (2023). We meat again: A field study on the moderating role of location-specific consumer preferences in nudging vegetarian options. *Psychology & Health*, *25*, 1–15.

Verbeek, P. P. (2006). Materializing morality: Design ethics and technological mediation. *Science, Technology, & Human Values*, *31*(3), 361–380.

Volden, J., & Hansen, A. (2022). Practical aeromobilities: Making sense of environmentalist air-travel. *Mobilities*, *17*(3), 349–365. https://doi.org/10.1080/17450101.2021.1985381

Wallenborn, G., & Wilhite, H. (2014). Rethinking embodied knowledge and household consumption. *Energy Research & Social Science*, *1*, 56–64.

Warde, A. (2005). Consumption and theories of practice. *Journal of Consumer Culture*, *5*(2), 131–153. https://doi.org/10.1177/1469540505053090

Warde, A. (2014). After taste: Culture, consumption and theories of practice. *Journal of consumer culture*, *14*(3), 279–303.

Warde, A. (2016). *Consumption: A sociological analysis*. Springer.

Warde, A. (2022). Society and consumption. *Consumption and Society*, *1*(1), 11–30.

Weis, T. (2013). *The ecological hoofprint: The global burden of industrial livestock*. Bloomsbury Publishing.

Welch, D. (2016). Social practices and behaviour change. In F. Spotswood (Ed.), *Beyond behaviour change* (pp. 237–256). Policy Press.

Welch, D., Halkier, B., & Keller, M. (2020). Introduction to the special issue: Renewing theories of practice and reappraising the cultural. *Cultural Sociology*, *14*(4), 325–339. https://doi.org/10.1177/1749975520954146

Wendler, M. (2023). The social challenges of not eating meat: How social interactions shape the role of meat in everyday food practices. *Consumption and Society*, *2*(1), 24–41.

Wendler, M., & Halkier, B. (2023). Dietary transition requires work: Exploring the practice-transition processes of young Danish meat reducers. *Food, Culture & Society*, 1–19. https://doi.org/10.1080/15528014.2023.2193501,

Wethal, U., Hansen, A., & Sandnes, T. (2024). *Swamped in dinosaurs with LED lights: Negotiating sustainability in a high-consumption society* (pp. 1–22). Consumption and Society. https://doi.org/10.1332/27528499Y2024D000000008

White, S. K., Ballantine, P. W., & Ozanne, L. K. (2022). Consumer adoption of plant-based meat substitutes: A network of social practices. *Appetite*, *175*, 106037.

Whitmarsh, L., O'Neill, S., & Lorenzoni, I. (2011). Climate change or social change? Debate within, amongst, and beyond disciplines. *Environment and Planning A*, *43*(2), 258–261.

Wiedmann, T., Lenzen, M., Keyßer, L. T., & Steinberger, J. K. (2020). Scientists' warning on affluence. *Nature Communications*, *11*(1), 1–10.

Wilhite, H. (2008). New thinking on the agentive relationship between end-use technologies and energy-using practices. *Energy efficiency*, *1*(2), 121–130.

Wilhite, H. (2012). Towards a better accounting of the roles of body, things and habits in consumption. In A. Warde & D. Southerton (Eds.), *Collegium. Studies across disciplines in the humanities and social sciences, The habits of consumption* (Vol. 12). Helsinki Collegium for Advances Studies. content (helsinki.fi).

Wilhite, H. (2014). Insights from social practice and social leaning theory for sustainable energy consumption. *Flux*, *2*(96), 24–30. https://doi.org/10.3917/flux.096.0024

Winders, B., & Ransom, E. (Eds.) (2019), *Global meat: Social and environmental consequences of the expanding meat industry*. MIT Press.

CONTESTED IMAGINARIES OF PREFERABLE FOOD FUTURES: A COMPARATIVE ANALYSIS OF THE DIGITAL FOOD PROVISIONING PLATFORMS ODA AND REKO-RINGEN

Marie Hebrok and Nina Heidenstrøm

Oslo Metropolitan University, Norway

ABSTRACT

This chapter examines prevailing Western imaginaries of future food consumption by identifying two distinct imaginaries. The first imaginary revolves around a technology-enabled efficiency regime, characterized by affordable prices, convenience and a diverse range of familiar food items. The second imaginary centres on a community-enabled quality regime, emphasizing ethics, sustainability, co-creation, nutrition and variation in food offerings. The imaginaries are illustrated through a comparative study of two Norwegian food provisioning platforms: the online grocery store ODA, representing the efficiency imaginary, and the alternative food network REKO-ringen, representing the quality imaginary. Drawing from a combination of qualitative interviews and online ethnography, this chapter provides an analysis of the socio-technical imaginaries embedded in ODA and REKO-ringen. This chapter shows how the contested role of technology is shaping future visions of food consumption. ODA adopts an ambitious approach, seeking to pioneer the future of food provision through extensive technological innovation. In contrast, REKO-ringen faces resistance against technological advancements within its organization. By shedding light on divergent imaginaries of future food consumption, this chapter contributes to a deeper understanding of the socio-technical dynamics influencing food choices and provisioning. The

Consumers and Consumption in Comparison
Comparative Social Research, Volume 37, 215–229

Published under exclusive licence by Emerald Publishing Limited
ISSN: 0195-6310/doi:10.1108/S0195-631020240000037010

findings have implications for policymakers, industry stakeholders and consumers as they navigate the evolving landscape of food consumption.

Keywords: Food consumption; food provisioning; food technologies; food acquisition platforms; food systems

INTRODUCTION

The digitalization of society has innovated the way consumers can source their food. Accompanied by a dramatic change in our food systems during the last decades, driven by innovations along the value chains, we are now in an era of convenience, speed and efficiency (Colatruglio & Slater, 2014, pp. 37–55). At present, a large number of online platforms and pipelines for food provisioning have been established across European countries (Oncini et al., 2020), increasing the options consumers have, not only the ways in which they can acquire their food, but also in the breadth of food products available. There is great diversity in the various sources of consumer food items. While some merely represent online versions of physical stores (i.e. online grocery stores), others aim for more transformative impacts on food consumption. Some platforms seek to remove the perceived burden of planning and preparing meals (i.e. box schemes), while others seek to reduce the distance between producers and consumers (i.e. alternative food networks). Currently, most new platforms operate at the margins of the more commonplace food procuring practices in Europe, which is still the physical visit to grocery stores and markets. Seen from a Western perspective, while 'we have never been so far removed from the food we eat' (Colatruglio & Slater, 2014, p. 37), we have also never before in history had as many options at our fingertips.

In theory, the sustainability potential of these new platforms can easily be acknowledged. Reducing food waste, increasing consumption of ecological and local food and reducing consumption of meat are often used as arguments in favour of the services (Heidenstrøm & Hebrok, 2022; Samsioe & Fuentes, 2022). However, there are significant differences in how they find their place within the everyday food practices of European consumers, or whether they do so at all (Fuentes & Samsioe, 2020; Heidenstrøm & Hebrok, 2022; Samsioe & Fuentes, 2022). The main problems these platforms face are that of upscaling; to increase the number of consumers that use the platform on a regular basis.

One important barrier for upscaling is the ways in which the different platforms imagine our food future to be. Current expressions of sustainable food futures are dominated by techno-centric visions – imaginaries – of how we will cope with the major challenges of our era (Davies, 2014). Techno-centric imaginaries of food exist not only in our collective imagination but are already materializing and being performed in the present. In parallel, less technology-intensive imaginaries evolve through the labour of food producers and consumers – envisioning, performing and materializing alternative food futures.

In this chapter, we compare the imaginaries embedded in two food acquisition platforms in the Norwegian market, the online grocery store ODA who represents a techno-centric vision of the future, and the alternative food network REKO-ringen who represents a less technology-intensive vision. We use data from 20 at-home interviews with households who use these platforms, and an online ethnography of the two platforms' websites. Insights from 'socio-technical imaginaries', as formulated by Jasanoff and Kim (2015), is used to understand the role of technological innovation as well as social communities and consumer practices in food imaginaries. Socio-technical imaginaries of sustainable food consumption are produced, reproduced and changed by providers as well as consumers of food, and in the interactions between them. These imaginaries hold views of our desired and feared food futures (e.g. the needs and wants of consumers), our food moralities (e.g. what is healthy, good, high quality, sustainable food), and of the measures from which the food system itself can become more sustainable (e.g. the role of technology and community). However, sustainable food imaginaries might not be shared, in fact, we tend to take our own imaginaries of the future as natural, even objective, and thus expect others to have the same view as ourselves, even though most imaginaries vary between actors in different positions. The aim of this chapter is therefore to compare the food imaginaries of ODA and REKO-ringen, to identify (i) how they imagine a sustainable food system in the future? and (ii) what the roles of consumers and providers in the imagined future system are? In doing so, we demonstrate how different imaginaries shape present food practices in different ways, how they affect the potential of upscaling sustainable food acquisition alternatives and the power relations between imaginaries.

SOCIO-TECHNICAL IMAGINARIES OF FOOD FUTURES

The Indian novelist Amitav Ghosh is often cited for his critique of the imaginative shortcomings in dealing with climate change (Ghosh, 2018). He calls it 'a crisis of imagination.' This crisis of imagination refers to society's ability, or inability rather, to imagine future worlds without simply reproducing present trajectories. In fact, most imaginaries are reproductive in the sense that they reproduce and reinforce dominant ideologies (Ricoeur, 1976). In order to increase our understanding of the impact expectations of the future have on the present, sociological research, and science and technology studies have increasingly been engaging with the future as a site for exploration (Borup et al., 2006; Brown & Michael, 2003; Jasanoff & Kim, 2015; Mische, 2009).

How we imagine the future to be – our imaginaries – projects new socio-material structures, new ways of doing and living into existence (Ricœur, 1976). Imaginaries are powerful because they also affect how we organize society today. When we have an idea of what the future will look like, we plan our actions accordingly. Imagined futures then become mobilized in the present, and they might materialize as new services, products, technologies and innovations. They also infuse new knowledge regimes and ideologies and create conflict and controversies. Some imaginaries are dominant, while others are given little attention. In the case of sustainability and climate change, imaginaries of the utopian power of technology are vastly dominating (Davies, 2014; Dolejšová et al. 2020; Tangeland et al., 2016).

We study the role of technology in imaginaries of food futures as socio-technical imaginaries defined by Jasanoff and Kim (2015) as 'collectively held, institutionally stabilized, and publicly performed visions of desirable futures, animated by shared understandings of forms of social life and social order attainable through, and supportive of, advances in science and technology' (Jasanoff & Kim, 2015, p. 4). An important point made by Jasanoff and Kim is that there is a multitude of imaginaries encompassing collective beliefs about how the world works and should work in the future, which leads to the rejection of a linear path towards a single future. In this view, futures become plural and contingent on how imaginaries act on the present. Socio-technical imaginaries are not only located in our imagination or in our mind – they can be found all around us in the material world (i.e. technology and infrastructure), in culture (i.e. literature, art, media and film) and in the way we do things (i.e. social practices) (Jasanoff & Kim, 2015).

As ideas of green growth dominate political and industrial agendas towards mitigation of climate change, techno-optimism grows in Norway and other western countries (Tangeland et al., 2016). Meaning that people are looking more and more towards technology to solve the big challenges. Perhaps without demanding substantial changes in lifestyles. The politics and industry of food, as one of the most basic consumer goods, is heavily influenced by these techno-centric imaginaries of future food consumption (Davies, 2014). These imaginaries fuel the development of, for instance smart and precision farming, personalized nutrition and technological solutions aimed at the reduction and prevention of food waste (i.e. Ciccullo et al., 2021; Finger et al., 2019; Zeisel, 2020). Online food delivery services are positioning themselves in Europe, with promises of saving both time and money and reducing waste – all enabled through innovations in technology and logistics. Some expect the development of an 'Internet of Food', enabling efficiency and sustainability (Holden et al., 2018). With this follows extensive use of big data and tech-devices to monitor and record food choices and health, and also considerable risks and loss of human agency and control, shifting the power balance in favour of big business (Verma et al., 2021). These are just some examples of how technology-driven imaginaries of food consumption shape our present, and so our futures.

In parallel to the above-described examples of techno-visions of food consumption exists what can almost be said to be the complete opposite – namely the visions of alternative food networks (AFN) driven by local communities without the extensive use of technological innovations. However, the boundaries between AFNs and mainstream retail blur, as the changes in perception of quality as embedded through means of production, absence of toxins, presence of nutrients and animal welfare and the willingness to pay for such qualities has led to an integration of AFN products in mainstream retail – not solely to the benefit of AFN producers who are subjected to the pressures of cost/price relationships pushed by supply chain management (Goodman et al., 2012). Nevertheless, the socio-technical imaginaries that guide the existence of alternative food networks are still clearly distinct from those shaping big retail.

METHODS AND DATA MATERIAL: A COMPARATIVE STUDY OF FOOD IMAGINARIES

Contested sustainable food imaginaries are studied by comparing two food service providers in Norway, the online grocery store ODA and the alternative food network REKO-ringen. The data material consists of 1) qualitative interviews with users and 2) online ethnography of the websites of ODA and REKO-ringen.

In 2020, qualitative interviews were carried out with 20 Norwegian participants who actively engaged in the use of ODA, REKO-ringen or both, on a monthly basis. Ten interviews took place in-person during home visits, while the remaining ten were conducted digitally via Zoom,[1] adapting to the constraints imposed by the Covid-19 pandemic. The Norstat Recruitment agency was responsible for recruiting the families, with the goal of ensuring diversity across age groups, family compositions and gender. All the informants signed a written consent form either at the time of the visit or via email. Each interview was conducted with a primary informant, but other household members joined in sporadically. The interviews were conducted in an unstructured fashion, fostering informal discussions about food consumption. This approach allowed informants to guide the conversation towards their unique perspectives, enabling the exploration of broader narratives, as highlighted by Spradley (2016). All interviews also included a digital walk-through of the service(s) the informants used. In the digital walk-through we accompanied informants through video call when using the platforms of ODA and Reko-ringen as well as when looking into fridges and cupboards in their kitchens. For more information about the interviews see the article *Towards realizing the sustainability potential of digital food provisioning platforms* (Heidenstrøm & Hebrok, 2022).

The digital ethnography of the websites of ODA and Reko-ringen was conducted in 2023 to study the digital communication on the sites in terms of images and text, to elicit key messages. All pages were analyzed for content, and key messages and quotes were noted and categorized. Digital ethnography is not a research method per se, but rather an approach to explore digital sites as part of everyday life practices in various ways. We have applied this approach to observe how socio-technical imaginaries shine through the narratives told by different actors online. This includes visual elements accompanying textual messages on the websites including a visual ethnographic approach (Pink, 2007). Images used in marketing produce specific atmospheres through the aesthetic experience the consumer undergoes (Böhme & Thibaud, 2016). This experience is influenced by the composition in images, use of colour and materials, symbols, as well as the inclusion of people, objects, nature and backgrounds, and how the viewer is positioned in relation to these elements (Ledin & Machin, 2018). Aesthetic devices also often support an underlying narrative, which helps shape the consumer's perception of the product and brand. They are also usually a product of ideology (Ledin & Machin, 2018). The analytical strategy in the context of the digital ethnography included grouping key messages, quotes and images. Central keywords were future, technology, efficient, time, quality, fair, ethical, sustainable and social.

ODA AND REKO-RINGEN: CONTESTED IMAGINARIES

To clearly illustrate the contested nature of present imaginaries of food consumption, we have chosen to compare the grassroots innovation network (Seyfang & Smith, 2007) REKO-ringen with the conventional online actor ODA. REKO-ringen was founded as a response to the detrimental effects of conventional industrial food systems by food producers offering food produced in a more sustainable and ethical way and consumers engaging to ensure the availability of such food (Ehrnström-Fuentes & Leipämaa-Leskinen, 2019). ODA, once known as kolonial.no, which was founded at the same time, represents the online version of conventional retail in food. By conventional retail we think of the kind that is reliant on 'industrialised methods of food production and processing, where the distribution and trade is organised in long supply chains with anonymous actors and there is a concentration of the negotiating power in large retailers, and where success is measured by operational efficiency and not based on the social or environmental impacts of food production, distribution and consumption' (Tregear, 2011, p. 419 as cited in: Ehrnström-Fuentes & Leipämaa-Leskinen, 2019, p. 4137). When comparing ODA and Reko-ringen we find two distinct imaginaries of preferable food futures. The first is a technology-enabled efficiency regime providing low prices, convenience and wide selections of familiar food items. The second is a community-enabled quality regime focused on dimensions of ethics, sustainability, co-creation, nutrition and variation in food items.

ODA – Building the (Technological) Future of Grocery Shopping

ODA is the largest Norwegian online grocery store founded in 2013. Many Norwegian consumers increased their use of ODA's service during the pandemic, to avoid getting infected in the store. This also led to many new customers and might have sped up the significant upscaling of the business. The company defines itself as a 'technology and logistics company that delivers to private individuals and businesses in Eastern Norway.' All quotes from ODA's online presence in this chapter can be found by accessing the about section and the sustainability section of their website https://www.oda.com/. The quotes were accessed in January 2024. ODA communicates three strategies through which it is working to minimize its own and its customers' environmental footprints through its website; 1) to influence suppliers, 2) to reduce the impact of their own operations and 3) to make it 'easier' for their customers to 'live healthy and sustainable lives.' Seeing their position as particularly influential in sitting between customers and suppliers being able to 'motivate change in both directions.'

The company presents clear future-oriented statements on their web site conveying ambitious goals of using *technology to create the grocery experience of the future*, creating *a retail system that consciously contributes to a sustainable future* and *building the most efficient retail system in the world.* The company invests heavily in its technology and has for instance developed its own route planner, the Navigator, for the most efficient distribution of groceries. The technology that goes into the online platform and the logistics of the whole system of warehouses and distribution is substantial. The company's self-representation online is imbued with ambitions of combining cutting-edge technology, efficiency and sustainability. One of their slogans is: *We exist to build the world's most effective retail system to create a society where people have more space for life.* A win-win situation that creates more time and 'space for life', makes it 'easier to live healthy and sustainable lives', in fact making 'life simpler and easier' in general. ODA has recognized the value of time for certain consumer groups and claim to save time for their customers: *With most of the entire tech world chasing to increase the time their users spend with their products, we optimize for the opposite; minimal time spent. In fact, we save our customers 60+ hours in stores each year.*

Features that are built into the platform to enable this saving of time are for instance the page *Dinner in 1-2-3!*, which shows recipes with few ingredients made in only three steps. All the recipe titles start with the word quick. For example, *Quick meat-free lasagne.* The ingredients can be put in the shopping basket with only one click. Other features such as suggestions for weekly menus, lists of frequently bought items and saved shopping lists, are all there to help consumers save time and do their shopping most efficiently. Perhaps also relieving them of some of the mental load included in food practices. Advantages voiced by the study informants are related to easy overview of products and special offers, storing shopping lists and frequently bought items, planning from home and being able to take stock while shopping. Some use Oda to buy staples in bulk (i.e. rice, pasta, cereals, etc.), and go to other stores to get higher quality products such as organic fresh meats, vegetables and grains. In this way, they combine the efficiency they get from ODA, with less easy access products from delis, farms and other physical stores. One of the informants gave us an example of the difference between steaks at ODA and their local butcher:

> 'When you buy a steak labelled Gilde (at ODA), it doesn't taste nearly as good as a steak from Nordvold Farm. There are several farms around here that supply the butcher we use, so we have a lot of locally sourced meat and fish. It's partly about the taste and also about supporting those in the local area.' (Household 4, ODA)

Online shopping is similar in some ways to physical shopping in stores. You have the same food items, choose and put them in a basket, pay and get them to your kitchen. Nevertheless, the online experience strips away most of the potential distractions and temptations, it is easier to keep track of what you already have and what you probably need, and you do not have to move either yourself or the food items to complete the purchase. Some even experience this as a close-to-automated practice of food provisioning:

> My shopping has almost become automated, I go straight to the shopping list that is there (saved online), put everything in the shopping cart, and then add what we need in addition or remove what we don t need. (...) What we buy in the (physical) stores is just what we cannot find at Kolonial (now ODA). "(...) you have the list of what you bought on the previous order, and then there are these small pop-ups saying 'we think you need this'. (...) So, I actually use all these three to decide what to order". (Household 7, ODA)

Having more control over distractions and temptations also makes it easier to avoid overspending, like this informant talks about: *(...) You should buy what you need, (...) we are trying to cut down on impulse buying (...) and went from 6,000 (NOK) to 4,000 (a month spent on food after starting to do grocery shopping online) (Household 6, ODA)*. All in all, ODA builds an imaginary of food provisioning as something that should be efficient, and technology-enabled. This is a focus that largely overlooks other qualitative aspects of food provisioning such as the ecological, social and ethical dimensions of how food is produced, distributed and consumed.

However, ODA also communicates a strong focus on sustainability, in this way, they adopt many of the same arguments that we will meet when looking at REKO-ringen in the next section. On their website, there is an extensive page called Bærekraft (Sustainability) on which ODA explains how they address issues of animal welfare, food waste, reduced plastic consumption, energy consumption, local suppliers, carbon and emissions. ODA claims to be *building the store of the future:*

> We are building Norway's most efficient grocery store. Our goal is for it to also be the most sustainable. Fortunately, we have committed customers on our team. On this page, you can read about how we work with climate-friendly transportation, food waste, improved packaging, and local producers. In addition, we want to help our customers live a little more environmentally and climate-friendly, even in a busy everyday life. (https://sustainability.oda.com/)

As such, it seems that ODA is bringing both the benefits of efficiency through technology, and offering sustainable ways of eating as well. At least, this is how they present themselves, while consumers seem to be mostly concerned with the value of efficiency and time saved that ODA serves them with.

Images on the ODA website are of course mainly of food items and dishes; however, there is also a considerable amount of images of neighbourhoods and families that underline the communication directed at families with children that are pressed for time. Many depictions of ODA facilities and staff project an image of a technology-oriented organization. In doing so, they construct a socio-technical imaginary that blends 'soft' values such as family and community with 'hard' technological innovation. Moreover, their emphasis on environmental concerns, animal welfare and support for local farmers suggests the possibility of achieving a holistic approach. This entails an efficient technology-enabled food supply system that not only saves time and effort but also mitigates our environmental impact and fosters an ethically sound food system. Transitioning to our next case,

REKO-ringen, we encounter an organization primarily focused on the latter aspect, albeit facing challenges in its relationship with technology.

REKO-ringen – Building a Fair and Sustainable Future of Food Consumption and Production

While ODA explicitly communicates their ambitions for the future, and sell their business as part of a larger ideological view of the future of food consumption, REKO-ringen does not mention the future at all on their website, apart from a quote by Thomas Snellmann who started REKO in Finland in 2013: *I have received many awards, for which I am grateful, but the best feedback has come from rural producers. Producers have contacted me and said that before REKO, they had no future – but now there is one* (https://www.rekonorge.no/produsent1). However, this does obviously not reflect a lack of ideology behind REKO-ringen, but rather it underlines the different natures of the organizations. While ODA is a commercial business employing marketing professionals, REKO-ringen is driven by enthusiasts on low budgets that do not allow for the kind of communication coming from ODA.

REKO-ringen is a sales channel for local food organized through Facebook. Customers pre-order food items by commenting on the ads put out on the group feed by local producers. They later pick them up at a predefined location on a specific date and time. REKO is an abbreviation for the Norwegian 'rettferdig konsum', which means fair consumption. The concept was first developed and implemented by Thomas Snellman in Finland in 2013 (the same year as the foundation of ODA). The purpose was to create a sales channel that could link producers and consumers together directly (Ehrnström-Fuentes & Leipämaa-Leskinen, 2019). There are no intermediaries in this way of trading food, only a direct link between producers and consumers. In this way, the producer receives 100% of the sales price. According to the Norwegian REKO-ring website the first REKO-ring in Norway was established in November 2017. As of February 2022, there are over 140 rings spread across large parts of the country. There are around 500,000 customers associated with the REKO-rings, and over 600 manufacturers who sell food (rekonorge.no, 2024). Many of the food producers are too small to receive subsidies from the state and are also denied access to the big retail chains because they cannot compete with bigger players on price, volumes and logistics. For them, the REKO-rings become an important platform for selling their food products.

For consumers, the network gives them access to food products of certain qualities that would be hard to come by without. The qualities do not solely pertain to the intrinsic aspects of the food items themselves, but also to where, by whom and how they were produced. One of the informants explains the qualities of REKO-ringen:

> So that's why Reko-ring is so fantastic, because then you'll be told which suppliers are coming (. . .) and then you can order, and then you get ingredients that are often organic. Animals that have had a good life if you want meat. And then there is a lot, both drinks and bread and food which may be a little more expensive than in normal shops, but then I think that it is better to

> have quality than quantity. (...) then I support a local producer, (...) support young people who may have sold everything they owned to take a chance on this. (...) it's worth a little extra then (...) and I get clean food (...). (Household 1 REKO)

The visual content presented on the Norwegian REKO-ringen website predominantly features depictions of farms, livestock and sales outlets, serving to show the operational dynamics of the concept. This imagery underscores the primary objective of facilitating direct transactions between local food producers and consumers, thereby enhancing market access for small-scale producers. Noteworthy is the absence of any reference to technological advancements, innovation or future-oriented perspectives within these visual representations.

From how the REKO-ringen presents itself online it is clear that it is a grassroots organization driven by the work of producers and consumers combined. The first statement on the website is *Local food – completely without intermediaries.* Then you are asked: *Do you want to buy good, short-distance food from your area? Do you want to contribute to increased food production in your district? Do you want to buy quality products directly from the manufacturer?* On the REKO Instagram account, there are numerous images of happy animals and people, lush vegetables and small-scale farms. On the blog these headlines can be observed: *Is REKO-ringen a joint project? Is it the responsibility of the consumers to support small-scale food producers? REKO-ring's clockwork – the volunteer administrators, A new ordering solution for REKO?*

To keep the ordering system on Facebook or develop a new separate system for sellers and buyers is an ongoing debate in the REKO-ring community. Some experience the present system as vulnerable, and the personal transaction as both nice and challenging. On the one hand, being able to buy ethically produced food directly from the farms, and to see and communicate with the people producing the food is highly valued, on the other the personal encounter can become uncomfortable if for instance somehow you are prohibited from showing up, as exemplified in these quotes:

> Yeah, you get to say hello, it's often the same people, so they might recognize you a bit, I don't know. It's definitely very nice to see who has produced the food you're eating. I think that's a very big plus. When I bought the lamb roast, I got a lot of instructions on how to best roast it. Like some info about, there's often some cartilage and some glands inside this meat that you should avoid and such things. So I got a lot of good information about the preparation of the food. (Household 8, REKO)

> I'm not really a fan of the ordering system because it operates through Facebook. You're a member of this group, and then there are announcements. Different producers participate each time and advertise what they're selling for that Sunday... they've already started posting for the next one, in two weeks. So they tend to start quite early. And then you have to comment on the posts what you want to order. And then they confirm the order, and then you've sort of committed to showing up and picking up the order. If you don't do that, it creates a bad atmosphere. They can actually demand money from you, it's part of the rules. Because they often bring goods that may stay frozen on the way down but maybe not on the way up. So it's vulnerable. (Household 8, REKO)

There are both significant benefits and challenges associated with relying on Facebook as a platform for communication and ordering between providers and consumers. To deal with the challenges there have been attempts at developing digital solutions and new order and delivery concepts outside Facebook in Sweden and Finland. However, these solutions have often lacked resources to sustain themselves, and fail to preserve the social aspect of the REKO-ring ideology (Hagolani-Albov & Ehrnström-Fuentes, 2023). The main advantage of the Facebook system is that it is completely grassroots-driven without any intermediaries extracting financial resources from any transactions between providers and consumers. However, the concept is entirely reliant on a platform controlled by the interests of a multibillion company that does not advocate for the interests of REKO-ring specifically (Hagolani-Albov & Ehrnström-Fuentes, 2023). Moreover, consumers are prompted to share their private information with the platform owners (Meta). Consequently, there exists a privacy cost that is not explicitly accounted for in the transaction. This hidden cost and intermediary benefiting from the activity generated by the REKO-ring groups on Facebook constitutes a dilemma that cannot easily be resolved. In general, the principle of avoiding an intermediary making a profit on transactions between buyers and sellers fuels the resistance against developing a new digital platform within the REKO-ring community. At the same time, dwindling sales point towards a need for change.

DISCUSSION

The most striking contrast between the imaginaries conveyed by the two platforms for food provisioning moves along the dimensions of technology, efficiency and convenience versus ethical, social and sustainable food consumption. ODA tells a story of technological innovation and efficiency that will contribute not only to sustainability but to improving the lives of people by reducing the time spent on buying and cooking food. Customers validate this story by choosing the platform to save time – and make time for other valued activities. REKO-ringen on the other hand, tells a story of ethical food consumption where producers get fair pay for their products and consumers get access to local healthier, and diverse food. Customers validate this story by repeating it as motivation for using this platform of provisioning. In contrast to ODA, many members of REKO-ringen have been sceptical of introducing new technology to make the trade run smoother. The main argument is against an intermediary (a platform owner) who would undermine the basic concept of direct contact between consumers and local producers. Yet, it seems unavoidable to involve an intermediary that profits from the operations facilitated by REKO-ring. Currently, consumers exchange their privacy details, a requirement for accessing Facebook.

The role of technology is contested in the two future imaginaries of food consumption that the platforms convey. ODA has a strong ambition to build the future of food provision through extensive innovations in technology, while REKO-ringen is still held back from technology by internal resistance. This resistance towards technology seems to add to the work consumers need to put in to participate in this specific alternative food network. As such, it promotes the opposite of the convenience that ODA offers. Nevertheless, problems appear when AFNs are integrated into convenience regimes of big retail, such as producers not getting the same fair price for their products. This dynamic is a barrier against making local food more available to the average consumer – demanding more effort to be put in to access certain food qualities. In this way, the convenience, technology and efficiency offered by ODA become an antonym to the ethics, quality and diversity offered by REKO-ringen. Or ODA (as representing big retail) becomes the antagonist in a story of big tech versus small people. Although people might be drawn to the imaginaries REKO-ringen represents, they soon get pulled back into the interconnected practices of modern life, that have increasingly been shaped by imaginaries of efficiency, technology and convenience during the last century (Southerton, 2020).

Our comparison shows that what constitutes a preferable future of food production, distribution and consumption is clearly contested. Moreover, some actors hold more power over what imaginaries of food futures manifest in the present than others. The most scalable and actionable imaginaries are those that align with present dominant socio-technical imaginaries of progress enabled by technological innovation and efficiency. Thus, ODA, has had significantly more success in terms of scale and revenue, than REKO-ringen. Moreover, ideas of technological progress as in the digitization of food provisioning in combination with efficiency goals is a force that suppresses alternative imaginaries of sustainable food futures who cannot compete with the benefits of everyday life convenience. Imaginaries of food futures cannot be isolated from wider imaginaries of what it means to live a good life. As shown by sociological inquiries into consumption, change is, not only a matter of developing infrastructure, technology and competencies, but also to a great extent driven by imaginaries of what a good life is (Jensen et al., 2022).

The convenience and efficiency we seek is of course also a result of how life is lived and organized as a whole. We are living our lives in a way that demands us to remove as much resistance and time-consuming tasks as possible to get it all done. In this regard, it might seem common-sensical that the most efficient and convenient solutions are those that become scaled and successful. The problem with this mechanism is that alternatives that could be better, more sustainable, are becoming marginalized and overrun. Thus, the power of dominant imaginaries and their consequences for present and future food consumption should not be underestimated or taken as given. However, it is challenging to create change initiatives aimed at changing imaginaries of what a good life is, if it demands fundamental changes to present societal imaginaries (Milkoreit, 2017). As described by Jasanoff and Kim (2015, p. 4)

> Multiple imaginaries can coexist within a society in tension or in a productive dialectical relationship. It often falls to legislators, courts, the media, or other institutions of power to elevate some imagined futures above others, according them a dominant position for policy purposes. Imaginaries, moreover, encode not only visions of what is attainable through science and technology but also how life ought, or ought not to be lived: in this respect they express a society's shared understanding of good and evil.

To ensure democratic and dispersed power structures there should be continuous questioning of dominant imaginaries and their alternatives, in particular the forms of values they represent. In the cases of ODA and REKO-ringen, we can see that they are driven by different primary values where convenience and price stand in contrast to values connected to ethical and sustainable production.

CONCLUSION

This chapter has delved into the embedded imaginaries within two distinct food acquisition platforms within the Norwegian market: the online grocery store ODA and the alternative food network REKO-ringen. Through this examination, two divergent imaginaries of sustainable food consumption have emerged, underscoring the contested nature inherent in envisioning preferable food futures within Western society and how these dominant imaginaries influence our food practices. The socio-technical imaginaries in which ODA and REKO-ringen are situated reveal clear disparities. ODA projects an image centred on efficiency, affordability, convenience and familiarity, while REKO-ringen embodies an imaginary heavily grounded in ethics, quality, sustainability and diversity. Currently, dominant imaginaries emphasizing efficiency through technology tend to reinforce power structures favouring actors like ODA, often overshadowing alternative models such as REKO-ringen. Further research avenues could explore the sociopolitical implications of these competing imaginaries, investigating how they influence consumer behaviours, market dynamics and policy frameworks. Moreover, exploring the potential for hybrid models that integrate elements of both efficiency and ethical considerations could offer insights into fostering more inclusive and sustainable food systems.

NOTE

1. We used a version of Zoom that was authorized by the Norwegian Agency for shared Services in Education and Research (Sikt). The conversation was recorded after approval from the informant.

REFERENCES

Böhme, G., & Thibaud, J.-P. (2016). *The aesthetics of atmospheres*. Routledge.

Borup, M., Brown, N., Konrad, K., & Van Lente, H. (2006). The sociology of expectations in science and technology. *Technology Analysis & Strategic Management*, *18*(3–4), 285–298.

Brown, N., & Michael, M. (2003). A sociology of expectations: Retrospecting prospects and prospecting retrospects. *Technology Analysis & Strategic Management*, *15*(1), 3–18.

Ciccullo, F., Cagliano, R., Bartezzaghi, G., & Perego, A. (2021). Implementing the circular economy paradigm in the agri-food supply chain: The role of food waste prevention technologies. *Resources, Conservation and Recycling*, *164*, 105114. https://doi.org/10.1016/j.resconrec.2020.105114

Colatruglio, S., & Slater, J. (2014). Food literacy: Bridging the gap between food, nutrition and well-being. In F. Deer, T. Falkenberg, B. McMillan, & L. Sims (Eds.), *Sustainable well-being:*

Concepts, issues, and educational practices. Education for Sustainable Well-Being Press (ESWB Press). ISBN 978-0-9939534-0-8. www.ESWB-Press.org

Davies, A. R. (2014). Co-creating sustainable eating futures: Technology, ICT and citizen–consumer ambivalence. *Futures*, *62*, 181–193.

Dolejšová, M., Wilde, D., Altarriba Bertran, F., & Davis, H. (2020). Disrupting (More-than-) human-food interaction: Experimental design, tangibles and food-tech futures. *Paper presented at the Proceedings of the 2020 ACM designing interactive systems conference*. Association for Computing Machinery.

Ehrnström-Fuentes, M., & Leipämaa-Leskinen, H. (2019). Boundary negotiations in a self-organized grassroots-led food network: The case of REKO in Finland. *Sustainability*, *11*(15), 4137.

Finger, R., Swinton, S. M., El Benni, N., & Walter, A. (2019). Precision farming at the nexus of agricultural production and the environment. *Annual Review of Resource Economics*, *11*, 313–335.

Fuentes, C., & Samsioe, E. (2020). Devising food consumption: Complex households and the socio-material work of meal box schemes. *Consumption Markets & Culture*, *24*(5), 492–511. https://doi.org/10.1080/10253866.2020.1810027

Ghosh, A. (2018). *The great derangement: Climate change and the unthinkable*. University of Chicago Press.

Goodman, D., DuPuis, E. M., & Goodman, M. K. (2012). *Alternative food networks: Knowledge, practice, and politics*. Routledge.

Hagolani-Albov, S. E., & Ehrnström-Fuentes, M. (2023). The REKO model: Facebook as a platform for food system reconnection. *International Journal of Food Design*, *8*(1), 61–87.

Heidenstrøm, N., & Hebrok, M. (2022). Towards realizing the sustainability potential within digital food provisioning platforms: The case of meal box schemes and online grocery shopping in Norway. *Sustainable Production and Consumption*, *29*, 831–850.

Holden, N. M., White, E. P., Lange, M. C., & Oldfield, T. L. (2018). Review of the sustainability of food systems and transition using the Internet of Food. *NPJ Science of Food*, *2*(1), 1–7.

Jasanoff, S., & Kim, S.-H. (2015). *Dreamscapes of modernity: Sociotechnical imaginaries and the fabrication of power*. University of Chicago Press.

Jensen, C. L., Oldin, F., & Andersen, G. (2022). Imagining and co-creating futures of sustainable consumption and society. *Consumption and Society*, *1*(2), 336–357.

Ledin, P., & Machin, D. (2018). *Doing visual analysis: From theory to practice*. Sage Publications.

Milkoreit, M. (2017). Imaginary politics: Climate change and making the future. *Elementa: Science of the Anthropocene*, *5*, 62.

Mische, A. (2009). Projects and possibilities: Researching futures in action. In *Sociological forum* (Vol. 24, No. 3, pp. 694–704). Blackwell Publishing Ltd.

Oncini, F., Bozzini, E., Forno, F., & Magnani, N. (2020). Towards food platforms? An analysis of online food provisioning services in Italy. *Geoforum*, *114*, 172–180.

Pink, S. (2007). *Doing visual ethnography: Images, media and representation in research*. Sage Publications.

rekonorge.no. (2024). Hva er REKO? https://www.rekonorge.no/hva-er-reko

Ricoeur, P. (1976). Ideology and utopia as cultural imagination. *Philosophic Exchange*, *7*(1), 17–28.

Samsioe, E., & Fuentes, C. (2022). Digitalizing shopping routines: Re-Organizing household practices to enable sustainable food provisioning. *Sustainable Production and Consumption*, *29*, 807–819. https://doi.org/10.1016/j.spc.2021.07.019

Seyfang, G., & Smith, A. (2007). Grassroots innovations for sustainable development: Towards a new research and policy agenda. *Environmental Politics*, *16*(4), 584–603. https://doi.org/10.1080/09644010701419121

Southerton, D. (2020). *Time, consumption and the coordination of everyday life*. Palgrave Macmillan.

Spradley, J. P. (2016). *The ethnographic interview*. Waveland Press.

Tangeland, T., Heidenstrøm, N., & Holst, H. T. (2016). Teknologioptimisme - en behagelig hindring for bærekraftig forbruksutvikling? [Technological optimism -$a convenient obstacle for sustainable consumption?]. In G. Vittersø, A. Borch, K. Laitala, & P. Strandbakken (Eds.), *Forbruk og det grønne skiftet* [Consumption and the Green Shift]. Novus Forlag.

Tregear, A. (2011). Progressing knowledge in alternative and local food networks: Critical reflections and a research agenda. *Journal of Rural Studies*, *27*(4), 419–430. https://doi.org/10.1016/j.jrurstud.2011.06.003

Verma, S., Sharma, R., Deb, S., & Maitra, D. (2021). Artificial intelligence in marketing: Systematic review and future research direction. *International Journal of Information Management Data Insights*, *1*(1), 100002.

Zeisel, S. H. (2020). Precision (personalized) nutrition: Understanding metabolic heterogeneity. *Annual Review of Food Science and Technology*, *11*(1), 71–92. https://doi.org/10.1146/annurev-food-032519-051736

INDEX

Printed and bound by CPI Group (UK) Ltd, Croydon, CR0 4YY

15/09/2026

14962483-0005